The Makers of
HEAVENLY ROSES

The Makers of

HEAVENLY ROSES

ROSES

Jack Harkness

SOUVENIR PRESS

To
ELIZABETH, ROBERT and PHILIP
with love

First published 1985 by Souvenir Press Ltd,
43 Great Russell Street, London WC1B 3PA
and simultaneously in Canada

ISBN 0 285 62654 X

Filmset in Monophoto Garamond by
Northumberland Press Ltd,
Gateshead, Tyne and Wear
Made and printed in Great Britain by
Richard Clay (The Chaucer Press) Ltd,
Bungay, Suffolk

Contents

List of Illustrations

Black and White Illustrations

Preface

In writing these seventeen short biographies, I have succeeded in educating myself, if nobody else. At times I felt like the compiler of *Lives of the Saints*, except that my subjects are of more earthy character, not obvious candidates for canonization, although to be sure they have performed their own miracles, and suffered their own trials.

The chosen cast presents seventeen facets of a story which, like a plant, is in continuous growth. Others have fair claims to be included, but I shall not argue about that, no, I shall peacefully agree with every critic who says I ought to have left out A and brought in B. The names Lacharme, Lambert, Lammerts, De Ruiter, Swim, Mallerin, Lens and Cant roll out like a litany in which I, as a man with written words to cry on the market place, scent another book.

I acknowledge with gratitude the ready response I received from those to whom I applied for information and pictures; especially I thank L. Arthur Wyatt and Betty Harkness. Those two have been in the making of the book all the way through, and have magnified the pleasure I got from writing it.

JACK HARKNESS

1

Guillot

Monsieur Pierre Guillot was a professional rose grower in Lyon, residing, appropriately, in the district called La Guillotière. The soil of that area, combined with the brilliant sky and high temperature, made a favourable environment in which to grow rose plants for sale. In consequence Lyon had become a centre for rose growing in France, with an abundance of rose nurseries, including some of the most renowned in the country. Agreeable this no doubt was to most people, but for Pierre Guillot it posed the problems of competition and of how to raise himself to a similar eminence.

On his side, he had the assets of his own skill and industry, and the presence in his home of a promising lad, his son, Jean-Baptiste.

The work was hard but rewarding, provided one was in love with roses. Much of the year was spent in making and tending cuttings of those roses which could be propagated by that means. Some roses, however, had to be budded or grafted; they demanded that roots be provided for them. The host roots came from the wild roses growing in the district, which meant going out into the countryside and bringing home a load of briar shoots from which to make more cuttings.

Spring was a time for planting and hoeing, summer a time for budding and hoeing, autumn a time for more planting, and for digging up rose bushes and selling them.

Pierre Guillot had started his nursery in 1829. He lived in a time of change, during which few things were changing more quickly than roses. The rose world of his experience saw the establishment in popular favour of many new types of rose, notably China (which to Guillot was 'Bengal'), Tea-scented, Bourbon, Hybrid Perpetual and Noisette. William Paul wrote in 1848: 'How has such a change been wrought? We reply, Simply by a long course of careful and systematic culture. What was the Rose, comparatively speaking, fifty, or even thirty years since?'

It occurred to Pierre Guillot that, as new varieties were being produced at a quite amazing rate, and as a new rose commanded for a while a premium on its price, he should become a raiser of them. It would not be too much extra work and Jean-Baptiste, fortunately, would be interested; and for once, it would put to useful employment the thousands of insects that had their being upon the nursery.

The method of raising new roses then in practice was an ideal partnership with Nature. She was left entirely alone to produce the seed. When she had done so and the hips were ripe, they were gathered, preferably after an autumn frost, mixed with soil or damp sand and kept in boxes or pots, over which a sheet of glass was placed to keep mice out.

Early in spring, the hips were taken out of the sand and the seeds extracted from them. Some hips were still hard, others were decomposing and messy. The seeds were sown in a well prepared bed, preferably near a path where they would be seen on the daily nursery round. They stayed in that bed for two or three years, by which time one could assume most of them had germinated and flowered.

When they flowered, most proved worthless, and the nurseryman pulled them up like weeds; or, if this could not be done without disturbance to others, he cut them off below the ground. Some looked better, and were left to prove themselves. A few were thrilling, and were propagated with hope and joy.

Such is the variation in hybrid roses, that practically every seedling was distinct and different. Twins were as common as among people in the market place.

As a general rule, nobody bothered to identify them, nor asked what the parents were, nor wrote any labels for them. Time enough for those details when there should be a variety worth such attention. Why waste time and money labelling rubbish?

The first introductions from the house of Guillot came in 1842. They were only mildly successful, but one never forgets one's first offerings, and it is to be supposed that, even on his death bed, the word 'Lamartine' would sound sweetly in Pierre Guillot's ears. It was a Bourbon, in the right colour for a rose — that is red; but it had an unfortunate cast of blue, and to judge by the lack of references to it in the publications of that era, its career was brief. Never mind, Guillot had made his mark as a rose raiser, and the consequence was most gratifying: he was entrusted with the introduction of an important, successful rose. Let us try to indicate its importance.

The most striking feature of the new roses of the early nineteenth century was their ability to flower in the autumn as well as in summer. The rose had previously, with a few exceptions, been a flower of the summer; by August it was finished for the year.

Once autumn flowering roses were obtained, the raisers selected varieties with large, double flowers, admittedly without the high centres we are familiar with today, but quite clearly forerunners of them. A perceptible class emerged, known as Hybrid Perpetuals in England, *Rosiers Remontants* in France. Its main shortage was a decent red.

Monsieur Nérard had such a rose, named 'Géant des Batailles', and he entrusted Monsieur Guillot with the introduction of it, which took place in 1846. It was welcomed within two years in William Paul's book as 'a broad step in the right direction' and as 'a beautiful Rose'. It was still being offered for sale half a century later.

Then came 'Mme Bravy', destined to run as long or longer than 'Géant des Batailles'. This came from a Monsieur Guillot of Pont-de-Chéruy. He had named

1. 'Géant des Batailles', Hybrid Perpetual (Nérard 1846).
Drawn by Betty Harkness, after The Rose Garden *by William Paul, 1848*

it 'Danzille', and he assigned it to Guillot of Lyon in 1846, presumably keeping it in the family. The name was changed, and the rose was introduced as 'Mme Bravy' in 1848, though some say 1846, leaving the date uncertain.

'Mme Bravy' belonged to the popular class of Tea-scented roses, which descended in the main from two varieties imported into England from China in 1809 and 1824. Their chief characteristics were large and elegant double flowers (according to the standards of that era), their tea scent, their refined foliage and their ability to grow and flower repeatedly as long as there was the moisture and temperature to allow it. Had there been no winter, they had not stopped growing. This brought with it a handicap, for they were not trained to expect frost, and great were the losses of them in hard European winters.

'Mme Bravy' was a creamy white rose, with a blush of pink at the centre, the flowers 'absolutely globular, like an incurved chrysanthemum', according to one writer who used to exhibit it. He added that they drooped so much, they 'can only be seen in perfection when artificially supported'. Another says the scent was like 'expensive face-cream'.

Imitation's well known relationship to flattery was proved in convincing style by at least two varieties which were introduced during the subsequent fifteen years and proved to be indistinguishable from 'Mme Bravy'. Harsh things were said in England about the honesty of the French raisers, especially by those who imported new roses only to receive duplicates of previous introductions. Making every allowance for misjudgement and eagerness, we must say that to introduce a rose which is not distinct from another man's is, at the least, sharp practice. Guilty in this case were Claude Pernet who, as a fellow citizen, should have known better, with 'Mme de Sertot' in 1859; and Monsieur Lartay of Bordeaux, with 'Alba Rosea' in 1862 or 1863.

At least Pierre Guillot was now a man to imitate; and almost the next thing that happened was the departure of Jean-Baptiste who had already, at the age of twenty-two, altered the future of the rose industry. The practice had been to make briar cuttings into root-stocks for the roses, a slow and tedious task with a poor success rate. In 1849, Jean-Baptiste demonstrated that if one collected the seeds of briars, both Dog Rose and Sweet Briar, the briar seedlings would prove better and cheaper root-stocks than cuttings. The Guillots were the first rosarians to adopt this method, which was in due course followed all over Europe and beyond.

As to his move, we have the mere fact that in 1850 he started his own business in the Monplaisir district of Lyon. The probability is that it occurred upon his marriage, and that the family agreed that the one holding would not support two families.

Thenceforth Pierre Guillot was always known as Guillot Père, and Jean-Baptiste as Guillot Fils. When full of years, the latter was Guillot Fils and Old Guillot at the same time.

As all rose breeders have found, so Jean-Baptiste learned that some years must pass before he could produce a variety of his own from a new beginning. While he is doing so, let us follow the last years of his father's career.

Possibly to console his son-shorn wife, although we cannot be sure because the lady is not positively identified, he introduced 'Mme Guillot' in 1851. It was a rose-pink Hybrid Perpetual; one can imagine it appropriately feminine.

He supported one of France's allies in the Crimean War with 'Lord Raglan' in 1854. Whether appropriately or not, as historians may decide, the rose was a seedling of 'Géant des Batailles'; so in this instance Guillot Père had either used a label in his seedlings at last, or else guessed the progenitor by the appearance of the child. It was a Hybrid Perpetual, crimson, and poor Lord Raglan can never have seen it, for he died of dysentery in the Crimea early in 1855.

In 1856 (some say 1855), he introduced 'Impératrice Eugénie', which is worth mentioning because it was a Moss Rose, light pink in colour, and listed for many years as 'perpetual'.

Guillot Père introduced a winner in 1859, the red Hybrid Perpetual 'Sénateur Vaïsse'. The colour was very bright, the growth strong, and the petals resistant to rain. It came from the seed of 'Général Jacqueminot' and was a popular rose

2. 'Mme Falcot', Tea (Guillot 1858).
Drawn by Betty Harkness, after the Deutsches Rosen-Buch, *1889*

for the rest of the century. There we may leave him, for although his roses continued to appear up to about 1869, we have mentioned the more notable successes out of the eighty or so varieties he introduced. It is time to ask how Jean-Baptiste had fared.

The answer is, very well indeed, for in 1858 he opened his career as a raiser with a triumph comparable to that of a batsman scoring a century in his first Test Match. His rose was a Tea-scented one, 'Mme Falcot'. Thirty years on it was still earning praise: 'its beautiful buds and its dark leaves entitle it to one of the first places among Tea Roses.' 'A lovely bud, the exterior of the outer petals having often the most charming combinations of red and yellow, the inner petals being of a beautiful self-yellow.' So said, respectively, the *Deutsches Rosen-Buch* in 1889 and the Reverend A. Foster-Melliar in 1894. It was a deeper, brighter version of 'Safrano', and its sweet buds earned forgiveness for the pendulous flower stalks and the somewhat untidy middle it showed when the buds opened.

Jean-Baptiste Guillot is described by an English visitor as 'a small, spare man.' It is a puzzle to look back a century, wondering, what sort of a man was this? When he and his contemporaries died, the record closed; the firsthand witnesses had testified and sworn to precious little. What dare we add to the 'small, spare man'?

I think we can say he was bright and brisk in manner, a challenging man to meet, intelligent, with a hint of fiery temper better left unprovoked. He wore a generous moustache, apart from which his face was clean shaven. His garden was not large, but his self confidence abounded, as witness his introduction of 1861, 'Triomphe de Guillot Fils'; this at the start of his career! It was a Tea-scented rose, with enormous flowers, blush with a touch of pink and yellow. He received a tribute in the same year from Eugène Verdier, a distinguished

3. Jean-Baptiste Guillot. Raiser of the first Hybrid Tea, 'La France', and the first Polyantha, 'Pâquerette'.
Photo: Roseraies Pierre Guillot

Parisian raiser, who named a Hybrid Perpetual 'Jean-Baptiste Guillot'. The colour is described as violaceous purple, and perhaps accounted for a marked lack of interest in that rose by subsequent writers.

In the same year, according to the best authority (although another puts it as 1868), Jean-Baptiste produced 'Catherine Guillot'. Her rose was a purple-pink, fragrant Bourbon. After Jean-Baptiste's death, his son Pierre introduced 'Souvenir de Catherine Guillot' in 1896 and 'Souvenir de J. B. Guillot' in 1897. It seems likely that he was commemorating his parents.

When 'Horace Vernet' came out in 1866, Jean-Baptiste was already absorbed in a greater project, involving a pink rose of great promise. That, no doubt, did not detract from his pleasure in 'Horace Vernet'. It was a red Hybrid Perpetual, one of the most beautiful flowers ever shown, 'grand in the extreme in every way on the exhibition table, equalled by few, surpassed by none; but to be avoided by those who grow Roses for ordinary garden purposes. The plant is of a weak constitution; and often cannot be kept in health or strength beyond a year or two.' Thus Foster-Melliar wrote about 'this most noble rose'.

In 1865 or 1866 — the date is uncertain — Jean-Baptiste received a visitor from

England, a clergyman, who at an earlier stage in his career had been Curate of Bray, and had had the good sense to move before promotion came to him. He was the Reverend Henry Honywood D'ombrain, and although born in London, he was in a sense returning to his fatherland, for he came of a Huguenot family.

D'ombrain's great interests, outside his calling, were gardening in general, and roses in particular. He is described as having an appearance that defied distrust; as a man who made friends wherever he went.

Before he left for France, he had been commissioned by a Mr Bull of Chelsea to enquire about a yellow Hybrid Perpetual, supposed to have been raised by François Lacharme in Lyon; and if he thought well of it, to offer any sum up to £200. The rumour proved groundless; there was no yellow Hybrid Perpetual.

Jean-Baptiste welcomed his visitor and they walked round the roses, arriving in due course at the one its owner cherished.

'There,' said Jean-Baptiste, 'is one I think highly of, not only for itself, but as being possibly the beginning of a new race.'

The rose was different from any that D'ombrain had seen. The colour was no surprise, being pink, with the outer surface of the petals rather deeper than the inner. The flowers attracted one not so much by their colour, but by their shape and carriage. It owed the carriage to the plant. D'ombrain studied the plant. How beautifully it held the blooms, on straight stems; it was a plant with the vigour of a Hybrid Perpetual and the refinement of a Tea. As if a surgeon had been at work, the coarseness of the one class had been taken away and the droopy limbs of the other reinforced. The blooms had the delicacy of a Tea rose, with the new pointed centre, and yet some of the substance of a Hybrid Perpetual.

'Monsieur,' asked D'ombrain, 'how did you obtain this rose?'

'It came among my seedlings,' replied Jean-Baptiste, 'and although it differs from all the rest, I regret it is not possible to trace which parent gave birth to it.'

It occurred to D'ombrain that Mr Bull's two hundred pounds could be invested advantageously in this pink rose. He accordingly made the offer to Jean-Baptiste who, he later reported, 'was proof against it.'

During the summer of 1867, the Society of Horticulture of Lyon formed a judging committee. It was an enormous panel of fifty members whose task was to assess new roses of French origin, and to recommend one worthy of the name 'La France'. They judged more than a thousand varieties, and selected Jean-Baptiste's pink rose as the most distinctive of them all. They added a rider, that it was the first of a new class, and from it no doubt interesting developments would arise.

The rose made its debut at the Paris Universal Exhibition of 1867, its triumph a foregone conclusion. Alas, the time of judging came, but not the judges. This was a serious matter, because a good exhibitor selected those blooms which would be at the peak of perfection at the moment of judging. This was hard luck on the visitors who came subsequently, but it was the way to win. As the time passed, so Jean-Baptiste's pink rose became less perfect. The judges eventually arrived two days late and gave it nothing.

It was introduced in 1867, as a Hybrid Perpetual despite the talk of a 'new class', and under the name 'La France'. Thirteen years later, the French agreed between themselves that a new class had indeed appeared, and because it apparently arose from a marriage between Hybrid Perpetual and Tea-scented roses, they named it *Hybrides de Thé*. After another thirteen years of argument, the British National Rose Society followed suit, and so Hybrid Teas were established and in due course became the dominant roses of the twentieth century.

By common consent, 'La France' is taken to be the first of them, and Jean-Baptiste Guillot is thereby assured of a prominent place in rose history as long as it remains in human memory.

The forecast of ample progeny from 'La France' was not fulfilled, due to a fact hidden from the eyes of those clever rosarians. Within its cells, 'La France' had twenty-one chromosomes instead of the normal fourteen or twenty-eight, a variation that severely restricted its ability to breed.

Jean-Baptiste's first love among roses must surely have been the Tea-scented, the epitome of elegant delicacy. If so, that sentiment was expressed and gratified by 'Catherine Mermet' which he introduced in 1869. This sweetly scented pink rose was destined to delight millions of people, because the cut rose growers planted it in their glass-houses all over Europe and the United States. Looking back on it from 1882, one commentator summed up its praises, bluntly and un-equivocally, 'The finest of all Teas'.

In Lyon at that time lived an intelligent horticulturist named Jean Sisley. He tried to convince French rose breeders that their methods should be improved, but the greater number of them, in which Jean-Baptiste must be included, saw no point in changing a successful system and burdening themselves with work Nature did free of charge. Jean-Baptiste was well acquainted with Monsieur Sisley, with important consequences, as we shall see. He named a cream Tea-scented rose 'Marie Sisley', introduced in 1868; a purple red one 'Aline Sisley', followed in 1874.

Jean Sisley, perhaps out of gratitude for the rose named after Marie, gave Jean-Baptiste some interesting seeds from his garden. They had come from a rose plant sent from Japan to England in 1865 by Robert Fortune, a plant explorer who considerably influenced international economics by introducing the tea plant to India.

The plant from Fortune's consignment had been sent from England to the Mayor of Lyon, and planted in the Parc de la Tête d'Or, the pride of the city. The municipality was not particularly grateful and decided to discard it, whereupon Jean Sisley obtained it and planted it in his own garden.

In Japan there was a wild rose with very strong growth, rough looking leaves and small white flowers. It was known to the French for many years as *R. poly-antha*, although its correct name is now agreed to be *R. multiflora*. Seeds of the

4. 'Catherine Mermet', Tea (Guillot 1869).
Drawn by Betty Harkness, after the Deutsches Rosen-Buch, *1889*

typical wild rose had already been grown in Lyon, having been sent to the Mayor, who appears to have been a target for horticultural offerings, by a Monsieur Coignet in 1862. That gentleman was a French engineer, employed by the Japanese government.

Robert Fortune's discovery was a dwarf variety of that wild rose. It grew about two feet high, and showed its little white flowers in the summer.

Whether from Jean Sisley's seeds, or more likely from a subsequent generation, Jean-Baptiste produced a double white rose with small flowers and an enchanting low habit of growth. He called it 'Pâquerette' and introduced it in 1875. It bloomed with extraordinary freedom, and in retrospect was taken to be the first of the new class of Polyantha roses, giving the family of Guillot the honour of being first in two important developments.

The new class was augmented by Jean-Baptiste in 1880 with the light pink 'Mignonette'; and again in 1887 with 'Gloire des Polyantha', which not only confirmed the French in the use of the term Polyantha, but also brought a deep pink colour into the race.

Success with his beloved Teas attended him to the end of his life. In 1887 he nearly achieved the dream of a yellow Tea rose with 'Mme Hoste'.

To obtain a yellow Tea or Hybrid Perpetual in those days was as elusive an ambition as the hope of flying. Consequently a rose such as 'Mme Hoste', which could more honestly be described as yellowish-white, was welcomed as the best yellow Tea rose of the time. In the first year it came out, the famous English rose nurseryman, Benjamin Cant, showed the Rev. Foster-Melliar 'a tiny bud on a grafted plant, with a prophecy, which has been amply fulfilled, of its future value and popularity.'

Jean-Baptiste's closing years were attended with the respect of the rose world,

5. 'Pâquerette', Polyantha (Guillot 1875).
Drawn by Betty Harkness, after the Deutsches Rosen-Buch, *1889*

and the knowledge that his son Pierre should succeed him. He was elected Honorary Member of the National Rose Society in London, one simple honour to add to the many he held.

In summing up his career, D'ombrain said, 'The only other raiser who I think at all approaches him is Ducher'; Henry Ellwanger placed him second to Lacharme out of all the raisers in the world, saying, 'In "La France" and "Catherine Mermet", he has given us new types of wondrous beauty.' Thus he was saluted far beyond the borders of his native France, by an Englishman and an American.

He died in 1893, having raised about eighty roses, among them some of the most beautiful in the world. Seventy-four years later, on the centenary of his historic 'La France', I exhibited flowers of that variety in London at the summer show of the Royal National Rose Society, as a tribute to the rose, to its raiser and to France.

2

Bennett

When Henry Bennett picked up his newspaper, that journal was in pristine condition, because nobody in the house was permitted to read it until the master had done so.

The house was Manor Farm, in Over Street, in the village of Stapleford, about six miles to the north-west of Salisbury in the County of Wiltshire. It is a pleasant village, nestling in the Wylye Valley, not exposed to the rigours of the Salisbury Plain as some strangers suppose.

Henry Bennett was the tenant farmer, engaged in growing wheat and raising cattle. The newspaper, therefore, would not set his mind at ease, with its accounts of the government's free trade policy, and misgivings as to its effects upon agriculture.

His family was growing. He had married Emma Rebbeck in July 1852, and the twelve years since that ceremony had been regularly punctuated by births, as witness the presence of John and Charles and Maria and Francis and Mary. Emma's pregnancies prevented her on occasions from riding to hounds, but the farm kept horses all the same. They were essential not only for work and transport, but also for those important pursuits from which country people got their leisure and social life: riding and hunting. The warm breath of horses was one of life's pleasures.

Manor Farm was a prosperous, Victorian household, firmly governed by the father of the family. He was responsible for its well being, and he was ill at ease.

If one could see into the future, all problems would be easy to solve. That being impossible, one must make the best possible forecast. Henry Bennett judged that lean years were coming to farmers, years during which the earnings, laboriously accrued in the past, would be increased with great difficulty or, worse still, might be whittled away by losses.

Such a prospect demanded action. Most farmers grumbled — an agricultural habit — but showed no intention of changing their ways. If they wished to stick in their farm mud, there was no reason for Manor Farm to keep them company. On Bennett's farm, a new source of income should be found, possibly leading to a new career. If wheat and cattle don't pay, then plainly it is not business to continue with them.

He made up his mind to cash in on the craze for roses. All over the country people were talking about them, growing them and holding rose shows at which prizes were keenly competed for. These activities had come to a climax in 1858, when a Grand National Rose Show had been held in St James's Hall in London. It moved to the Crystal Palace, where in 1860 it was visited by 16,000 people. There was already a rose grower in Salisbury, named John Keynes.

Henry Bennett began a special study of roses in 1865. He bought plants of the best varieties, planted them at Manor Farm and diligently applied his mind to the problem of making money out of them.

Most of the roses bore French names, because the best originators of new roses in those days were French. It occurred to Henry Bennett that the novelties of one year were not so different from those of the last, a kind of eternal repetition of the Tea-scented and Hybrid Perpetual roses, the most popular classes wherever roses were grown. To the Victorian rose world in general, the progress was evident, exciting and inevitable. To one impatient newcomer, there was little progress, little improvement; it occurred to him that by judicious cross breeding, greater advances were possible. His practical knowledge of cattle had taught him something about breeding.

During the summer of 1868, he worked hard among his roses, copying the French methods he had read about, but with an important difference. Whereas they left the wind and the insects to carry the pollen from one flower to another, Henry Bennett did it by hand. The French, in consequence, permitted most of their flowers to be self pollinated, because the pollen often falls from the stamens before the petals unshield the female parts. This gave the raisers no concern, because the seeds of almost every garden rose grow into plants different from that which bore them, in contrast to the seeds of wild roses which, having no stranger's blood in their heredity, faithfully come true to their mother.

If we may use the analogy of cattle, which cannot have failed to cross Henry Bennett's mind, the seed-bearing flower was the cow, and the donor of pollen the bull. Suppose the aim was to change the beautiful flowers of 'Mme Bravy' from creamy blush to glowing red, then if 'Mme Bravy' were the cow, the noble, red 'Géant des Batailles' could possibly be the bull. The old method left the choice of pollen to chance; in the new method there was purpose. Although we call it the 'new' method, it had been known for at least twenty years, and was practised on a small scale by some raisers. Most, like the farmers, preferred to keep to their familiar routine.

The subsequent operation was simple: remove from 'Mme Bravy' her petals and stamens before she could fertilize herself; of her flower, leave only the female parts exposed; take to her a flower of 'Géant des Batailles', and shake the Giant's pollen on to her; a few months later, when the seed is ripe, collect it, sow it, and hope that among the seedlings that grow may be found the one that was planned.

Alas for such hopes! That summer Henry Bennett operated on thousands of flowers in his rose garden, but his labour was wasted, because he obtained in the autumn only a few unripe seeds. He sowed them, and tried again in 1869, with no better success. The few seedlings he raised proved worthless.

During this time, three more children had been born: Arthur, Charlotte Emma and Edmund; but one of them was lost, because Charlotte, who was baptised in 1867, died in 1868.

The venture into breeding roses had run aground, and was further discouraged by a paper Henry Bennett read in July 1869: 'Improvement of Plants by Selection, Hybridising and Cross-breeding, having Special Reference to the Hollyhock and the Rose.' That piece with the long-winded title was the published form of a lecture delivered at the Manchester Horticultural Congress. It dealt with hollyhocks in detail, those flowers being much fancied, to the extent of supporting specialist hollyhock growers until the rust fungus destroyed their livelihood.

Nothing remarkable so far, thought Henry Bennett. Then, after the hollyhocks were dealt with, came a statement about roses, one which surprised him: 'With the Rose the case was somewhat different. It had been experimented on by clever and industrious men in France for a number of years, and doubtless I was here traversing ground which some of them had exhausted long before.'

Could this be true? If true of the lecturer, did it apply also to Henry Bennett? Was he wasting his time, trying to breed roses in England? He knew that the French breeders, Victor Verdier and J. P. Vibert, had broken away from the traditional routine and raised some roses by the deliberate transfer of pollen.

If the raisers across the Channel were truly as clever as the lecturer said they were, then Bennett might as well give up; but he thought there might be a little ground left unbroken by the French. He must make sure he was not walking in the footsteps of others. He decided to visit all the principal French raisers to see for himself what they were doing. This was a decision typical of his energy, thoroughness and determination.

From 1870 to 1872 he paid visits to France, where he carefully inspected the nurseries of Lyon, which he took to be the home of the rose. His character and his interest in roses must have impressed the French raisers, because his visits were succeeded by roses being named in his honour. Antoine Levet introduced 'Henry Bennett' and 'Mme Henry Bennett' in 1872, both pink Tea-scented roses. François Lacharme named a red Hybrid Perpetual 'Henry Bennett' in 1876. Another red Hybrid Perpetual was named 'Mme Bennett' in 1876, this time from Gilbert Nabonnand, a prolific raiser of roses, who introduced more than 200 varieties in his career, nearly all of them Tea-scented roses. Monsieur Nabonnand lived at Golfe Juan in the Alpes Maritimes, from which it may be supposed that Bennett did travel to all the leading French raisers as he had determined, and not only to Lyon, which he mentioned no doubt as the most important centre.

It is not every visitor whose calls bring such responses. Evidently there was power in Bennett's personality.

Bennett summed up his visits to France: 'I failed to detect any scientific means of raising roses by an artificial process. I could see plainly that Rose raising in Europe was like cattle breeding in Mexico, or horse breeding in the New Forest, simply leaving Nature to herself and selecting the best of her produce.'

In France, he made a friend of Jean Sisley. Sisley, an amateur rosarian and expert horticulturist, had been trying in vain to persuade the rose raisers of Lyon to adopt the methods Bennett believed in. Sisley spoke English fluently, and was related to the impressionist painter, Alfred Sisley. His family was connected with the silk industry in Lyon. Apart from his influence on French rosarians, his contribution to horticulture included the raising of double zonal and improved ivy-leafed pelargoniums. He hated standard roses, which he ironically called 'broomsticks'. This 'much-esteemed friend', to use Bennett's own words, convinced him of what in his heart he was already sure of: that he was right.

His visits to France taught Henry Bennett to fear nothing from the French raisers. He was more certain than ever that rose breeding ought to be formed on an intelligent choice of parents, and by observing the influence, good or evil, transmitted by parents to their offspring. The awkward problem of raising seed remained, but he now had ideas on that subject. He began to set up in Stapleford a modern, go-ahead, scientifically controlled rose breeding station, one in keeping with the great contemporary era of progress, one to yield products of which its owner would be proud and possessive to an almost offensive degree.

Because the British climate had failed to ripen seed for him, he ceased to rely on it, and 'tried an entirely new mode of culture' which, he bluntly said, 'self-interest compels me for the present to keep secret'. There spoke Bennett the business-man; helping competitors was no policy for him. The 'secrets' suggested he was ahead of the others, and excited curiosity.

His new mode of culture was to use a glass-house, and to heat it. The roses he chose as parents were planted in pots. Given heat, the Tea-scented roses in particular would flower almost without stopping, and consequently a plant could be fertilized over a longer period than had been possible out of doors, and could carry many more seed pods through having borne more flowers. In due course this practice was followed by other rose breeders in Britain. Breeding began each year not in the summer, but in March; the one breeder who still does this in 1983 declares that the best, most fruitful pods are got from the crosses made early in the year. Bennett's problem of producing seed was triumphantly solved.

The glass-house brought other benefits, by excluding three hazards suffered by hybridizers who worked out of doors: rain, wind and most of the insects.

The years of failure had postponed the date when Henry Bennett could introduce his own roses. He therefore bought a rose from Joseph Schwartz, a well known breeder in Lyon. The variety had been given to Schwartz by its breeder, Monsieur A. Dunant. It was a pink Hybrid Perpetual, which Bennett named 'Duchess of Edinburgh' and introduced in 1874. The Duchess was the wife of Queen Victoria's second son, Alfred, the first of several aristocrats to be favoured with roses by Bennett.

Rose breeders had to be quick to earn their money, because once a variety left their hands, were it only a single stem dropped at a flower show, it was grown by others. While they themselves were the only source of supply, the breeders

6. Henry Bennett, 1823–1890. 'The man who transformed a profession'.
Photo: by courtesy of Charles Quest-Ritson, who obtained it from Henry Bennett's great-granddaughter

could sell their plants for half a guinea — about £15.65 when translated into 1984 values. When their rose came into general circulation, the price descended year by year to about sixpence.

They therefore propagated their new roses with the utmost speed, by grafting in hot beds. This started in January. A seedling plant, selected during the previous summer, supplied about ten grafts. By March, the grafted plants had grown sufficiently to offer about ten more each; the hundred grafts made in March could be multiplied to a thousand in May. Those would in due course be potted up, and sold. The plants were small and spindly by modern standards, but they were acceptable because most purchasers bought them as a source of stock for propagation. Testing the roses for their worth as garden plants was minimal. The flower was everything, to be exhibited or grown for cutting.

Whatever successes lay ahead, Emma Bennett was not destined to share them. She died on 25 May, 1875, as the result, so the Bennett family say, of a riding accident. She and Henry had been married nearly twenty-three years, from the day at Ebbesbourne Wake when he had taken Emma Maria as his lawful wedded wife. When she died, the youngest child, Edmund, was six years old. Maria and Mary, then sixteen and eleven, eventually took over the running of the house.

In the following year, on 7 December, 1876, the National Rose Society was formed. It was the first rose society in the world to cater for an entire nation. Its founders were men of high principle, not one of whom accepted credit for the origin of the idea, but ascribed it to another. The mainspring appears to have been the Reverend H. Honywood D'ombrain, who became Secretary. Canon S. Reynolds Hole, whose charming *A Book about Roses* had been published in 1869, became President. He had been the chief organizer of the first Great National Rose Show, eighteen years previously. We may safely assert that had it not been for Anglican clergymen, the Society would not have been born at that time.

Henry Bennett had been churchwarden at Stapleford, a post that ought to have accustomed him to the clergy; he was a rose breeder, a calling that should relate him to rosarians. These twin advantages failed to establish a proper sympathy between Bennett and the chief officers of the new society. Bennett was a commercial man; they were idealists to the point that some of their followers thought it demoralizing to compete for prize money at rose shows.

The reverend gentlemen in pursuing their hobby had not forgotten their calling. They believed that men and women of all degrees would benefit from roses, for were not these flowers the most beautiful of God's works? Canon Hole, in particular, saw the rose as a magnet to draw the working classes from their taverns to their allotments. One of his favourite stories told of working men who grew roses in Nottingham: ' "How do you afford," I inquired from another, "to buy these new and expensive varieties?" and I would that every employer, that every one who cares for the labouring poor, would remember the answer, reflect, and act on it.

' "I'll tell you," he said, "how I managed to buy 'em — *by keeping away from the beershops!*" '

Henry Bennett was not an outstanding example to the labouring poor in this respect. He was a hard worker, a man who had to go and see for himself, to get up and work with his own hands, to discover what others were doing and then push himself towards a more difficult target, to rule his roses, farm and home, to take strain. He had lost his wife. He was drinking too much.

In 1878, he introduced four varieties which he had obtained from other breeders. 'Mabel Morrison' was a white sport of the Hybrid Perpetual 'Baronne Adolphe de Rothschild'. It had been found by a man named Broughton, who noticed among the pink flowers a stem bearing a white one. On propagating it, he found the accident of nature continued. 'Mabel Morrison' became a popular white rose.

The other three roses were French, the best of them, 'Lord Beaconsfield', a red Hybrid Perpetual raised by Joseph Schwartz. The human Lord Beaconsfield was Benjamin Disraeli, who had recently received the honour of that title.

From Bennett's point of view, these roses, even Disraeli, were pot-boilers to tide him over until he could introduce his own Stapleford roses. He showed some of them during 1878, but held his fire until 1879, when he laid down a barrage that reverberated through the entire world of roses.

He chose to introduce ten varieties, lavishing on them all extravagant praise which time, in no great measure, disproved. He claimed 'greater perpetuity as regards blooming, greater depth of petal, and that they are altogether different in type from any Rose before seen.' If there was a vice, his roses didn't have it: no mildew, no rust, no fading, no freezing, no dullness; they were virtue all the way.

He stated that his roses had been raised in a scientific manner, by experiments conducted by himself with the greatest care. He published the parentage of his roses, and said he could guarantee it correct. No raiser of roses had made such claims before. Nobody had made so definite a point of crosses between two classes, the Tea-scented and the Hybrid Perpetuals.

It is one thing to make a statement, like a man holding a nail to a piece of wood, but it is another to drive the nail home. His farming life had put a sledge-hammer slogan into his mind, and he introduced his ten roses as:

PEDIGREE HYBRIDS OF THE TEA ROSE

Pedigree, a word taken out of the cattle ring and tossed into the rose world, made a crystal of his claims in eight shining letters. Its immediate effects were to impress the public, and to invite critics to attack it. Its results were profound; it was a reproach and a goad to raisers of roses all over the world. The gentle advice of Jean Sisley had been repeated in the *Journal des Roses* of March 1877, but still the traditional methods persisted. After Bennett's Pedigree Roses appeared, the old ways were ended. Rose raisers made haste to follow him, and could hence-forth be rightly called rose breeders.

Against the attacks of his critics, Henry Bennett defended himself with much vigour and little appeasement. His defence was one of prompt counter-attack, in which two weapons were used, the evidence of his experiments, and the amaze-ments that he should reveal in future. One of the forthcoming wonders was the first yellow Hybrid Perpetual, a cross between 'Victor Verdier' and 'Isabella Sprunt'; but it never came forth.

He described how he took his favourite Teas, 'Alba Rosea', which was another name for 'Mme Bravy'; and 'President', which was more correctly called 'Adam'; and raised most of his new roses from their seed.

To confound his critics, he took plants in pots, and covered with hips, to a show in South Kensington in the autumn of 1879, to demonstrate to the Scientific Committee of the Royal Horticultural Society the nature of his experiments. The Committee reported that 'the results were not only interesting from the scientific point of view, but practically valuable in the production of what is virtually a new race of roses of great beauty and vigorous habit.'

What of these ten historic roses? Their careers were not illustrious. According to George Paul in 1895, the main survivor was 'Duke of Connaught', a red rose with beautiful buds, then still being used to produce cut flowers in the winter in England. The Duke had been Prince Arthur, the seventh child of Queen Victoria, and was a distinguished soldier. He died in his nineties, in 1942. His wife, who was a Prussian princess, also had one of the roses named after her. 'Duchess of Connaught' was a pink rose, somewhat similar to 'La France'.

The 'Duchess of Westminster' was also pink, but with little scent and poor form, unfortunate lady. 'Hon. George Bancroft' was red, but not an attractive colour, and the pretty buds opened to disappointing flowers. The Hon. George was, to Bennett, potentially a valuable introduction to the American market. He was a distinguished American historian who served as Minister to Great Britain, from 1846–49. He was also a great rose enthusiast.

Some critics found 'Michael Saunders' one of the more valuable of the ten introductions. It was pink, with coppery red shading. The pink 'Nancy Lee' was praised for perfume and beautiful buds, but damned for its delicate habit. Ellwanger wrote: 'our commiseration is excited along with our regard.' 'Pearl' fell into much the same category.

The main disaster was 'Jean Sisley'; what a shame that the 'much-esteemed friend' received a rose which was roundly condemned for its muddy lilac rose colour, inability to open properly, scentlessness and mildew.

The other two bore Wiltshire names: 'Viscountess Falmouth' had been bred from the Tea rose 'Adam' crossed with pollen from a Moss rose. It was pink, fragrant, thorny and interesting. An echo of home was heard in 'Beauty of Stapleford'; but it is to be feared it got its name as a last resort, Bennett having run out of aristocrats; it was deep lilac pink; there was no scent but plenty of mildew.

Within one year, Benjamin Cant wrote in his catalogue: 'Bennett's Hybrid Tea Roses have turned out with me to be perfectly worthless. It is as well to give them a trial for another year before throwing them away, which I expect will be their ultimate fate.' In 1881, the *Gardeners' Chronicle* complained: 'They grow well, come freely into bud, and there they stop; they will not expand.' But by then, Bennett's mind was engaged in future projects, and no amount of criticism could diminish the value of his achievement. George Paul later wrote: 'Though not immediately successful, his original ideas were right, and he made for himself a name as a successful and original raiser of Roses by a process involving method and skill.'

The response from Lyon to the Pedigree Hybrids was practical and immediate, as if that city had been stung by a bee. In the spring of 1880, Bennett was invited to a meeting of the Horticultural Society of Lyon. Its most important business was to ask what one should call those new roses, which were neither Teas nor Hybrid Perpetuals, but something in between. With decisive common sense, that provincial society declared that a new class existed, and that it should be called *Hybrides de Thé*.

The reputation of Lyon was sufficient for this to be adopted in France; in 1883, Paul & Son of Cheshunt followed suit in their catalogue; then Hugh Dickson of Belfast in 1884. The National Rose Society did not agree, owing to a reluctance to interfere with the schedules for their rose shows, those exhibitions being the main reason for their existence. This attitude led them into more difficulties than it solved; for example, a rose would be disqualified for being shown as a Hybrid Perpetual at one show, but a few days later would win a silver medal as the best Hybrid Perpetual at another. After much argument, the society adopted the Hybrid Tea class in 1893. It cannot be doubted that during the years of indecision, Bennett made the society free of his unwelcome opinion.

There were no introductions from Henry Bennett in 1880 and 1881, because he had given up Manor Farm and was busy moving from Stapleford to Shepperton, a village in Middlesex, outside London. It had recently become the terminus of a railway line; communications were therefore good. He leased and moved into Kilmiston House at Shepperton in 1882; Henry's farming days in Wiltshire were over, and he was henceforth a rose breeder.

He was back in business that year with six new roses, of which the most famous was a pink Hybrid Tea, 'Lady Mary Fitzwilliam'. Its fame came from the hands of a Frenchman, Joseph Pernet-Ducher, who used its pollen in raising 'Mme Caroline Testout'. Through that rose, 'Lady Mary Fitzwilliam' appears in the family trees of thousands of Hybrid Tea varieties. It was no great plant, but grew a little, then stopped still to produce such huge flowers as to exhaust the bush. The flowers were light pink, very fragrant, and of a fine shape, especially when half open. It was raised from a Tea rose found in Plymouth in 1838, called 'Devoniensis'; crossed with the deep pink Hybrid Perpetual, 'Victor Verdier'.

One of the functions of a rose society is to commend the best roses to its members, to prevent them from planting inferior sorts, and this is especially important in respect of new roses. The National Rose Society instituted in 1883 a Gold Medal to be given to outstanding new varieties exhibited at its shows. One of the roses entered was from Henry Bennett. It was named 'Her Majesty'.

One can almost hear him chuckling over that rose. It was a whopper. As it produced its fat buds, he resolved to show it in thirty-sixes, several of them. In fact a thirty-six consisted of two boxes of eighteen set together. The boxes were designed to display specimen blooms to the best advantage. The blooms were shown in a level plane on short stems, each in a tube. The tubes were set in fixed positions, in three rows, and six inches apart. A box of eighteen was thirty-three inches long and eighteen inches wide. The surface of the box, beneath the flowers, was covered with the freshest, greenest moss one could find.

As the enormous rose pink flowers unfolded at Shepperton, they brought agony instead of joy, because they were too early. By the time of the show, they were past their best, but Henry Bennett took them to the Crystal Palace, with these results, later described by Foster-Melliar:

'As to sensations produced by particular Roses, I think nothing has ever equalled the first Exhibition of Her Majesty for the Gold Medal by Mr Bennett. Several great boxes of thirty-six were shown, every bloom being fully expanded; and

7. 'Her Majesty', Hybrid Perpetual (Bennett 1885).
Drawn by Betty Harkness, after the Deutsches Rosen-Buch, *1889*

such a large Rose, that showed no eye even when it was expanded flat, had never been seen before.'

The first Gold Medal went to Henry Bennett, 'granted by acclamation'.

Those who had acclaimed were much disappointed to be informed, when they sought to buy 'Her Majesty', that the entire stock had been sold to an American nurseryman. They were obliged to wait for it until 1885, when there was a large demand for plants at half a guinea each.

They were not amused at being placed at the back of the queue for the first Gold Medal rose, nor did they appreciate the commercial attitude of the breeder. He was, after all, considered more or less an amateur, but had the disconcerting habit of behaving like a tradesman. Some people questioned the parentage, which Henry Bennett had declared to be the white Hybrid Perpetual 'Mabel Morrison' crossed with Guillot's Tea, 'Canary', neither of which had many petals. Quite plainly, they said, there is no want of petals in 'Her Majesty', nor any sign of Tea; she is Hybrid Perpetual through and through. When they finally grew 'Her Majesty' themselves, and showed younger flowers than Bennett had been able to exhibit, they criticized his lack of judgement as an exhibitor. And after they had paid their half-guinea and put 'Her Majesty' in their gardens, they found it a dreadful rose. The blooms were admittedly magnificent and long lasting, but were extremely shy in appearing. According to Foster-Melliar, one did well in the summer to get one flower per plant, 'while the Autumnal flowering was much worse.' As for mildew, she was, said Alexander Hill Gray, 'a whole syndicate in herself'; he saw her some years later in France, 'overwhelmed with the original sin of mildew'. She was indeed notoriously subject to that ailment, thorns and leaves and all. Foster-Melliar concluded that Mr Bennett might in consequence revise his ideas, and consider 'chance still as likely to be successful as the careful choosing of seed-parents.'

Henry Bennett went about his business, and took a box of twenty-four 'Her Majesty', the same twenty-four flowers, to four different shows, winning a first at each. Let the critics stuff that in their pipes and smoke it.

He atoned in 1884 with 'Grace Darling', a cream and pink Hybrid Tea, which lacked the size required for exhibiting, but grew beautifully. It was in retrospect recognized as one of the earliest 'garden roses'.

In the same year he pulled off another American deal, by selling a red Hybrid Tea to Mr Evans, a grower of cut flowers in Philadelphia, for the sensational sum of five thousand dollars. Put that in 1984 values, and it is over £37,000. The rose was named 'William Francis Bennett', after his elder brother.

This rose provided a good example of his breeding, because the seed came from the blush Tea, 'Adam', and the pollen from the dark red Hybrid Perpetual, 'Xavier Olibo', resulting in a red Hybrid Tea. Whether it proved a good bargain for Mr Evans is a matter of some doubt.

8. 'William Francis Bennett', Hybrid Tea (Bennett 1884).
Drawn by Betty Harkness, after the Deutsches Rosen-Buch, *1889*

The National Rose Society did not award its Gold Medal in 1884; but in 1885, the exquisite form and sweet perfume of 'Mrs John Laing' won everybody's admiration. This beautiful, pink Hybrid Perpetual is the best rose Henry Bennett raised; it won the society's second Gold Medal, giving Mr Bennett a regular corner in that award. *The Garden* said, 'Had Mr Bennett only given us Mrs John Laing, rose growers would have been grateful.'

The flowers spread wide, the shape is regular, the plants grow well. It is a beauty, and was acknowledged 'a still greater triumph for Mr Bennett and English-raised Roses ... it is everybody's Rose, with perhaps fewer imperfections than any other.' It was not introduced immediately, but in 1887. No pollen parent was recorded by the pedigree breeder, who said merely that it was a seedling of 'François Michelon'.

It appears that Henry Bennett had been sending some of his roses to the United States before they were introduced in England, in the hope of reaping an introducer's rewards in two countries instead of one. The *Deutsches Rosen-Buch* states that 'Mrs John Laing' was awarded a Gold Medal in New York in 1885; and in the case of 'The Puritan', which was a white Hybrid Tea bred from 'Mabel Morrison' crossed 'Devoniensis', the Germans reported, whether accurately or not I cannot say, that flowers were cut in New York, shipped across the Atlantic, and shown at an exhibition of the National Rose Society in South Kensington. It also won a Silver Medal, the highest award, at the Pennsylvania-Massachusetts exhibition. It was introduced in 1888.

About this time, when most men of his age would have thought twice about it, Henry Bennett sailed the Atlantic to study rose growing in America. He was, so the *Gardeners' Chronicle* assures us, warmly received by our transatlantic cousins.

His last rose, out of the thirty-eight introductions he raised, had not, according to one report, flowered at the time of his death. His youngest son, Edmund, introduced it in 1893. It was 'Captain Hayward', a crimson Hybrid Perpetual, which was considered a magnificent red and was grown for many years. Edmund spent his life in roses, at William Paul's nursery in Waltham Cross, and then at Bide's in Farnham, Surrey. In 1911 he emigrated to Australia, where he grew roses for cutting in Queensland. He died in his nineties, from a chill he caught as the result of volunteering to chop down a hedge for a lady.

Henry Bennett died at Shepperton on the twelfth of August 1890, from cirrhosis of the liver. He was sixty-seven. He was taken back to the churchyard he knew so well in Stapleford, and there lies buried. The tribute to him from the National Rose Society spoke volumes of omissions: 'Rosarians have to regret, too, the loss of Mr Henry Bennett of Shepperton. He never, it is true, took kindly to the Society, and it is as a raiser of new Roses that he will most be missed.' Regret has been more poignantly expressed.

History has put him on the pedestal he deserved, as the father of the Hybrid Teas, the man who transformed a profession, and the mainspring of British rose breeding.

3

Pernet-Ducher

The year 1870 was one of disaster for France. The Prussians surrounded Paris for four months, until the city surrendered. France sued for peace, and paid dearly for it in land and money. Many Frenchmen hoped for the day when the rôles should be reversed, when their honour, land and francs should be returned with interest.

One of them was a small boy of Lyon, who, at the age of twelve, was then starting his working life. His name was Joseph Pernet, son of Claude Pernet, rose grower; and his employment was at the nursery his father had founded in 1845.

After a year or two, his father arranged an apprenticeship for him with M. Alégatière, a rose grower of good repute and a raiser, in a modest but skilful way, of new varieties. We may imagine young Joseph reporting for duty on the first day of his apprenticeship at a rose nursery in Lyon.

First of all, he would see the nurseryman's house; then the shed for potting and packing and storing. Nearby was the glass-house, with its coal hole and heaps of fuel, providing warmth to enable one to graft roses or grow them from cuttings. Conveniently at hand were the frames, where the young plants were acclimatized on their graduation from warmth to open air. No doubt he would spend many an hour lifting and replacing their cumbersome glass lights in response to the changes in the weather. Finally, a patch of ground in which plants grew until they could be sold. The entire area of a typical rose nursery was less than three acres. It probably contained the nurseryman's chickens, vegetables, fruit trees and any other manifestation of his interest.

He needed no telling that the least glamorous tasks would all be his, and that if he had to wash a thousand pots, then the sooner he did it, the sooner Monsieur would find him something else to do, possibly something more interesting. He was a Pernet, and the day would certainly come when Monsieur would place a knife in his hands and set him grafting. That was the apprentice's equivalent to graduation. Joseph could attain it only on merit, having been sent away from the protective privileges of home to work among people who would grant him no favours.

Other boys might go to academies, but Joseph had the advantage of them, by practising his chosen profession from the age of twelve. He would be a master of his career before they started theirs.

In that place he worked and learned for the next few years, accumulating a debt to M. Alégatière for those inestimable treasures, knowledge and experience.

When his apprenticeship was nearly served, he sought more experience, and asked for a post with the firm of Ducher, which was one of the most respected in Lyon.

Claude Ducher, a talented raiser of new roses, had started his business in 1835. He had taken a leading part in the first great rose show in Lyon, on 16 June, 1845, an exhibition which subsequently became an annual opportunity for the Lyonnais rosarians to show their wares.

Lyon was the home of some of the world's greatest rosarians, such men as Guillot, Levet and Lacharme, and it had produced some of the world's greatest roses, for example 'La France', 'Maréchal Niel' and 'Souvenir de la Malmaison'. The rose growers of Lyon looked upon the Parisians as provincials, the foreigners as far-behind followers, themselves as the leaders and the centre of the rose world.

Joseph Pernet knew that the household contained a shrewd lady, Mme Ducher; and an interesting daughter, Mademoiselle Marie. These two had both enjoyed the pleasure of lending their names to roses, in Madame's case twice over, with a third to come in the future.

The Duchers were far from prolific in the matter of raising roses compared with other French raisers, some of whom sent out hundreds of new varieties. On the contrary, their list was short, but marked with such high quality as to show that Joseph had entered a house of excellent judgement and taste. Their Noisette roses, 'Rêve d'Or' (1869) and 'Bouquet d'Or' (1872) were to outlast nearly all of that class. Their two great successes in Teas were 'Marie van Houtte' (1871), one of the strongest growers in the class, and 'Anna Olivier' (1872); and in Hybrid Perpetuals, 'Antoine Ducher', red (1866). In the future other great roses were to come, including the orange-yellow climber, 'William Allen Richardson, (1878); it had, admittedly, a provoking habit of producing white blooms instead of orange. There was also one other sweetheart, which is loved to this day, as shall be seen.

Claude Ducher died in 1874, and his widow took over the business. It was common among French nurseries, that when the proprietor changed, the name of the business followed suit. The firm took the title of Veuve Ducher, which means the widow Ducher. The ability of Joseph Pernet, and the trust in which the Ducher family held him, are evident from his being made their foreman, a post he is known to have held at the age of twenty-two. It was at that age, in the year 1880, that he received an invitation to attend a meeting of the Horticultural Society of Lyon.

The cause of that meeting was an English farmer named Henry Bennett. He had visited Lyon during the previous years, to examine the practices of French rose raisers. He said bluntly that he found them wanting, even in the rose capital of the world.

Bennett believed, as we have seen, that the right way to raise new roses was to envisage the offspring, and then deliberately to mate the two parent roses most likely to produce that child. The French knew this theory, but preferred in practice to forego the labour and take the seeds as Nature had fertilized them. Bennett brought a cattle breeder's background into the business of raising new roses, and his ten new 'Pedigree Hybrids of the Tea Rose', exhibited in London in 1879, had had their pedigree specified, emphasized and advertised. He was the scientific rose breeder. All others, in contrast, were made to seem out of date.

It was a shock to the rose raisers of Lyon that their supremacy should be challenged by, of all men, an English farmer; and from, of all places, the obscure, unheard of village of Stapleford in Wiltshire. All credit to them that they responded with immediate interest, and invited Henry Bennett to their meeting.

Henry Bennett, a man of forceful character in his late fifties, made a deep impression on the young Joseph Pernet. The meeting had a good tangible result, in declaring the existence of a new class, *Hybrides de Thé*, on the evidence of Bennett's deliberate crosses. It proved the reputation of Lyon, that this pronouncement by a local society was accepted with little question in France; and later, with more questions, in other countries.

The intangible result of the meeting was greater; it was to be demonstrated in the life of Joseph Pernet, and it influenced virtually every other rose raiser in the world.

Joseph went away, and asked himself what offspring he desired and how he could choose the best parents to get it. He had been a rose raiser; he would become a rose breeder. But first he had private matters to settle.

His relations with Mme Ducher and Marie had reached the stage where he requested of the former her permission to marry the latter. It was all arranged in a prudent, sensible, French way. Madame should retire, Joseph should take over her interest in the business and be a good husband to Marie. To preserve the Ducher name among rosarians, and not to waste the value it might have, he should suffix it to his own, and become in future Joseph Pernet-Ducher.

This was not an uncommon arrangement in France, although we may note with interest that the surname applied to one generation only. The children of Joseph and Marie were all to be known as Pernet, without the Ducher at all.

They were married in 1881, and immediately had the pleasure of introducing one of the last of the Ducher varieties, one of the most beautiful and individual roses ever created. It was 'Mme Cécile Brunner', usually known just as 'Cécile Brunner'. The Americans called it, most appropriately, the Sweetheart Rose, on account of its thimble-sized flowers, small but exquisite in shape, in light shades of pink. It has been loved for a century, and shows no sign of losing man's affection. One may regard it with all the more pleasure, in the knowledge that Marie and Joseph knew it when they too were sweethearts.

In the year after their wedding, the Pernet-Duchers had a son. They christened him Claudius.

Joseph ordered Henry Bennett's roses, regarding them as the foundation of his breeding stock.

In those days, the favourite roses were Teas and Hybrid Perpetuals, and if we could go back in time and see them in bloom in the Pernet-Ducher nursery, we should immediately notice a deficiency of yellow. There were no yellow Hybrid Perpetuals, and what yellow the Teas offered was buff or cream or suffused in red, and in each case fleeting. The best yellow roses in those days were Noisettes of a climbing nature, of which 'Maréchal Niel' was the supreme example; and hybrids of the Austrian Briar, Lutea Hybrids they called them. 'Maréchal Niel' was a flower for a florist to grow under glass. The Lutea Hybrids bloomed only for a short time in early summer, without the form, size and refinement of the Teas and Hybrid Perpetuals.

In the famous park of Lyon, Le Parc de la Tête d'Or, grew a double form of the Austrian Briar called 'Persian Yellow'. That was the parent for Joseph. He decided to use the pollen of that bright yellow, shapeless rose, no matter how short its flowering season. On Bennett's principles, he had only to fertilize Hybrid Perpetuals, or Hybrid Teas or Teas with it, to get a bright yellow colour into those classes.

Others, including Bennett himself, had the same idea, and one by one they discovered that 'Persian Yellow' had next to no pollen at all. Bennett was quoted by Lord Penzance as having made hundreds of crosses, but without any success. One of the Lyonnais breeders, Joseph's former employer, Monsieur Alégatière, informed the Horticultural Society of Lyon: 'There is a total incompatibility between the beautiful wild yellow roses and remontant garden hybrids; the two will never combine.'

It is a thankless task to pollinate roses when one cannot see the pollen, and sooner or later those who attempted the task abandoned it. Joseph, however, kept stubbornly at it for five seasons, from 1883 to 1887, and in the end all he got were a few seeds which he sowed in 1888. They did not flower in that year, nor the next, so he put the plants in a border. 'Persian Yellow' looked like labour in vain, and there were more pressing things in life.

One was his second son, Georges, who was born in 1886. His arrival was celebrated with a little rosy peach Polyantha rose, named after him and introduced in 1887. It was one of the earliest in its class. Although Joseph raised this, and the rosy white 'Mlle Bertha Ludi' (1891), claimed by some to be the forerunner of the Floribundas, his heart was not in these cluster flowered types of roses. He was a Hybrid Tea man. And he had a beauty to introduce in 1890.

It was the famous 'Mme Caroline Testout', which he got by crossing the Tea, 'Mme de Tartas' with pollen from one of Bennett's roses, 'Lady Mary Fitzwilliam'. It was 'Caroline Testout' (the Mme was usually dropped) more than any rose which made Hybrid Teas into bedding roses. Its flowers were satiny pink, of good size and substance, the outer petals readily opening to show a firm if slightly rounded centre. It beat all records in flower production, and was lavishly planted all over the civilized world. The famous record, which has often been quoted, was in Portland, Oregon, where 'a person can walk for hours along the streets of the city beside hedges of Caroline Testout. Mile after mile of the parking between the sidewalk and the roadway is filled with bushes of this glorious Rose.' News-papers put the number planted in Portland at 'upwards of 3,000,000', but we know how to divide their figures. A more sober estimate, by the American rose grower E. G. Hill after a visit to Portland, ventured 450,000, which is still an extraordinary number of one variety.

The success of the rose was gratifying not only to Joseph, but also to the lady for whom it had been named. She came from Grenoble and was in the fashion business, with interests in Paris and London. As Lyon lies between Grenoble and Paris, and was a centre for silk, which was her business, and roses, which were her pleasure, it is to be understood that Mme Testout combined the two in that city. She saw the rose as an extension of that combination, in short as an advertise-ment for her business.

It is tempting to imagine the transactions between this capable and sophisticated customer, and the serious young rose grower. She was, no doubt, a very difficult lady to say 'No' to. He had only a few plants of the variety, and at the time was not fully certain of its merits; the proposed deal was a novel one, and from it might arise inconvenient responsibilities to supply flowers and plants. His doubts were dealt with by Madame Testout, on his tongue if not in his mind, and the rose made its debut in her London showroom in the spring of 1890.

During 1891, Joseph noticed that one of the seedlings from his 'Persian Yellow' pollen was flowering in the border. It was a long way short of the yellow rose of his hopes. The flowers were semi-double, pink and yellow. They smelt like 'Persian Yellow' and flowered for just as short a time. Its seed parent had been a red rose raised by his father-in-law, 'Antoine Ducher'.

He left it where it was.

His reputation grew in the next two years, due to the quality of his new roses, for 'Caroline Testout' was not his only success. Famous rosarians caught the tram, and arrived at his door. He was described by nearly all of those who recorded their experiences as kind, courtly, patient. He listened to their advice, allowed them to believe that he had taken it, and continued inflexibly on his own course.

One such friend was Ernest Viviand-Morel, the editor of *Lyon Horticole* and a prominent member of the French National Society of Horticulture. The talk turned to 'Persian Yellow', which everybody had found mulish. Joseph remarked that he had a seedling from applying its pollen to 'Antoine Ducher'. His friend, knowing from expert opinions that those two would never combine, replied that he would believe it when he saw it; Joseph promised to send along a few blooms when they were available. In due course he went to cut them. It was the early summer of 1893.

The 'Antoine Ducher' seedling was flowering. As he bent to cut a few blooms, he noticed a different flower, double and orange-yellow, where the other had been semi-double, pink and yellow. Further examination showed that a small plant had grown from seed, which presumably had fallen from the larger plant. It was unbelievable. For ten years he had dreamed about a yellow rose, and failed to get it. Here it was, a free gift from Nature; not quite yellow, perhaps, but of a ruddy yellow colour far in advance of any Hybrid Tea. He grafted it, and watched it with the greatest interest.

In 1895, Joseph Pernet-Ducher introduced the famous 'Mme Abel Chatenay'. This was a light pink rose with a deeper centre; the colour, in its cast and combination of shades, was more subtle than it sounds, so much so that rosarians expressed it as 'Chatenay pink'. Although it posed problems to gardeners, particularly through being short lived, thousands upon thousands were planted before anyone found that out; even when they knew that fault, many people were prepared to enjoy the short but rewarding life of their bed of Chatenay.

'Mme Abel Chatenay' was happier in a glass-house than in the garden, and she must have dressed, fed and housed the families of cut rose growers all over the world. In the Lea Valley, north of London, it was reported in 1912 that practically half the money made out of cut roses came from this one variety. It was grown under glass there not by the hundreds, or thousands, but by acres. They reckoned to cut it for the whole twelve months of the year. Selected stems, a metre in length, were exported to Paris. One nursery planted a quarter of a million Chatenay, having started with three stems, and kept on grafting. The stems came from another nurseryman who had rashly decided to throw Chatenay out.

In the same year as 'Mme Abel Chatenay', Joseph introduced 'Antoine Rivoire'; those who know the lovely roses 'Ophelia' and 'Mme Butterfly' would see a family likeness to them in 'Antoine Rivoire'. Although proof does not exist, it is a generally accepted conjecture that 'Ophelia' was a seedling of this variety.

Each year, Joseph increased his stock of the ruddy yellow descendant of 'Persian Yellow', ever more conscious, as he saw it flowering, that he had such a rose as was never seen before. It was less responsive to propagation than most roses, therefore he needed more than the usual time to raise enough stock to meet a demand which, one could forecast, would be enormous. He had an excellent free growing rose in 'Mme Ravary', which the world would accept as an improved yellow, but only provided his wonderful ruddy yellow was not available. He therefore decided to introduce 'Mme Ravary' in 1899, and the exciting one in 1900. In fact, after he had followed that programme, 'Mme Ravary' proved a great success, because although the yellow in it faded quickly, the buds were charming, and its growth and freedom of bloom made it a splendid bedding rose.

In spite of his prudent programme, Joseph could not resist showing his new rose in advance. In August 1898, an International Horticultural Exhibition was held in Lyon. Here was the chance to show that the firm of Pernet-Ducher was the richest source of new roses in the future.

He chose the name 'Soleil d'Or', and took his flowers to the exhibition. Joseph, by that time, had grown the rose for six years, and knew it intimately. The world had never seen it, nor any rose like it for intensity of orange-gold colour. The first reaction was astonishment. 'Soleil d'Or' was the marvel of the show and received every honour that could be given. Those who attended that day were witnesses of a new page in the rose's history. The yellow of an Asiatic species had been channelled into the bloodstream of modern roses.

'Soleil d'Or' made its first appearance in Britain in 1901. There its reception was less enthusiastic. The flowers were stuffed with so many petals that they would not open easily in a British summer. They were neither large enough, nor so perfectly formed as to appeal to exhibitors. The plants, which Joseph had found slow to propagate, were also slow to grow. They died back in the winter, fell victim to blackspot, and received prompt discharges from the gardens they had hopefully entered. Blackspot shocked Joseph. He never saw it in Lyon, because the local chemical factories charged the air with fungicide.

The breeders seized 'Soleil d'Or' and started to work, but Joseph had some years' advantage of them.

Claudius Pernet was by now interested in roses, and was by all accounts a lively and likeable lad. He went to work in England, for the famous rosarian George Paul. Those who worked in the firm of Pernet-Ducher found Joseph a stern master, but kindhearted in a gruff way. Of those who trained under him, several went far in the profession.

The great roses continued to flow: 'Prince de Bulgarie' in 1900, 'Mme Mélanie Soupert' in 1905, and the famous 'Lyon Rose' in 1907. The latter was a descendant of 'Soleil d'Or' and inherited its pithy, tender wood; but it displayed a new kind of pink colour, described as shrimp pink or coral, with yellow shading. It was grown in great quantity. The seed parent was Pernet-Ducher's 'Mme Mélanie Soupert'.

The French National Society of Horticulture declared that roses like 'Soleil d'Or', which had been called Lutea Hybrids after the yellow briar they came from, constituted a new, distinct class, deserving a name of its own. The name of the class, in honour of the breeder, was Pernetiana. This was adopted in Britain in 1914, after years of protest that it was unacceptable for botanic reasons.

In Paris, in the gardens of Bagatelle, the world's first rose trial ground was opened. A Gold Medal was offered to the best rose in each year. In the first year, which was 1907, it was awarded to Pernet-Ducher's 'Marquise de Sinéty'. There was no award in 1908. 'Lyon Rose' won in 1909. In later years, Pernet-Ducher's varieties won the Bagatelle Gold Medal from 1916 to 1926, with the exception of 1918.

On 27 August, 1909, an Englishwoman boarded a Lyon tram at the Place Bellecour and travelled its south-eastward journey to the terminus at Vennissieux. The tram left the city, swayed past vineyards and open fields, and after an hour's journey stopped in the dusty little square of Vennissieux. The woman walked half a mile to the house and high walled garden of Monsieur Pernet-Ducher. He met her with a kind and courtly greeting. She was Rose G. Kingsley, an amateur rose grower who had recently written a useful book, *Roses and Rose Growing*. He was by now well used to visitors from England.

He had raised seedlings with the assistance of the pollen of 'Soleil d'Or'. One of them — it came from seed of 'Mme Mélanie Soupert' — was truly yellow, a shining colour, as much an advance upon 'Soleil d'Or' as that rose had been over its predecessors. He had sent plants to an English correspondent for an opinion, under his private code name, Canari. Here at home, it was now in flower, ready for introduction the very next year, its name chosen. It would be interesting to watch the expression of Madame Kingsley when she came to it.

He showed her around the nursery slowly, letting her spend some time among hundreds of 'Lyon Rose'; and eventually he led her to the yellow rose he knew she had never seen before.

'Marvel of marvels!' she exclaimed, quite startled by this sheet of shining yellow. 'What have you here, Monsieur? It is the yellow rose we have been waiting for these last twenty years.'

'It is true,' came the proud, quiet answer. ' "Rayon d'Or" is without doubt the best yellow rose that exists.'

They sent her home from Lyon a few days later, with a large and dazzling bouquet, including the incomparable 'Rayon d'Or'.

When it was shown in Regent's Park, there were scenes of excitement and amazement as soon as the blooms were taken out of their box. It won the Gold Medal of the National Rose Society.

'The year 1910,' said Joseph Pemberton, 'will be known hereafter as the year of "Rayon d'Or".'

Its career as a garden plant was not unlike that of 'Soleil d'Or'. That was disappointing, but of minor importance compared with its potency to breed the yellow roses we take for granted today. We owe those yellow roses to Joseph Pernet-Ducher.

Joseph was persuaded to enter a rose at Chelsea in 1912, in an unusual competition. The prize to the breeder was a gold cup and £1,000. The prize to the sponsor was that the winner be named 'The Daily Mail Rose', for it was indeed that enterprising and successful journal that was scattering largesse among rose growers, in the twin causes of interesting its readers and increasing its fame.

Unfortunately, the rose Joseph entered already had a name. It was 'Mme Edouard Herriot', who was the wife of the Mayor of Lyon. The rose was of a remarkable coral colour, and although the flowers were thin, they were spectacular.

When the judging took place, the entry from Pernet-Ducher was clearly in the lead, so much so that beside it there was none other in serious consideration. Then came the difficulty with the name. No pressure could persuade Joseph to change it. How could he treat the wife of his city's mayor in such a way? The *Daily Mail* was obliged to compromise with 'Mme Edouard Herriot or the Daily Mail Rose'. For once Baron Northcliffe did not get his own way.

Monsieur Herriot subsequently became France's Prime Minister.

Claudius, a patriotic Frenchman, became an officer in the military reserve. He

9. Rosarians in London, May 1912. Back four (l. to r.): A. Lamesch (Luxembourg), E. Gurney Hill (USA), Pierre Guillot (France), George Paul (England). Row of five (l. to r.): Mlle Pernet, Joseph Pernet-Ducher (France), Alexander Dickson II (Ireland), A. Soupert (Luxembourg), Adolph Farenwald (USA; he was President of the American Rose Society). Two standing front left: Peter Lambert (Germany), Mlle Guillot (France).
From the Rose Annual 1913, *by permission of the Royal National Rose Society*

was well liked by his English friends, who quizzed him about his father's methods. How, for example, could he be sure of the parentage? Did not insects fertilize the blooms in between the times of preparation and pollination?

He explained that this was prevented by a paper cone, which one slipped over the flower when its petals and stamens were removed. The cone was kept in place by a label strung round its lower end. One replaced the cone for a week or two after pollination, and the label was for the purpose of noting the pollen parent.

What about that famous Pernet-Ducher red rose, 'Château de Clos Vougeot'? Was there not some uncertainty about its parents?

Claudius smiled, and said that his father's paper work was not in every case as carefully tended as his roses.

One of his English friends described him as 'the beloved son'.

There was a rumour that Claudius fell in love with Marie, grand-daughter of the famous rose breeder Jean-Baptiste Guillot. Joseph and Pierre Guillot had quarrelled over some trifle, and then foolishly allowed the disagreement to grow into enmity. When the wedding was proposed, Joseph was inflexible. He would

41

not give his consent. This story was brought home from a visit to Lyon by the American rose grower, E. Gurney Hill.

Joseph Pernet-Ducher was fifty-six years of age; he had been a rose grower for forty-four of them, the head of his firm for thirty-three. The roses he had bred were the joy of mankind around the world. He had brought entirely new genes into garden roses. His sons were fine young men, his wife was still by his side, as were his three daughters. His business was prosperous and confidently efficient; when he advertised a new rose, he would offer: 'Samples Flowers will be sent free on application throughout all the European Continent.'

Honours and awards for his roses must have filled a large chest. He himself was made Chevalier de la Légion d'Honneur.

His career was at its peak. He had sons to follow him. The future was bright.

On Monday, 3 August, 1914, Germany declared war on France, and in a short time forced a way through Luxembourg and Belgium, on the way to Paris. It must have seemed like 1870 all over again. Claudius, too impatient to wait for the reserve to be called up, enlisted as a soldier of the 159th Infantry Regiment; and Georges joined the 357th. The government left Paris for Bordeaux on 2 September. Général Gallieni, who was military governor of Paris, sent his 'army of Paris' to the front in taxi-cabs.

Claudius Pernet was mortally wounded on 23 October, 1914, at St Laurent-les-Arras. The Germans had tried to break through, with the intention of isolating the British; but the French stood fast, and finally drove them back. Claudius died in hospital at Douai on 25 October, at the age of thirty-two, and was provisionally buried there.

Georges Pernet fell in the face of the enemy during the assault of La Fontenelle, in Vosges, after ten months of the war. He was twenty-eight.

Their grief-stricken parents, and their sisters Angèle, Marie and Louise, sent out a notice of this 'cruel loss' on 2 August, 1915. It ended with the words, 'Priez pour Eux!'

After the war, Joseph commemorated his sons with roses. 'Souvenir de Claudius Pernet' was a yellow rose, introduced in 1920. It was popular in countries with good climates, and became an important parent. 'Souvenir de Georges Pernet' was orange-pink. Both won Gold Medals at Bagatelle.

In 1924, he arranged for Jean Gaujard to take over the business. He died and was buried in November, 1928, at the age of sixty-nine.

Years before, they had called him the magician, and the Wizard of Lyon. The best evidence of his character he provided himself, when asked to address the International Rose Conference in London in 1912. Instead of claiming credit for his achievements, he contented himself by paying a tribute to Henry Bennett. It was Bennett who had shown him the way. Bennett's roses were the foundation of his breeding stock.

He, the Wizard of Lyon, knew little of science and genetics. He relied solely on his intuition.

4

Dickson

The Dickson Saga, we might call this, for it is the story of six generations of a family which, like many others, had migrated from Scotland — Perth in this instance — and settled in Ireland. They became Ulstermen and women.

An Ulsterman is a breed apart, neither English nor Scottish nor Irish. His more obvious ancestral qualities were industry, thrift and determination. These, having been exposed to an Emerald-Isle change, were overlaid with imagination, quick wits and charm, with the result, as history shows, of an outpouring of talented people disproportionate to so small a territory. The immigrants have absorbed great qualities from their chosen land, but have generally managed, whether intelligent or not, to preserve their obstinacy in virgin state.

Heaven defend us from ill-considered generalities! To illuminate the Dicksons I have tried to explain the stock they belong to, in elementary terms, with the benefit of having lived in their country for some years.

Alexander Dickson was born in Scotland in 1801. In Northern Ireland, he obtained employment in the gardens of Grey Abbey, and married a young lady by the name of McGredy. They had two rose-growing sons: George, who was born in 1832, and Hugh. Alexander started into business on his own account in 1836.

The family had settled in Newtownards, County Down. It was a charming town, elegantly laid out in the seventeenth century with wide streets, and situated at the northern tip of the peaceful and beautiful Strangford Lough. One could look over the fertile Irish landscape to the Mountains of Mourne. It was a splendid place to start a nursery, a sweet frame for the pretty flowers they grew, the sweet peas, dahlias, pansies, tulips and gladioli. The soft Irish rain made the plants grow like Jack's beanstalk, and the rich market of Belfast was only ten miles away to the west.

During the nineteenth century, Belfast was growing quickly; it was a town with an appetite for the flowers, vegetables and plants that nurserymen such as Alexander Dickson could send to market. Its developing industries, of which the most important were making linen and building ships, were owned by people of wealth, who lived in fine mansions, with estates and gardens to be filled with the best plants money could buy. In matters of horticulture, Ulster was one of the most sophisticated and skilful communities in the world.

There was a culpable difference between the rhododendron parks of the rich, and the rows of meanly built houses in which the labourers dwelt. Just a little more room would have given much more comfort; to save the extra cost, the families were instead confined and cramped.

The two boys, George and Hugh, learned the nursery business at their father's heels as a matter of growing up, and they learned it so well that in 1853 they became partners in the firm, which from that date was entitled Alexander Dickson & Sons. When Alexander died, the business was safely established, and the sons were well able to continue it, but Hugh decided to have a nursery of his own. He therefore withdrew in 1869, receiving one third of the value of the old business, with which he set up his new one in Belfast; a great success he made of it, but that is another story.

George Dickson was a man who welcomed ideas and people with enthusiasm. He must have saved himself a good part of his wages bill, because he had four sons and employed them all in the nursery. The eldest was Alexander, born in 1857. He entered the business in 1872, and it will perhaps aid clarity if we call him Alexander II. He and his brother George, whom we had better enter as George II, are the two out of the four brothers of interest to us, because of their future work in roses.

Roses had been just one of the nursery's many crops, but over the years and in response to the excitement of the public, Dicksons found themselves growing more and more. They propagated the roses both under glass, mainly by grafting, and in the open field. The method in the field was to plant under-stocks in rows twenty-seven inches apart. The under-stocks were usually cuttings of briar or 'Manettii' and, when the example of Monsieur Guillot became known, briar seedlings. These under-stocks were planted in spring, budded in summer at ground level; cut off, with a knife, just above the point of budding the following spring: and hey presto! a field of roses was in bloom a few months later, and ready to sell that autumn. It is the method practised, with some refinements, up to this day.

Dicksons had no idea of becoming rose breeders, because everyone knew the British climate would not allow it. One might as well try to produce Burgundy in Newtownards as breed roses. Both tasks were left for the sun-favoured French.

The falsity of this notion was apparent when Henry Bennett showed his 'Pedigree Hybrids of the Tea Rose' in London. He first exhibited some of them in 1878, whereupon George Dickson, ever receptive to new ideas, promptly started breeding roses in 1879. If a Wiltshire farmer could do it, so also could an expert Ulster nurseryman.

George and his two rose-minded sons became engrossed in this new venture, in the idea that they could determine the progeny by selecting its parents, so virtually creating new and better roses. They started in a small way, with a few of the best existing roses, which proved a dismal failure. They made the surprising discovery that their results were better with those sorts they considered second best. The best variety was not necessarily the best parent.

It had seemed a good idea to marry kinds of the same colour, in the hope

10. George Dickson I, 1832–1914. 'One of the most successful pioneers'.
From the Rosarian's Year-Book 1891, *by permission of the Royal National Rose Society*

of improving each. Alexander II reported, with regret, that 'the results were anything but what we had arranged for.'

Seven years later, in 1886, Alexander II took Dickson's 'First Set of Pedigree
Seedlings' (yes, they pinched Bennett's grand word, 'pedigree') to London.

The set consisted of three varieties which were first offered for sale in 1887,
the beginning, had the rose world known, of a river of beauty which would still
be flowing from Newtownards a hundred years on. All three were well received,
especially the red Hybrid Perpetual named 'Earl of Dufferin' after the Viceroy
of India. The others were 'Lady Helen Stewart', also red; and 'Miss Ethel Brown-
low', a pink Tea.

The 'Second Set of Pedigree Seedlings' followed in 1888; and so on each year
until 1892 when, owing to an unexpected business deal, they had nothing ready,
and announced that they were postponing introductions until 1893, 'to more
thoroughly test our Seedling Roses — so that our name may be identified with
Sterling Novelties only.' They were raising about 3,000 seeds per year about this
time. The rose field was now big enough to accommodate 200,000 root-stocks,
in other words going up towards ten acres.

11. Alexander Dickson II, born 1857. One of the sons of George Dickson, here aged about 38. He appears later in life in the photograph of Rosarians in London, page 41.
From the Rosarian's Year-Book 1896, *by permission of the Royal National Rose Society*

In response to their first failures, and as a result of their observations, Alexander II and George II evolved a system of in-breeding. It may briefly be explained by saying that a cross of Mother × Father = Seedling was followed by four more crosses, namely Mother × Seedling; Father × Seedling; Seedling × Mother; Seedling × Father. From the progeny, those nearest the ideal were selected, and the process was continued, if the line appeared promising, and within the limits of reasonable quantity.

This policy made a mockery of their published parentages, which they announced in a simplified form. For example, their white 'Mildred Grant' (1901) was stated to be from 'Niphetos' × 'Mme Mélanie Willermoz'. In fact, Alexander II admitted it arose from a seedling of those two roses, crossed with another seedling.

The younger Dicksons were hard-headed when it came to business. They were tempted to explore rose breeding out of scientific curiosity, but confined themselves to the practical business of trying to raise varieties they could sell.

46

Their father, George, quite carried away by the new science, endeavoured to cross summer and winter flowering heathers, by keeping the pollen of the one until the other was in bloom. He sealed it in goose quills.

They described their work in contradictory terms. It was a 'science of pure experiment'. It was 'chance'. It was 'a systematic course of in-breeding'. The only thing they could be sure of was 'the absolute uncertainty of what our results would be'.

One can scent Ulster in those statements, the Dicksons getting an idea in their heads one fine morning, pursuing it for the fun of it, convincing themselves by bedtime, and doing the same thing tomorrow with a contradictory notion.

Alexander II married, and became the proud father of George III. In 1893 another son was born and, out of habit, one supposes, became Alexander III. The third son was named Thomas.

In 1892, they showed a pink Hybrid Tea rose, 'Mrs W. J. Grant', and were immediately awarded the National Rose Society's Gold Medal for it. This rose was of interest for several reasons. It was the first Hybrid Tea to win the Gold Medal, the first of note to be bred from 'La France', allowing that Dicksons were right in saying it came from 'La France' × 'Lady Mary Fitzwilliam'. It had a magnificent flower, but such poor growth that keen exhibitors budded it every year, to cut flowers from maiden bushes, reckoning that by its second year it would already be fading away. Finally, it embroiled Dicksons in some of the odium which had been familiar to their great exemplar, Henry Bennett.

This happened, much as in Bennett's case, because an American nursery, Siebrecht and Wadley of New York, made an offer for the entire stock, successfully tempting the Dicksons. 'Mrs W. J. Grant' was wafted away from the eager English exhibitors, across the Atlantic, where it was renamed 'Belle Siebrecht'. Dicksons did not offer it in England until 1895, which, said Mr A. Piper, was 'adverse fortune, which would not have occurred had the raisers kept this grand Rose in their own hands.'

Loyally following their agreement, they advertised it in 1895 as 'Belle Siebrecht', but the National Rose Society were not having that. They 'naturally restored the original name under which it had been shown and received the Medal'; Dicksons had to conform, and in 1897 'Mrs W. J. Grant' appeared in their list once more, and remained there a surprising time, considering its weakness.

As the century neared its close, it was plain that the decision to breed roses had transformed Dicksons from a little Ulster nursery into a national pride. No longer was Britain almost entirely dependent on Frenchmen for new roses; she could now, thanks chiefly to Dicksons, produce as good or better. The continentals were often content with colour, and would accept a bright rose of poor form; not so the British, led by exhibitors. To them the form of the flower was its greatest beauty. Dicksons agreed with this national sentiment, and their roses were living evidence of it.

Their rose fields extended to twenty-five acres. They exported 100,000 plants to the United States. They held the Royal Warrant of Queen Victoria. In 1897, while on a state visit to the North of Ireland, the Duke and Duchess of York visited Dicksons nursery. They were the future King George V and Queen Mary.

Dicksons travelled to rose shows in England, Scotland, Wales and Ireland, by steamer and train, with all the difficulties of loading and unloading at each changing place, and of working out the time-tables for the journeys. They arrived tired and hungry and dirty, and often late, and proceeded to challenge or defeat the home growers, 'without ever putting in a flower not at its best'.

Alexander II was by now recognized as the moving spirit in the enterprise, but the strain was great and affected his health for some years. In 1895 Dicksons therefore bought some land at Uplands, Ledbury, in Herefordshire, and put in charge of it a man called Walter Drew, whose task was to grow roses for the English shows.

In 1900, Dicksons became a limited company, with George as chairman and his four sons as directors. The Ledbury branch justified itself handsomely that year, by providing flowers that won the National Rose Society's Championship. It was the first time the championship had been won by an Irish firm; up until then it had been the preserve of Messrs Paul, and Cant, and Harkness. Dicksons were to repeat this success from time to time in future years; but the Trophy, during one of its sojourns in Ireland, disappeared. It was replaced by a new one; nobody knows what became of the original.

Although Dicksons could already boast, or advertise, more Gold Medals for new roses from the National Rose Society than any other breeder, they failed to win one in 1900 for one of the most important varieties of the era. It was a red rose, 'Liberty', from 'Mrs W. J. Grant' × 'Charles J. Grahame', or at least so they said. The flowers were not big enough to please the judges, but the cut flower trade found them just right, especially in the USA, from which country Dicksons reported a 'phenomenal demand, almost 80,000 booked'.

The last years of George's life were passed in peace and success. His white beard, flowing moustache, clear eyes and complexion, bore witness to a long and healthy life. Dicksons had not abandoned their other crops in pursuit of roses, but on the contrary now had a seed warehouse in 55 Royal Avenue, Belfast; and in 1901, they opened another one at 61 Dawson Street, Dublin. Liking Dublin, they established a branch nursery at Oakley Park, Blackrock. A Dublin girl named Olivia Austin went to work at Dawson Street; she was later the mother of the author of these pages.

One great Dickson rose followed another: 'Bessie Brown' in 1899, 'Mildred Grant' in 1901, 'Lady Ashtown' in 1904, and that evidence of good taste in Newtownards, the single 'Irish Elegance' in 1905. Finally, in 1912, George's sons introduced an enormous red rose, one destined to stay at or near the top of the list for years. They named it 'George Dickson', their tribute to their father. The National Rose Society awarded him its highest honour, the Dean Hole Medal, in 1912, he being only the third recipient of it, and the first professional. The

1 (above) 'Mme Bravy' *Tea* Guillot of Pont-de-Chéruy 1848   2 (below) 'La France' *Hybrid Tea* Jean-Baptiste Guillot 1867   3 (above right) 'Grace Darling' *Hybrid Tea* Bennett 1884   4 (below right) 'Mrs John Laing' *Hybrid Perpetual* Bennett 1887

5 (above left) 'Cécile Brunner' *China* Ducher 1881   6 (left) 'Caroline Testout' *Hybrid Tea* Pernet-Ducher 1890   7 (below left) 'Antoine Rivoire' *Hybrid Tea* Pernet-Ducher 1895   8 (above) 'Soleil d'Or' *Hybrid Tea* Pernet-Ducher 1900   9 (below) 'Lyon Rose' *Hybrid Tea* Pernet-Ducher 1907

10 (above) 'Shot Silk' *Hybrid Tea* Alexander Dickson 1924   11 (below) 'Silver Lining' *Hybrid Tea* Alexander Dickson 1959   12 (above right) 'Dearest' *Floribunda* Alexander Dickson 1960 13 (below right) 'Grandpa Dickson' (Irish Gold) *Hybrid Tea* Pat Dickson 1966

14 (above) 'Precious Platinum' (Red Star) *Hybrid Tea* Pat Dickson 1974   15 (below) 'Pot o' Gold' *Hybrid Tea* Pat Dickson 1980   16 (above right) 'Peek-a-Boo' (Brass Ring) *Floribunda* Pat Dickson 1981   17 (below right) 'Beautiful Britain' *Floribunda* Pat Dickson 1983

citation described him as 'one of the most successful pioneers in the scientific hybridisation of roses'.

George died in 1914, in his 82nd year, leaving the nursery in the care of his sons, Alexander II and George II; the two similarly named sons of the former were just the right age to be soldiers. Young Alexander III, after being educated at the Coleraine Academical Institute, had been packed off to the Royal Horticultural Society's gardens at Wisley. A training at Wisley was the horticultural equivalent of a soldier going to Sandhurst. Perhaps Sandhurst would have been more use to him, because he had little time at home to show what Wisley had taught him, before he was learning how to put on puttees and slope arms in the Royal Irish Rifles.

The Great War was less stringent to the civil population and more terrible for the services than the Second World War. Dicksons introduced new roses year by year, the great ones being 'Mrs Wemyss Quin' in 1914, the best yellow rose in existence then and for many years after; the biscuit-white 'Clarice Goodacre' came in 1916, with small but quite charming blooms. Fortunate they were to be small, for even so the flower stalks could not hold them straight. 'K. of K.', semi-double and blazing red, named for Kitchener of Khartoum, came out in 1917.

By the end of the war, their English nursery had moved from Ledbury to Marks Tey, near Colchester.

When Alexander III returned from the war, almost too thin and spare and quiet to pass for a soldier, one might have thought, it was to a different Ireland. For many years the Irish had demanded independence, or Home Rule as it was called, and the British had resisted or evaded those demands, in an endeavour to keep the British Isles together as a United Kingdom. When the British were finally obliged to concede, because an unwilling Irish nation was impossible to administer, the Protestants of Northern Ireland, led by Sir Edward Carson, proved as implacably opposed to being ruled by the Irish, as the Irish were to British rule. By the outbreak of war, this had led to a shipload of arms being procured to arm the Protestants, a provisional government in Belfast, and a Home Rule Bill passed through Parliament.

The Great War suspended further action for a time, or so the British thought. But the tide that had started to flow could not be stemmed; the Easter Rising happened in Dublin in 1916; the Irish formed a parliament in Dublin after the election of December 1918, and declared their independence. The British tried to stop them, in the guerilla war associated with the Black and Tans. Eventually it was agreed that twenty-six counties should form the Irish Free State, and six of the counties of Ulster should become Northern Ireland, a part of the United Kingdom with its own parliament.

The Dicksons got on with their work, being gentle and decent people who saw nothing but trouble in politics, and who preferred to pursue their avocation of growing and breeding roses.

Alexander III was made manager in 1920, and his first big disaster was a fire, which destroyed the firm's breeding records in 1921. This was a serious loss but it relieved them from awkward questions about parentages, and it was pretty to see the blithe expressions on their faces when they blamed the fire for the lack of information, which lack even extended on occasion to varieties bred after the blaze. Alexander said that they tried to reconstitute the records, but were not very successful.

Alexander III was married in 1922, the year in which 'Betty Uprichard' was introduced. This was one of the most popular garden roses of the time, being easy to grow, with abundant flowers in lively carmine and pink. The lady herself lived nearby, and was noted for her fondness of hunting, at which she was eventually thrown from her horse and killed.

If it were possible to raise a better garden rose, Dicksons did it by introducing 'Shot Silk' in 1924. The cherry red and orange pink of it were brilliantly suggested by the name; the shiny green leaves added lustre to a truly sparkling rose.

Rose breeders are optimistic folk, with so great a trust in Nature that they expect her some day to produce a blue rose. They all hope she will have the goodness to give it to them, rather than to one of their rivals. Nature in return teases them with imitations of lilac or purple in their pink and red roses. Alexander

12. Alexander Dickson III, 1893–1975. The yellow rose 'Grandpa Dickson' was named after him.
Photo: Pat Dickson

III had found such a 'blue rose' in his seedlings; he took it to London, and showed it in 1925.

He returned, quite pleased with himself and his strange rose, to encounter stern disapproval from his father who demanded to know what Dicksons were coming to, showing such a monstrosity? The old man, for Alexander II was then a year or two short of seventy, insisted that every plant of the 'blue rose' be dug up and destroyed. He was obeyed.

At the same show, Dicksons had competed in one of the classes against an able exhibitor named Elisha J. Hicks, of Hurst, Berkshire. The judges placed Dicksons second to Mr Hicks. However, there was also a special award to the most meritorious exhibit in the show, determined by a separate team of judges, who gave it to Dicksons, so causing much amusement back in Newtownards.

The fifth generation of rose-growing Dicksons arrived in 1926, was duly named Alexander, but was called by his second name, Patrick. Perhaps this was more convenient to the family, which already had two Alexander Dicksons to distinguish. Patrick was the second child, his sister Shirley being the elder; his birth was followed by those of George and Jaçon.

The year of Pat's birth was also that of the introduction of 'Dame Edith Helen', a huge pink rose with glorious fragrance. It was named after the Marchioness of Londonderry whose estate was nearby. A rose of her name already existed, having been introduced by Dicksons in 1893 to honour a former holder of the title; to avoid having two roses of the same name, the lady chose to be known in her rosy form as 'Dame Edith Helen'. Her husband, the seventh Marquess, was to be Secretary of State for Air during the early 1930s, and to preside over the development of those country-saving aircraft, the Hurricane and Spitfire.

Alexander II retired in 1930. Of his two sons, Alexander III took over the roses and George III attended to the rest of the business, which consisted mainly of glass-houses producing carnations and other flowers for market, and the Belfast seed store, which had become a profitable shop.

The 1930s were marked by more fine Dickson roses, notably 'Barbara Richards', light in colour and of thoroughbred form, in 1930; 'Trigo', an interesting shade of orange, in 1931, named after an Irish horse that won the Derby; and 'Colonel Sharman-Crawford', a popular red rose, in 1933.

The year 1936 was their centenary, and as they had more gold medals than they knew what to do with, they caused them to be melted down, formed into golden roses, mounted, and presented with due ceremony in 1937 to the Borough of Newtownards as a mayoral chain.

Two years afterwards, the Second World War began, and not only were soldiers, sailors and airmen mobilized, but also every acre of land. Of the hundreds of thousands of rose bushes ready for sale that September, many were burned; and the under-stocks, already budded to be ready for sale in 1940–41, suffered a similar fate. The annual production was limited by governmental direction to ten per cent of what it had been, and Dicksons were directed to grow food.

The hybridizing was stopped for the duration of the war. This was a calamitous decision, as shall be seen.

Pat left school and went straightway into the Royal Ulster Rifles, from which Regiment he was posted to the Glider Pilot Regiment. He was a bright and adventurous young man; like his father he was slim and spare, a little below medium height, with brown eyes and hair. He had the energy and enthusiasm typical of the family. Fast cars and motor races were his idea of fun, and students of military matters will not be surprised that he was posted to machines without engines.

Pat left the Army in 1945 and was sent to one of the largest glass-house nurseries in the country, Lowe & Shawyer of Uxbridge, Middlesex, to learn how to grow flowers under glass, particularly carnations and chrysanthemums. In 1949, he went for a season to Walter Bentley & Sons at Wanlip, Leicester, for a summer's work in the rose fields. Bentley's grew roses to sell them wholesale to other nurseries. The man in charge of their growing operations was Ken Bentley. One of the most skilful wardens of rose soil in the business, Ken produced wonderful crops, no matter how many times he grew them on the same land. He was a large man, by nature gentle and patient.

During the war, Dicksons had relinquished their branch nursery at Marks Tey. They replaced it in 1949 with one at Stoke Goldington, Buckinghamshire, and followed the tradition started at Ledbury over half a century before by placing in charge a member of the Drew family.

Bob Drew was a fine rose grower, slow of speech but quick in thought, with a droll sense of humour. His stories took some time to arrive at their point, because he could not resist exploring each side-shoot that occurred to him. When he got to the point, it was as often as not yet another case of poor Bob getting egg on his face. This truly wonderful man was not only entrusted by Alexander III with the English nursery; he was also given the task of bringing up Pat to be a rose grower; and off to Stoke went Pat.

Dicksons soon realized that the French, Dutch and Americans had all been breeding roses during the war; and to a lesser extent, even the Germans. It was only in Britain that the business had been entirely laid aside. The cost of that sacrifice was great, because from the time breeding began again, seven years must be expected to pass before varieties were selected, tested and increased to the point of introduction. It was equivalent to giving one's foreign competitors a free lead for thirteen years. During the twentieth century, and thanks in large measure to Dicksons, British roses had dominated the home market, without excluding worthy foreign introductions. Now it was the turn of the French, with 'Peace'; the Americans, with 'Masquerade'; and the Dutch, with 'Spek's Yellow'.

Dicksons made the best of a bad job by arranging to introduce American roses in Britain. They started with the famous salmon Floribunda, 'Fashion', in 1949, a variety raised by Eugene Boerner of Jackson & Perkins. Meanwhile, Alexander III, feeling like a beginner all over again, with his ideas some years out of date, slowly and painfully rebuilt his rose breeding department.

Pat was enjoying life at Stoke Goldington. He had married a Newtownards girl named Anisley Black, and the two of them were as bright as fireworks and deeply happy in their English home. He still enjoyed cars, and maintained that you would never be had up for speeding, provided you went so fast the police wouldn't see you.

There was an old pig sty on the nursery at Stoke Goldington, and it occurred to Pat that it would serve as a lean-to glass-house, if its roof were removed and a little ingenuity used. He was soon putting roses in it, and in that small way he started his career as a rose breeder.

His first results were disastrous. He did not know how to get a crop of seed, nor how to grow it when he got it, nor how to choose parents that would make it worth growing anyway.

Pat reflected that Meilland, by his annual successes, must have the answers to all those problems. He asked the firm to pay for him to visit Meilland in the South of France.

He returned full of admiration for what he had seen; the Stoke Goldington pig sty was not in the same league. He built a better glass-house, and sought his father's advice as to which roses were best planted for parents, for in that respect he had gained little knowledge in France. This time, he was confident of success. When one is pollinating roses, one sees reasons why every cross should produce a winner.

And then, next year, one tries to reason why the winners have not arrived. This disappointment was yet again Pat's fate, and he was brave enough to find the right answer, which was to doubt the advice of that father who had been one of the leading lights of the profession. He did not express it that way, his Ulster obstinacy would not permit such a thought. His father's advice was no doubt good, and in the paternal hands would prove fruitful. The truth of the matter, he decided, was that no rose breeder should try to give effect to other people's thoughts, he must on the contrary formulate his own lines.

Pat's conclusions, although characteristically vague, were sound. Alexander III was indeed breeding good roses again, and may be forgiven the unfortunate introduction in 1955 of a pink rose which proved unworthy of its illustrious name, 'Sir Winston Churchill'. Floribundas, which had not interested him before the war, were now an important part of his work. He brought out a beauty in orange and red in 1958, with the excellent name 'Shepherd's Delight'. In the same year, he introduced the blazing orange red 'Dickson's Flame', which was the first British variety to win the supreme award for new roses, the President's International Trophy, instituted by the National Rose Society in 1952. The award was perhaps unexpected, because Dicksons had insufficient plants to supply their would-be customers, and printed an apology for the shortages in the 1959 *Rose Annual*. In that issue they offered a first class pink Hybrid Tea, 'Silver Lining'.

In 1958, Pat returned to Newtownards where he was put in charge of the rose breeding. Alexander III did not retire completely, but at the age of 65 kept his

13. Pat Dickson, born 1926.
From the Rose Annual 1972, *by permission of the Royal National Rose Society*

own breeding programme in being, as a pleasant way of passing the years. Father and son, each in his own domain, were happy rivals, learning from one another.

Pat was not so happy with the elderly glass-houses. They had been the pride of the nursery, the mothers of carnations and chrysanthemums for the flower market, of roses for Chelsea Show, and of tomatoes during the war. They had been built on low-lying ground, for warmth; the hedges and trees and buildings around them had grown too high, shutting away the refreshing currents of air, and thereby inviting botrytis to enter, to form its mould on rose hips, and to destroy them. Worse still, those members of the family responsible for the market flowers naturally demanded precedence for their crops over the roses. The flowers were positive income; the rose breeding could promise no certain profit.

Comparing Dicksons with the foreign rose breeders he had visited, and with whom he was in competition, Pat concluded that he might as well enter a pre-war Rover of sedate and gentle character in the next Grand Prix. It was essential to build a new nursery and to dispose of the old one.

In the matter of profit from rose breeding, his brothers had a good point. The business had changed. Before the war, when Dickson and McGredy were the great breeders, roses were cheap, and in such abundance that most growers were resigned to a nasty bonfire of unsold plants at the end of the season. The advantage Dickson and McGredy had out of their own breeding was large numbers of plants at a higher price than their rivals could command on their stocks of older varieties.

After the war, such was the demand for roses that there were no more bonfires. The higher prices were no longer the privilege of British breeders, but of those firms who introduced foreign roses, prominent among them Wheatcroft of Nottingham; and only then for a short time, because the varieties were being circulated with amazing speed by Dutch and British propagators. The period in which a rose breeder could benefit from his variety was whittled away by those propagators, who needed only a plant or two, in order to supply the whole trade with propagating wood the following summer.

Unless there was some prospect of a definite profit from new roses, it might well be better to use the glass-houses in other ways.

Pat, who had been brought up by Alexander III and Bob Drew, defended his roses. He made plans for the new nursery. He travelled abroad, both to learn and to engage foreign agents to introduce Dickson's varieties, and to pay him royalties. He became a propagandist in Britain for some form of rose copyright or patent, such as authors and inventors enjoy.

When the results of Pat's first crosses were in flower, they showed that the lines he had chosen were promising. Pretty apricot and orange roses were there in plenty. Good, strong plants were growing. Absent, admittedly, were the huge flowers of perfect form in the Dickson tradition; but as those blooms were notable for having very little bush beneath them, Pat was pleased to have his own strain without them. He felt quite proud, and fetched his father to see them.

They walked through the roses, and stopped at a bright orange Floribunda. Alexander III shook his head, and said: 'Your grandfather would consider beauty of form to be of more importance than colour. Nowadays all that people ask for is bright colours.'

Pat admitted himself 'dazzled by colour, but not blind to form'. He was never allowed to forget the family tradition.

When he went away on his visits, his path was marked by parties and laughter and high spirits. If Pat Dickson were in the company, and most of all if the Speks of Boskoop were also present, it was headaches all round the next morning; some expert witnesses doubted whether Jan Spek's head ever ached, arguing that he was impermeable to all libations. The Jan Spek nursery acted as testing station, propagator and Dutch agent for the Dicksons. Jan's son, Hette Spek, became one of Pat's closest friends, one to rely on for sound common sense, good advice, honest dealing and laughter. There was the day Jan Spek met Pat in Amsterdam, driving a new Citroën, and before they went to bed next morning, a pig had walked through the windscreen.

Plant Breeders' Rights were passed by Parliament in 1964, in time, fortunately for Pat, to catch his varieties in full tide. He introduced 'Sea Pearl', shell pink with peach, in 1964, a Floribunda of excellent form. His 'Scented Air', 1965, was less popular, owing to its colour being half way between red and salmon; but it was a plant with superb bushy growth.

In 1966, Pat achieved his outstanding triumph, with a large yellow Hybrid Tea of noble form. It battled for the highest honour in the Royal National Rose Society's trials, and after a close contest with its rival, which was 'Ernest H. Morse', it received the President's International Trophy. It was named 'Grandpa Dickson', after Alexander III, who was indeed a Grandpa by this time, nine times over. Pat and Anisley had contributed two in the persons of Colin and Adrian.

'Red Devil' followed in 1967, the perfect example of the traditional Dickson flower on the modern Pat Dickson plant. It was so successful in the hands of exhibitors, that people got quite tired of seeing it looking so insufferably good and unbeatable all up and down the show benches. It was a wartime name; airborne soldiers of the British Army were called 'Red Devils'.

The best red rose in the world is what every breeder hopes to raise, a dark one, with scent. It is difficult to find the ideal. 'Crimson Glory' brought true contentment in the 1930s, and 'Ena Harkness' in the 1940s, but all the others have fallen short. Pat set out to breed one on a strong plant, and although he introduced 'Red Planet' in 1970 and 'Precious Platinum' in 1974, for all their virtues they are not the end of the search.

There followed a strange hiatus in Pat's breeding, a time when, if there was some accident that could befall his seed pods or his seedlings, it duly happened. The new nursery was established at Milecross Road, and the rose breeding moved to it. Nearby, Pat built himself a house. The administration of plant breeders' rights was a continual headache, the more so as the nation's industry had over-reached itself by producing far too many bushes, with a disastrous effect on prices.

In 1972, Pat took action to remove one worry, by suggesting to other breeders that they should co-operate in administering their rights. Alec Cocker, of Aberdeen, and I both responded. We three met in Alec Cocker's house to spend some days in conference, the result of which was the British Association of Rose Breeders, founded in 1973. Pat was its first President, serving for five years, and he imbued it with his sense of honour and his willingness to work for the common good.

Alexander III died at home on 15 October, 1975, aged 82. He held the Dean Hole Medal of the Royal National Rose Society, the Victoria Medal of Honour of the Royal Horticultural Society and the honorary degree of Master of Arts (Agriculture), which had been conferred upon him by Queen's University, Belfast.

The rose trade was still struggling with the difficulties brought about by over-production, and Dicksons were not exempt from them. Their plight was worse than that of their English and Scottish rivals.

Everybody knows the trouble there has been in Northern Ireland, although few can sort out the rights and wrongs of it, and nobody can at present propound a solution satisfactory to all parties. What can truthfully be said is that most people, whether Irish, Northern Irish or British, are disgusted by murder. Among British gardeners, many were so disgusted that, failing to distinguish between the innocent and the guilty, they damned all things Irish and stopped ordering roses from Ireland; they bought them from English or Scottish nurseries instead.

Dicksons were in a quandary. Jaçon and George were running a profitable retail business which would keep them comfortably, were it not making good the losses from Pat's roses. The answer was to split. Let Pat keep the roses, and make what he could of them.

The split took place, not without bruised feelings. Pat's firm became Dickson Nurseries Ltd. He continued to grow roses for a few years, but eventually decided to make his living as a rose breeder, using the spare glass-houses for shrubs and ground cover plants for sale to local authorities in Ireland.

This left him without a retail firm to advertise and show his varieties; to supply this deficiency, he came to an agreement with R. Harkness & Co of Hitchin.

Good new roses were coming again, after the lean years of so much difficulty. The free flowering salmon 'Memento' in 1978; the lovely yellow 'Pot o' Gold' in 1980; a charmer and delight in 1981, 'Peek-a-Boo', which is a small, compact bush, its apricot pink flowers opening thimble-sized; and in 1983, the orange-red 'Beautiful Britain', voted Rose of the Year by the professional growers.

In the hybridizing house, Colin is now at work, young, studious, industrious, a quiet Dickson like his grandfather. Dicksons are back as the leading British rose breeders. The principal awards in 1983 went to Newtownards, practically lock, stock and barrel. And from what I have seen over there, the best is yet to come.

Let Anisley add a postscript about Ireland. She has had a hard battle with her health, and more than once Pat's face has been grey with the fear of losing her.

'There I was in hospital,' she says, 'where there's always some poor soul worse off than yourself, and you fall in the way of companionship, until those who were strangers the day before turn into friends.

'Three of us, there were, used to spend the time together. One was a Roman Catholic priest from the Republic, and the other poor body was out of the poor part of the town, her husband as vigorous an Orangeman as you ever heard of.

'After a time, the priest told us he was being sent home, and although he did not speak it, we knew they could do nothing for him. Before he left, he says,

' "You've been good company, and I wonder if you ladies would like to join me in a wee prayer before I go?"

'So we agreed, although neither the two of us was much practised in praying, and there's him crossing himself, and us joining in, and when we'd done the Orangeman's wife looks at him and says,

' "And God bless you too, Father, if my old man hears of this he will give me a right thumping."

'The pair of them are both dead now, dear love them.'

5

McGredy

Samuel McGredy knew that promotion was all in the past for him. He had risen by arduous steps to the highest post his world had to offer. He was the head gardener.

As such, he commanded his little company of men and boys absolutely. He created the beauty of his domain, walks of azaleas, drifts of snowdrops; his glass-houses provided peaches and grapes for the house, flowers for the lady, button-holes for the master, cucumbers for the cook. His ears listened with deep respect to the horticultural hopes of his employers, and his wits circumvented those which were unsound.

He was fifty years old, and saw his future clearly. He could continue as head gardener until he was too old to work any longer, when he could retire with the uncertain hope that the money he had saved would support him during the remainder of his journey to the grave.

Or he could pack in his safe job, become his own master, and risk losing the security he had.

He had been born in 1828 and had two children, Samuel and Dorothy. They were now old enough to live their own lives; young Samuel, having arrived in 1861, was seventeen, growing into a big, enthusiastic man. It was a consideration that the boy's prospects in life would be all the better if between them father and son could establish a nursery of their own.

These thoughts led him to take up a lease on ten acres of ground just outside the town of Portadown. There was a small glass-house on the property. The firm of Samuel McGredy & Son, Nurserymen, opened there in 1880, their specialities being fruit trees and bushes, and show pansies.

In those days, pansies were much favoured. Pansy Societies organized exhibitions, at which the size, outline, flatness and markings of the flowers were the points in which excellence was seen. There were several hundred named varieties.

Portadown is on the river Bann, in County Armagh, about twenty-five miles south-west of Belfast. For a nurseryman's business, it had two great advantages: fertile soil and a railway. The first grew the plants, and the second transported them rapidly to Dublin and Belfast.

Samuel McGredy's decision was the right one. The former head gardener became respected in the community, being appointed a Justice of the Peace. When he died in 1903, he left behind him a good business, a son who was to become famous in the profession, and a small grandson six years of age.

14. Sam McGredy I, 1828–1903. *From the* Rose Annual 1951, *by permission of the Royal National Rose Society*

The second Sam McGredy had realized during his father's life that roses promised to be better business than pansies had ever been. The reason was simple: Hybrid Teas, and especially 'Caroline Testout'. This modern kind of rose was proof that everyman could enjoy beautiful roses in abundance and at low cost, however small his plot.

The McGredys, who had previously dealt in roses grown by other nurserymen, began to grow their own.

There was also the annoyance of the Dicksons, over in Newtownards, who had started breeding roses and were making quite a name for it. Unsure of finding his way in this new art, Sam McGredy made a modest start at breeding roses about 1895, regarding it as more of a hobby than serious business; he raised two or three hundred seedlings a year.

He married Margaret Davison, who bore a daughter, Ethel, a son, Samuel Davison, in 1897, and a second daughter, Ivy.

This man, with his young family at home, and the green fields and hills of Ulster assuring him that the world was beautiful and good, responded in full measure. He was exuberantly optimistic, as Adam would have been if he had seen the Garden of Eden the day before he was sent there. Nothing was ordinary, nor was anything accepted without comment; on the contrary, it was 'Did you ever see the like of that, now?' Laughter, delight and enthusiasm burst out of him, and surrounded those in his company with his own high spirits.

The two or three hundred seedlings a year gradually increased, as Sam began to see promise in his new roses, and to realize he might be in this business with some hope after all. It was galling, of course, to throw away hundreds for each one that seemed worth keeping, but that was the nature of the job. At last, in 1905, after about ten years' work, he decided to exhibit a few of his best ones in London, where new roses competed for that mark of excellence and approval, the Gold Medal of the National Rose Society. He would go to the show in hope rather than expectation.

Then began an experience which was to occur throughout his life, of cutting the flowers, travelling to the show, fussing over the boxes at each loading and unloading point, feeding porters with silver to ensure gentle handling, putting up his blooms on the show bench and then retiring while the judges cast their cold eyes over his roses. After the anxious wait, back into the hall, and joy of joys! Sam McGredy on his first venture won a Gold Medal for his salmon pink rose 'Countess of Gosford'.

The delight he showed was later described as 'unbounded'; he made no attempt to conceal it. Why should one hide a rejoicing heart? It was more his nature to wrap his happiness around everybody he encountered.

From that day, rose breeding was the main purpose of his life. He had to run the business, which depended on many kinds of plants; he loved his family; he had his hobbies, among which was the breeding of fox terriers; and his interests, among them freemasonry, which in Portadown in those days suggested one was at least sympathetic to the Unionist cause.

His breeding was done by growing his seed parents in pots, in a glass-house, heated so as to produce flowers in March and April. The flowers were emasculated and fertilized, and the hips were kept in peat or sand over winter. Early in the new year, the seeds were sown in large pots, and when they were about two inches high, they were transferred each to its own two-inch pot in which it could be expected to flower when about six inches high. From these flowers, the first selections were made, by discarding, or holding, or propagating.

Mildew killed many of the seedlings at the potting stage and was a sore trial to Sam, until he evolved his own cure for it. He named it 'Kuremil' and advertised it in his positive and optimistic way, without any cautious qualification: 'A Certain Preventative and Guaranteed Cure ... This Preparation, which we Guarantee, will prevent and cure Mildew on Roses grown outdoors or under glass, as well as ALL other plants subject to this disease.'

Such extravagant statements came from conviction, although they would more likely lead to it today, and from a wonder at every shining new thing the next glorious day would bring. His advertisements for his new roses were in similar style. In 1912, 'British Queen' was 'the finest white Rose in existence', but not for long, because he had 'Florence Forrester' to offer in 1914, and that was 'the grandest of all whites.'

'For 1915 we propose issuing the THREE most wonderful Roses the world has yet seen. Nothing to compare with these has yet been produced by any raiser, and we believe when known they will be regarded as the three greatest Novelties of the Century.'

The three, 'National Emblem', 'Cheerful' and 'Mrs Franklin Dennison', were succeeded twelve months later by five varieties for 1916: 'Nothing finer has ever been issued.' All eight were soon to be forgotten.

I am sure he believed every word at the time, and he infected others with his enthusiasm for roses. He was as generous with his praise of other men's roses as of his own, as on the occasion in September 1919, when he went with Courtney Page, Secretary of the National Rose Society, to see 'Mermaid' at William Paul & Sons of Waltham Cross. After looking at 'Mermaid', on a dewy morning of autumn mist, the Ulsterman turned to Arthur Paul, and said,

'I have seen the sight of my life, it's simply magnificent. I would not have missed it on any account.'

There spoke Sam McGredy. How much better a life it was, if as many things in it as possible were magnificent. What better appreciation of God's gifts could there be, than to be thrilled with every one of them?

He was the man, his contemporaries avowed, who was seen sitting absolutely still, staring at one rose for a full half hour.

He won Gold Medals regularly; among the great roses he introduced were the white 'Mrs Herbert Stevens', 1910; the yellow 'Golden Emblem' (Mildew proof!), 1917; and in 1918, the yellow 'Christine', the orange 'Emma Wright' and, in red and yellow, 'The Queen Alexandra Rose', the latter 'by special request named after our beloved Queen Alexandra'. She was the Royal Patron of the National Rose Society.

Emma Wright was to marry Fred Morse, of the Norwich rose growing firm, Henry Morse & Sons, with whom Sam was on friendly terms. He used to call her 'Mrs Emma Very Right But Not Always'.

He went to a show in Norwich in July 1919, with flowers of several good varieties, including 'Mrs Henry Morse', of which he claimed he had 'never raised or sent out a Rose with a feeling of greater pride.' The show was not without its difficulties. The hundred miles to Dublin, the steamer to Holyhead, the train to Euston, the motor to Liverpool Street and the train to Norwich conspired to set him down at the show at 12.30. Judging was at 1.30. Those exhibitors who had finished their work came to lend a hand. Courtney Page recorded: '. . . it was an interesting sight to see amateurs and nurserymen vying with each other arranging his novelties, while he calmly sat looking on.'

The volunteer helpers did very well for him, winning three Gold Medals and three Certificates of Merit. One of each was won by Dicksons, and as nobody else won anything at all, Ulster scooped the pool. One of the Gold Medals at

15. Sam McGredy II, 1861–1926. 'The Irish Wizard'.
From the Rose Annual 1922, *by permission of the Royal National Rose Society*

Norwich went appropriately to 'Mrs Henry Morse', a pink rose which had a very good run, until mildew finished it. Another was won by 'Mrs Charles Lamplough', a white rose with enormous blooms, which won prizes for exhibitors for many years; this rose was an important parent for Sam, producing, among many other famous roses, 'McGredy's Yellow'.

Sam's parentages, however, were not as simple as they seemed because, like Dicksons, he used many of his own seedlings. For example, 'Mrs Herbert Stevens' was supposed to be bred from 'Frau Karl Druschki' × 'Niphetos', that information being considered a fair enough guide to the general public. In fact, Sam admitted, it was only indirectly from 'Niphetos'; it was the result of six crosses with his own seedlings.

He was awarded the National Rose Society's Dean Hole Medal in 1921. Back in Portadown, he had become like his father, a Justice of the Peace. The rose world dubbed him 'The Irish Wizard'.

About this time, he was raising approximately 17,000 seedlings a year. The firm, in its advertisements, claimed to grow over 500,000 roses annually. In addition to roses, they issued catalogues of seeds, bulbs, fruit, shrubs, greenhouse plants and herbaceous plants.

After the show at Norwich, he got the reputation of sitting on his boxes and watching his friends and helpers stage his blooms. It was said that he got more pleasure from seeing others do it, than in doing it himself. However, the truth may be different. Shows are tiring occasions, and after a serious illness in 1922, he was probably glad to take things more easily. Sitting on a box while one's exhibit goes up is a great vantage point for meeting friends, journalists and customers, for having what Ulstermen call a 'good crack'.

Sam McGredy died suddenly in April 1926, while some of his finest roses still awaited introduction. His popularity is proved by the volunteers who helped him, as at Norwich, his skill by the roses he bred. He won the reputation of being a sporting and unselfish exhibitor, who enjoyed success but never grumbled at failure. The *Rose Annual*, in mourning his death, described him as 'one of the finest, most straightforward and conscientious Rosarians that ever walked'.

At this time, his son, Samuel Davison McGredy, was aged twenty-nine, and full of vigour and enterprise. He married Ruth Darragh, and in due time they had three children, Molly, Paddy and Samuel Darragh, who was born in 1932.

Under the third Sam McGredy, the firm expanded its production of rose plants, going up to 800,000 per year by 1928, and subsequently to a million, which would fill about forty acres of ground.

16. Sam McGredy III, 1897–1934.
From the Rose Annual 1951, *by permission of the Royal National Rose Society*

They had never, under Sam II, attached their own name to a rose, but that policy was changed in 1927, upon the introduction of 'Margaret McGredy', who was the mother of the third Sam. Thereafter the word McGredy frequently appeared in their rose names.

'Margaret McGredy', a carmine and yellow rose, was an excellent grower, but its colour and form lacked the appeal necessary for high public favour. It was a gift from McGredy to the rose world, because Meilland soon employed it, and in due time raised 'Peace' as a result.

The rose trade came to McGredy's assistance in September 1927, when the Portadown firm was late arriving at the Autumn Show in London, due to a delay on the railway. Their business rivals and competitors first agreed to an extension of the time allowed for staging, then helped to arrange their flowers, and did it so well that McGredy beat them all.

In 1928, the National Rose Society invited rose breeders to send plants to their trial ground at Haywards Heath. This was an important development of the Society's work and was well supported, for the rose breeders of the world submitted 279 varieties, of which eighty-two came from McGredy. A notable omission from the list of senders was the other great Ulster firm of Dickson, who did not overcome their mistrust of the trials until after the Second World War. When the first awards of Trial Ground Certificates were announced, in 1930, McGredy received twenty-four of them. The trial ground was helpful to them in discovering varieties which looked much better in England than in Ireland. It was responsible for bringing some good varieties on the market, which they might otherwise not have reached, among them the pink 'Picture', 1932.

Sam McGredy, having named a rose after his mother, naturally sought one for his wife, and showed her a few varieties he had in mind. She turned them all down, and indicated the one she would prefer, which the men apparently thought less of. It was a coppery pink rose destined to become famous under the name 'Mrs Sam McGredy'. It was introduced in 1929, the same year as the long petalled 'McGredy's Ivory'.

In 1933, they introduced one of the most beautiful of all, 'McGredy's Yellow'; with strange hesitancy, for their advertisement declared, '... the King of Yellows in our Rose grounds for the past twelve years.'

These were great days, in which the work of Sam II reached its climax in the hands of Sam III. Even the hobby of breeding fox terriers continued, and not content with roses and dogs, Sam III also bred budgerigars and parakeets.

Then, suddenly he had a heart attack, and died in November, 1934. He was only thirty-eight.

This calamity left the firm without a Sam McGredy to lead it, until the fourth one, then two years old, should come of age. A board of four trustees was appointed to run the firm until that time.

It was fortunate that Ivy, the sister of Sam III, had married a man named Walter Johnston. He proved able to take control of the business, and to discharge

18 (above left) 'The Queen Alexandra Rose' *Hybrid Tea* Sam McGredy II 1918   19 (below left) 'Picture' *Hybrid Tea* Sam McGredy II 1932   20 (above) 'Piccadilly' *Hybrid Tea* Sam McGredy IV 1959   21 (below) 'Elizabeth of Glamis' (Irish Beauty) *Floribunda* Sam McGredy IV 1964

22 (above left) 'Handel' *Climber* Sam McGredy IV 1965   23 (left) 'Sue Lawley' *Floribunda* Sam McGredy IV 1980   24 (above) 'Snow Carpet' *Miniature* Sam McGredy IV 1980   25 (below) 'Olympiad' *Hybrid Tea* Sam McGredy IV 1983

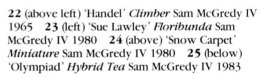

26 (above left) 'Dorothy Perkins' *Rambler*
Miller 1901   27 (left) 'Masquerade' *Floribunda*
Boerner 1949   28 (below left) 'Aloha'
Climber Boerner 1949   29 (above) 'Spartan'
Floribunda Boerner 1955   30 (below) 'Evening
Star' *Floribunda* Warriner 1974

31 (left) 'Moonlight' *Hybrid Musk* Pemberton 1913
32 (below left) 'Vanity' *Hybrid Musk* Pemberton
1920   33 (above) 'Penelope' *Hybrid Musk*
Pemberton 1924   34 (below) 'Cornelia' *Hybrid
Musk* Pemberton 1925

his trust with exemplary honour and efficiency. It is no discredit to any of the trustees, one of whom was the recently widowed Ruth McGredy, that the breeding began to be less successful. It takes a practised eye to be a rose breeder. Had the reverse been true, it would have suggested that anyone could do it.

They made a mistake in 1937, by seeking to commemorate 'the late Sam McGredy, Senior' by a huge light honey-coloured rose, 'Sam McGredy'. It would admittedly produce as large a flower as the rosarian could expect to see, but on the most miserable of bushes. When the next Sam McGredy grew up, he termed it 'an absolute dud, which should never have been given that name.'

As with other British rose nurseries, the Second World War obliged McGredys to burn roses and grow vegetables; there were mushrooms in the packing sheds and tomatoes in the glass-houses; after the war, Walter Johnston and his team brought the roses back into production again, with great sighs of relief. The trustees' task had run most of its course; it remained to be seen whether Samuel Darragh McGredy would join the firm, and whether he would be up to the job.

Young Sam had gone to boarding school at Enniskillen in 1939, at the age of seven. The standard of education in Northern Ireland has generally been better than that in England, perhaps due to the common sense of the teachers and the taught, a matter we can leave the experts to argue. Sam grew big, strong and bright, without at first a thought of being a rose grower. He knew less of roses than most rose-growers' sons, and vaguely saw himself as a journalist.

Towards the end of his schooldays, when masters began to talk earnestly of careers, he realized that there could only be one for a Sam McGredy, and from that time nothing could tempt him away from roses.

He won an exchange scholarship, under a scheme run by the English Speaking Union, to Mercersburg Academy in Pennsylvania, where for him 1948 was a happy and useful year.

Back at home, he went to Greenmount Agricultural College in 1949, where he studied under Crosbie Cochrane, a gifted teacher, expert horticulturist and a witty, perceptive man. From there he went to Reading University, the initials of which he apparently understood to mean Rugby Union, for playing football was nearly all the good he did there, and he left without completing his finals.

It was thought that some practical nursery experience was necessary, therefore he was sent to Slocock's, a large wholesale nursery at Woking, where the great speciality was the rhododendron. He was there over winter, and could not feel much advancement to his career as he packed parcels, burned rubbish and chopped firewood.

In 1952, he reported for duty in Portadown, knowing next to nothing about roses, his qualifications being his name and his character. His Uncle Walter led him to the breeding house, gave him the keys, and told him it was all his.

The prospect was depressing. Half starved roses sat in their pots. Sam was staring at the ruins of his father's and grandfather's work, neglected over the war, pushed aside for other crops, but just kept alive for tradition's sake. He wondered what to tell his staff. He had no idea what they ought to be doing, nor how to do it.

Well, there was only one answer: tell them to carry on, and learn from them. After all, the ruins before him were the famous McGredy breeding strain. He spent his first year learning, and concluded that the old strain was in need of invigoration. He added to it some stronger varieties, including Floribundas. After two years, he looked failure in the face, failure because the old strain was played out, the methods were antiquated, the pots shoved aside at chrysanthemum time, and about 90 per cent of the seeds failed to germinate. It was time to go out and learn more. He went to Germany, and was told by Kordes to cut out all the pots. Kordes planted his seed parents in the soil (that would be one in the eye for the chrysanthemums) and sowed the seeds straight in a bench, where they were allowed to flower without being transferred to pots at all.

The next vital information was about parents. Sam had discovered it was no use to follow the existing lines, he had to strike out on his own; but he needed some sound foundations. Eugene Boerner, from America, had been visiting, and was as helpful as breeders are liable to be on this subject, which most of them classify as 'most secret'. However, the persuasive young Ulsterman extracted more information than Boerner realized.

Finally, there was the matter of seed. Gordon Rowley, of Reading University, was his probable source of information. The answer was to keep the seed at 60°F until about Christmas. Rowley's actual advice was to shell it out upon harvesting, store it in moist vermiculite in the warmth, and then put it outside in a cold frame to experience temperature variations before sowing.

Armed with all this information, Sam demanded a chrysanthemum-free house, threw out the soil and replaced it with the finest loam and manure he could get. He planted his new parents, fixed up benches for sowing. He read all he could find about roses and breeding them, even keeping rose books handy beside the lavatory.

In 1954, his seed parents were in some cases carrying two hundred hips instead of the three or four of old. He sowed a fine crop of seed from them early in 1955, saw them germinating as never before, carried out his 1955 crosses, and went off to see roses in Europe.

From this account, it is clear that a man of vigour, purpose and intelligence had joined the family firm, a man who got things done like a typhoon in a hurry. He was a commanding person even when young, and he was also fun. He did not stay long in the company of solemn, reserved or self-important people, but preferred those who would respond to his wit; he created laughter and good fellowship, on a plane that few could emulate, and when he found a fellow spirit, he formed an iron bond of friendship.

Such a man was Niels Poulsen, who met young Sam at Copenhagen airport in 1955, bearing a bunch of blue roses which turned out to be the white 'Virgo' steeped in ink. Niels and Sam were both six feet three inches in height; another friend, Reimer Kordes, was taller still. They enjoyed going around with Jan Spek, the Dutchman, who was five feet two inches.

On his return to Portadown, Sam found Uncle Walter in the seedling house, looking at 20,000 seedlings, where before he had been accustomed to a thousand or fewer, 'scratching his head in amazement'. Sam's breeding programme had taken off.

The first rose he could claim as his own was 'Salute', a cherry red and yellow Floribunda, introduced in 1958. We might say it was a ranging shot. In 1959 the Floribunda 'Orangeade' hit the Gold Medal target. In 1960 the famous red and yellow Hybrid Tea, 'Piccadilly', deserved a Gold Medal but did not get it. Sam's first President's International Trophy was awarded in 1961 for the coral salmon 'Mischief', which received its name under the following circumstances.

Sam was beside his exhibit at a National Rose Society's show, when Major-General Naylor, then the Deputy President, asked what name was intended for the salmon rose? Sam replied that it had not been decided. The General suggested Mischief, which appealed to Sam we may suppose. Some time later, Sam discovered that the General had a little terrier, of which he was very fond, and that the new McGredy rose had been named after the General's dog.

'Paddy McGredy' was a great advance in roses. Named after the younger of Sam's sisters, this 1962 introduction flowered by the bunch of large blooms on one stem. It was rose red. At this time, Sam had in his employment Bob Aylwin, formerly the public relations man of Bertram Mills' Circus. Of all the brilliant stunts Bob performed for Sam, none outshone his effort to make 'Paddy McGredy' famous. The news reader on BBC Television wore it in his button-hole, and at the end of the news told the nation it was 'Paddy McGredy', straight from Chelsea Show.

The rose may be the Queen of Flowers, but to members of the National Rose Society in Britain, one lady is the Queen of Roses, namely Her Majesty Queen Elizabeth the Queen Mother. She visited the Society's shows, acted as its Royal Patron, and probably had a hand in recommending that it become the Royal National Rose Society, which title was approved on 26 February, 1965.

The Queen Mother had given Sam permission to name a rose for her, using the name 'Elizabeth of Glamis'. Her rose won all the major honours in 1963, including the top one, the President's International Trophy. Bob Aylwin had to tailor his Bertram Mills policies to the sober mien fitting to royalty; in Britain, to use the royal family as an advertisement just simply isn't done. He made the best of it by writing the royal order on a large envelope, lest he forget it, ''72 Elizabeth of Glamis — Royal Lodge, Windsor', and carried it about the show all day, tucked under his arm in an unobtrusive way, which nevertheless failed to prevent anyone from reading it. The rose was a lovely light salmon Floribunda, bred from 'Spartan' × 'Highlight'. It was introduced in 1964.

The rest of this book could be filled with evidence of Sam's brilliance as a rose breeder, of the honours he has won, and of his bold explorations of the genus. He has the breeder's eye to see possibilities which others had not dreamed

17. Sam McGredy IV, born 1932. 'He has the breeder's eye'.
Photo: Sam McGredy

of, and the imagination to uncover the way to them, through generations and
through disappointments. The prime example of this is his 'hand-painted' roses,
which started from his use of the Hybrid Scotch Rose, 'Frühlingsmorgen'. He
was looking for hardiness from that variety, but learned from the unpromising
seedlings it gave him that something else was possible. After much work, he
introduced in 1971 a rose with patterned petals in red and white, under the name
'Picasso'. It was completely new, his own creative contribution, and has been
followed by several others, including 'Matangi' in 1974 and 'Sue Lawley' in 1980.
The rose world has only seen the start of this journey.

The McGredy firm was a heady place under Sam. If other people said, 'The
sky's the limit,' then the sky was where McGredy began. Uncle Walter continued
to run the office, but his nephew caused him to do so in large premises, modern
to the point of bewilderment. Billy Douglas, a man devoted to plants and the
quality of them, convinced of the glory and the goodness of the world, if you
could follow his Ulsterine flow of words and idealism, was despatched to study
English garden centres; and on his return commanded to make the finest of them
all, together with a show garden at Derriaghy. Bright men were recruited to make
the McGredy firm effective, profitable and big.

They used to meet in Sam's office for coffee in the middle of the morning, careless of muddy wellingtons, and sitting on the desk and the floor when all the chairs were taken, together with any visiting rose people; the talk flowed. It was a Council of War in which the objectives were always being set further ahead, and the Irish wit flowing to roars of laughter. Sam's men also found that if things went wrong, he would be blunt and ruthless.

Sam was in his element walking through the rows of his seedlings in the rose field, preferably with companions who could criticize, counter, observe and suggest. His knowledge of roses by now was prodigious, and although his hands neither propagated nor grew roses, they bred them; his eye and his mind by now could understand a rose variety through and through.

He became engaged to Maureen McCall in 1959; she was a tall, dark and beautiful girl, employed as a fashion model. When they married, Reimer Kordes and Niels Poulsen acted as groomsmen. Sam built a house, all on its own on a hill among the rose fields. It was designed by Adair Roche, in modernistic style, with an eyrie at the top for Sam. Two daughters were born, Kathryn and Maria.

Sam was adamant that plant breeders should have rights on their varieties, and worked to that end from about 1955. He saw himself as a rose breeder, whose only return was to increase the value of his company's plants for a brief year or two, until his competitors caught up with him. It seemed ridiculous that a rose breeder could not earn his living except in association with his own nursery. Some British rose growers entered into 'gentlemen's agreements', to pay McGredy a royalty for three years; but most bought stock from professional propagators, both Dutch and British, even Bermudan for a time, and Sam had never a penny from them.

Major Gwilym Lloyd George was Home Secretary at the time. He and his wife greatly enjoyed their roses in their garden at Cottered in Hertfordshire. Sam met them, and put over his case with such conviction that the Government began seriously to consider plant breeders' rights. After much consultation and argument, an Act was passed in 1964. It was in time for Sam to secure rights on his beautiful climbers, 'Handel' and 'Schoolgirl'; and on Floribundas such as the yellow 'Arthur Bell', the carmine and white 'Molly McGredy' and the salmon 'City of Leeds'.

The major beneficiaries of such a decree were obviously McGredy and Dickson, as the leading British rose breeders. At this point, an unfortunate and unnecessary division of opinion, or rather a little war, occurred. Prudently taking legal advice, which in fact they might better have censored, and knowing more of the subject than their proposed licensees, Dickson and McGredy presented their terms.

The licensees, who were virtually the rest of Britain's rose growers, objected to detail after detail, convinced that in signing McGredy's and Dickson's agreements, they were ceding their freedom, liberty and independence. The more obstinate the licensees became, and the more Pat Dickson tried to explain, the more obdurate was Sam. He had the roses and the rights, and he was damned if he would give in.

He chartered an aeroplane to bring the British growers to Portadown, to show them the roses, to take their orders, to give them a day of McGredy roses and wine that should inspire them. When they were helped back into the aircraft that evening, there was a large box of chocolates on each seat, as a gift to the wives they had left at home.

Do it my way, he was saying, and we shall all prosper. If we do it your way, they were replying, you are King Sam, and we are your subjects. The result was a cautious compromise, more than they wished to give, and less than Sam hoped to receive, but after a few years a mutually satisfactory system was invented and implemented.

His travels to other countries had taught Sam that the climate of Ulster was of no great benefit to a rose breeder. He envisaged life in a sunnier land, imagined his roses growing so quickly that one year's work in the sun would almost be the equal of two in the clouds and rain. If the United States was his most important market, then the selection of roses for that country ought ideally to take place in a similar climate. To choose roses for America in Ulster was not much better than guessing.

If the grass be greener the other side of the fence, it becomes doubly attractive when one's own grass turns sour. The bitterness and murder in Northern Ireland reinforced Sam's thoughts of emigration. He arranged to go to New Zealand.

Before leaving, he made a last trip to England, to say goodbye to his friends there. He came to Hitchin, and we walked among my seedling roses. Someone had a bird scarer which made a bang every few minutes. It went off, and Sam jumped, asking, 'What the hell's that?' I told him, but when it banged again, he jumped again. I had felt like that in the war, until I learned to dive and emerge afterwards, as of habit. I was surprised and concerned to see my visitor from Northern Ireland so nervous.

It was a beautiful evening. Betty cooked a fine meal, and Sam sat down with our lively youngsters, Robert, Philip, Elizabeth and her fiancé, Peter. He started the chat flying across the table, lifting the company above its normal powers as only he, of all the men I have met, is able. It was an evening of wit and laughter. I thought at the time we had done him good. Afterwards, it occurred to me that he had done good to us, and I wondered, under the circumstances, what it had cost him.

Sam went to New Zealand in 1972, and is there breeding roses still, sending to his British representative, John Mattock of Oxford, a great variety of treasures, among them the creeping white Miniature, 'Snow Carpet', and the bold red Hybrid Tea 'Olympiad'. Sam tells me that about 750,000 'Olympiad' were budded in the United States in 1983. His third daughter, Clodagh, was born in New Zealand, but unhappily Sam and Maureen parted. Sam has since married again, and is now a New Zealand citizen. His second wife, Jillian, has turned out to be quite a rose breeder, helping him in the hybridizing house and critizing her husband's new roses.

I see Sam from time to time, always gladly. We met in Melbourne in 1975, and at his suggestion went into the Art Gallery there.

There's something sinister about an Art Gallery. You enter, see some pictures of great beauty, and assume that all the other exhibits must be admirable, for experts have assembled them. In an effort to appreciate, your own judgement is bludgeoned.

Sam and I reeled from one horror to the next, until we came to a large picture, which was plain black. A blackboard would have been more useful, because this exhibit had dribbles of paint on it such as one would not tolerate on a door or window frame. We could not imagine what had persuaded the Art Gallery to purchase and exhibit it, shook our heads, and wandered over to a free-standing sculpture. We were seriously debating its nature and artistic purpose, when the cleaning lady came and wheeled it away.

We thought it was time to go and have a beer.

6

Jackson & Perkins

Known to the rose world as J&P, Jackson & Perkins count their roses by the million, style themselves 'The World's Largest Rose Growers', and relate to most rose nurseries like the *Queen Elizabeth* among a fleet of fishing smacks. Yet they did not set out to be rose growers; a fortunate occurrence guided them.

The J was A. E. Jackson, the P was Charles H. Perkins. They started their nursery in 1872, growing grapes and raspberries as their main crops, in Newark in the state of New York. Newark is over 200 miles from New York City, close to Lake Ontario.

Among the company's employees was E. Alvin Miller. He was the research department when not required for other duties, and in the course of his work he attempted to breed roses. From the seed of a wild, oriental trailing rose, R. *wichuraiana*, he raised a rambling hybrid with pretty clusters of small, double, pink flowers. It was introduced in 1901 as 'Dorothy Perkins', and became one of the most famous roses in the world, the example of the rose at every cottage door.

J&P forthwith became specialist rose growers. Their nursery background was based on supplying to market rather than to retail customers. Accordingly they were 'wholesale only'. Their catalogues showed bundles of plants, and carefully stated how many shoots would be found on plants of first, second and third grade. Their customers bought J&P plants to sell them again. If every plant were saleable, and the quality consistent, then the business ought to grow.

Early in the century, J&P opened a branch nursery in California. In a country the size of the United States, it is better not to grumble at the weather, but to move to the climate one requires. The difference between the states of New York and California, in terms of rose production, is in the number of days per year when roses can grow and people can work. J&P calculate that their research department can work productively for eleven months in California, against five in Newark. Their first rose nursery in California was in McFarland, Kern County. By 1930, they were growing roses in the states of New York, Virginia and California.

The little research department had driven the company into roses, with profitable results; the management had the good sense to recognize its value, and to continue it. In succession to Alvin Miller, they employed a Frenchman who was up to that time working for a rival firm, the Conard-Pyle Co.

He was Jean Henri Nicolas, born in Roubaix, near the Belgian border, in 1875. In appearance, he was unlike one's mental picture of a Frenchman, being blond, tall and heavy: in fact six feet two inches tall and two hundred and ten pounds in weight. His career had been varied. After gaining degrees in both Arts and Science, he became a soldier in the peace-time French army. He was a Captain in the Artillery at the age of twenty-seven, but had to resign his commission because his eyesight became impaired. He then worked in the textile industry, and was appointed to a post that brought him from France to the United States as buying agent for raw cotton in New Orleans. In that city he met the lady whom he subsequently married.

During the First World War and despite his eyesight, he appears to have served as a liaison officer with the American Expeditionary Force. Details of his service are obscure but it must have been valuable, because he was made a Chevalier of the Legion of Honour. He was also elected an Officer of the Académie Française, a high distinction.

From his youth he had been interested in roses; after the war he settled in America and became a naturalized citizen. He turned to roses for his future career. A versatile man indeed.

Nicolas trained upon J&P's operations a studious and logical mind. The foundation of a rose bush is its root, which is that of a wild rose. Nicolas planted sufficient of the root-stocks then in general use, to enable him to bud upon them one hundred each of six commercially important Hybrid Teas of varied vigour and habit.

He sorted the resultant plants into four grades, calculated the wholesale value, which was then twenty-five cents for a first grade bush, and showed his employers the results. The best yield of plants out of six hundred was 510, on a selection of R. *canina*, 'Schmid's Ideal'; but many of the plants were small. The highest yield in value came from a selection of R. *multiflora*, which produced many plants in the higher grades. He called it 'Chenault', because he got it from a friend of that name in France.

The Research Department studied winter hardiness and many other rose problems, with benefit to the business. Under Nicolas, they produced some of the first roses sold in containers, 'canned roses', they called them. The idea came from a nurseryman named Wedge, who compressed the roots in peat moss, by a machine he had adapted from one that moulded blocks of cement. J&P bought the patent, went into production, and extended their sales season, especially in the colder parts of the country.

Nicolas was not under pressure to create new varieties, because J&P had new varieties to introduce from many other breeders, particularly from Europe. However, he was a wise and perceptive rosarian, and during his years with J&P, he raised some successful roses, among them 'Eclipse' and 'Rochester', the former so named because it was first seen to be good on the day of an eclipse of the sun in August 1932; it was introduced in 1935, a yellow Hybrid Tea, grown widely for many years in warmer countries than Britain.

'Rochester' has perhaps never received the credit due to it. It was a cross between the pink and white Polyantha, 'Echo,' and a yellow Hybrid Tea, 'Rev. F. Page Roberts'. The result was a buff double rose, flowering in clusters, and classified at that time as a Hybrid Polyantha. It may be argued that Kordes' 'Rosenelfe', usually thought to be the first of the type, was in fact preceded, in 1934, by 'Rochester'. The name came from a town some twenty-five miles west of Newark. We owe to Jean Henri Nicolas the suggestion that roses like 'Rochester' be called Floribundas.

He was known as 'The Doctor', a title he rightfully held from his qualifications; he was respected by rosarians in many countries. He died in 1937, shortly after a large, fragrant, pink Hybrid Tea had been named 'The Doctor' in his honour by a Californian rose breeder, Fred Howard.

To add up the rest of the rose world's indebtedness to him, we now turn to the successor he trained.

Eugene S. Boerner came from Cedarburg, in the cold state of Wisconsin, where he had been born in 1893. He was of German stock, and was proud of it. In 1911, he enrolled in the University of Wisconsin to study engineering, but after some months he was told to leave because his English was not up to standard. He went to the University of Illinois, where his studies were interrupted by the Great War. He served as a pilot for a short time, and afterwards passed his BSc in Horticulture. He joined J&P in 1920, and such was his progress that in 1927 he acquired a financial interest in the company. He succeeded Dr Nicolas as Director of Research.

Fate had a surprise in store for J&P. They decided to take a small stand at the New York World's Fair in 1939. From Kordes of Germany, they had a red Floribunda named 'Minna Kordes'. They proposed that in America it should be renamed 'World's Fair'. They set up their stand, prepared to sell roses to every businessman whose premises could possibly be used as a rose store.

The outcome was quite different. They were overwhelmed with orders, particularly for 'World's Fair', from the general public. A retail business by mail order was virtually presented to them by that one exhibition. They were not slow to take advantage of it, and as a result their breeding programme became of more importance to them.

Eugene Boerner was a heavily built man, with a jovial air and a strong sense of humour. His name, most felicitously for a rose breeder, was generally shortened to Gene. Having come from Wisconsin, where many roses were not hardy enough to survive the winter, he was ambitious to create roses both beautiful and hardy, so that people in cold climates could enjoy them. Following the examples of Nicolas, and of Poulsen and Kordes in Europe, he saw Floribundas to be those roses.

It is the reputation of Americans to outdo others in the size and scope of their undertakings; and of the Germans to be thorough. When those two characteristics were merged in J&P's Research Department, the result was the greatest labour ever put into rose breeding.

18. Eugene S. Boerner, 1893–1966. 'Papa Floribunda'.
Photo: Jackson & Perkins Co.

Gene's theory was 'applied population dynamics'; he applied it in this fashion: first, the breeder must recognize those features, not always obvious, that suggest a variety may be useful to breed with. He should then make a trial of it by mating it with several other varieties, and observing the resulting batches of seedlings. If one or more of those batches show promise, he should repeat the cross on so large a scale that the whole range of its potential will be exhibited in the progeny.

A simple proposition, one might think; but that would be to ignore the numbers involved in it. One may have a thousand plants of rose A, and fertilize every bloom with the pollen of rose B, and grow one hundred thousand seedlings of the cross between A and B, and still not come to the end of the possible variations.

They had to limit their applied population dynamics to practical numbers, but even so they produced a quarter of a million seeds in a year, and were prepared to grow 100,000 in order to select one good variety. Let J&P get hold of that one, and the World's Largest Rose Growers would sell it with such vigour and in such quantity as to reclaim all the money spent on research, and more besides.

They received from Gene Boerner a steady flow of excellent varieties. 'Goldilocks', in 1945, was plainly the best yellow Floribunda of its day, and Gene was already breeding from it before the date of its introduction.

Gene was friendly with the Kordes family in Germany; he was 'Onkel Gene'

75

to its younger members. From Wilhelm Kordes he received a rose named 'Rosen-märchen', which J&P eventually introduced in America in 1942 under the name 'Pinocchio'. This rose interested him; it was light pink with some touches of yellow, a double Floribunda. The feature that particularly intrigued Gene was that when the flowers were old, instead of fading, they became deeper in colour. He took 'Pinocchio' into his breeding programme, put its pollen on a yellow Hybrid Tea, 'McGredy's Pillar', and obtained a passable Floribunda with thin flowers, but sunny appearance. It was named 'Holiday', was introduced in 1948, and like 'Goldilocks' was in his breeding stock some years earlier.

He obtained a most extraordinary result from the mating, 'Goldilocks' × 'Holiday'. At first it looked like the yellow Floribunda one might expect from the cross; but as the flower aged, it became salmon, and then red, so that as the buds opened in succession, the cluster contained flowers of all three colours. No rose of that kind had ever been seen. The nearest to it was an old China rose, 'Mutabilis', a shrub which proceeded from buds of saffron to magenta in its old age. As the China roses are ancestors of Floribundas, it may be that the gene to cause so marked a colour change had suddenly asserted itself, perhaps through 'Pinocchio'.

The strange new rose was named 'Masquerade', and introduced in 1949, in harness with a rose of remarkable coral colour, 'Fashion'. In raising 'Fashion', Gene had been aiming for another target, a red version of 'Pinocchio', to achieve which he had fertilized that rose with the pollen of 'Crimson Glory'. He later said that it was a puzzle to him where the coral colour had come from; as both 'Pinocchio' and 'Crimson Glory' were raised by Wilhelm Kordes, the question was debated between Gene and Wilhelm on frequent occasions, but they were none the wiser.

With two roses of unique colour to sell, the J&P sales staff were as happy and effective as hungry dogs with a beefsteak each. It was easy work. They had roses to sell such as mankind had never seen before.

It is a strange feature of this story that it centres, not on the firm's principals, but on their employees. Of Jackson, we hear little but that he was co-founder. The Perkins family were in charge, in the persons of Charles Perkins, a nephew of the original, and his brothers Ralph and Clarence. Charlie was a man of decision, a cigar smoking tycoon with a difference, because unlike most tycoons he had muddy boots. He was a fine judge of roses and, when he saw a good one, he would invest heavily to ensure enormous sales.

J&P's success was causing production problems. They had opened a seventeen-acre show garden, which brought more orders; they were growing seventeen million roses a year. Charlie Perkins wanted vast areas of fresh land, in a climate where plants would grow fast and big and ripe. In 1952, he took 360 acres in the desert state, Arizona.

They sank a bore hole, striking water at 1,200 feet, irrigated the desert, and grew roses on it. The acreage increased, so that in 1963 they had 5,000 acres.

There they grew millions of roses, squares of green leaves and rose blooms surrounded by the desert and its great cacti. Sometimes the irrigation attracted flocks of geese, which paddled along the rows, eating weeds as they went.

Many of Gene Boerner's roses have names that are familiar. His rich pink climber, 'Aloha', is one of the best for a small garden; Hybrid Teas were not his speciality, although the buff yellow 'Diamond Jubilee', 1947, is a beauty. Floribundas galore came from him, 'Lavender Pinocchio', 'Vogue', 'Ma Perkins', 'Jiminy Cricket', 'Spartan' and 'Ivory Fashion' being just a sample of varieties that were internationally grown. 'Ma Perkins' was named after a broadcaster who told stories over the radio; she was not related to the Perkins of J&P. 'Spartan' was a great success, a salmon orange Floribunda. It was advertised at a cost said to be half a million dollars: the Charlie Perkins touch.

Gene Boerner had earned the affectionate title given to him in the rose world. He was 'Papa Floribunda'. When a young Ulsterman named Sam McGredy came to him for advice, he received him generously. Sam, who had been given the task of breeding roses, but had no knowledge of it, owned that Gene had been a kind of hybridizing father to him.

The J&P instinct for changing course at the right moment was shown by Gene's interest in roses for the cut flower growers. There was indeed a change in the business, shown by a fall in retail orders by mail. It had become more pleasant for the public to drive to a garden centre, bring home their roses, and plant them without further delay. The trade in cut roses was buoyant, and although the industry used only a few varieties, the quantities needed of each were great. A successful rose could earn for its breeder many royalties. Gene's most successful entry into this market was made with the orange red 'Zorina' in 1963.

'Papa Floribunda', a bachelor all his days, died on the fifth of September, 1966. In his will he left $120,000 for Cornell University to support graduates working on rose research.

In the same year, the bugles of big business were blowing in the ears of J&P, with the result that the company was acquired by Harry & David, of Medford, Oregon. They are a firm with interests in cold storage, fresh fruit and food. The decision was taken to move the whole firm out west. Newark was closed down, Arizona phased out. The growing operations were concentrated at Wasco, in the San Joaquin Valley, California. The plants were despatched from Medford; and the Research Department was moved to Tustin, California. Its new head was a quiet, dark haired man, William A. Warriner, usually known as Bill.

Bill Warriner had been at the Michigan State University when the Japanese bombed Pearl Harbour, thereby diverting him from lecture room to the US Marines. He returned after the War, took his BSc, and went to California to work for a well known firm of rose growers and breeders, Howard & Smith. He had a good tutor there, in Fred Howard. In 1956, Bill went into business on his own account; he accepted an offer to join J&P in 1963, and was made Director of Research on the death of Gene Boerner.

19. Bill Warriner. He succeeded Eugene Boerner at J&P.
Photo: Jackson & Perkins Co.

He soon produced a number of roses which were successful in America, including the Hybrid Teas 'Golden Gate', in 1972, and 'Medallion', in 1973, yellow and apricot respectively. In 1980, he had a remarkable triumph. In the United States, there is an organization called All-America Rose Selections, which tests new roses prior to introduction in a number of different places. Up to three varieties are given the AARS endorsement each year, with such publicity that it is a brave nursery that fails to grow them. In 1980, Bill Warriner won all three nominations, with the roses 'Love', 'Honor' and 'Cherish'. They are a red and white Floribunda to 'Love'; a white Hybrid Tea to 'Honor'; and a coral Floribunda to 'Cherish'.

Bill's roses must be bad sailors, because they do not always cross the Atlantic well. J&P sell millions of them in the States, but it is not so in Britain. 'Evening Star' is one of the best of his roses in this country, a fine white rose of beautiful form. It is Floribunda, officially, but some of its flowers are as good as those of Hybrid Teas. 'Pristine', a charming Hybrid Tea in pearly white, also does well.

J&P are now part of a huge concern. It reads like a nursery tale. J&P became a part of Harry & David. Harry & David became a part of Bear Creek Corporation; Bear Creek became a part of R. J. Reynolds Industries.

As a result, J&P are now in a business empire that includes tobacco, wine, exploration for energy, Del Monte canned fruit and Kentucky Fried Chicken.

It seems a long way from 'Dorothy Perkins' at the cottage door.

7

Pemberton

This is the story of a rose breeder who was born, not a son of the soil, but into a prosperous Victorian home, so dear to him that he lived in it all his days.

Joseph Hardwick Pemberton was born on 5 October, 1852, the son of Joseph and Amelia Elizabeth Pemberton, of Havering-atte-Bower, Essex.

The family house followed Victorian style by providing shelter to three generations, from grandmother to little Joseph; and from time to time various uncles and aunts and cousins as well. It defied architectural custom, because it had been built to a circular design, and was indeed known as The Round House. It stood, among trees and shrubs, in three acres of garden.

When Joseph was five years old, he met the companion of his life in the person of his sister, who was born on 1 December, 1857, baptized Amelia Florence, and known ever after as Florence.

To the children the garden was a world to explore, a world hidden by overgrown

20. The Round House, Havering-atte-Bower. The home of the Pembertons.
Photo: Graham Thomas

shrubs, made mysterious by winding paths, and ready to show its treasures, as when one came upon a glorious rose, relic of some old plantation.

On Sundays, the family went to church, dressed in their Sunday best. For little Joseph, this meant a light coloured, belted, Norfolk jacket, with large buttons of mother-of-pearl down the front; below that he wore petticoats, in the fashion for little boys at that time. When the family entered the church, a woman walked along the aisle in front of them, opened the door of their pew, and closed it when they were all inside. The pew was boxed in, with seats around it, where the family sat facing one another, the children unable to see very much of the church until it was time to stand up. Then they could stand on the seat, see over the pew, and Joseph could carry out what from his point of view was the most memorable part of the ceremony. He had come prepared for it.

There was a gentleman in a neighbouring pew, who wore a black coat, in the button-hole of which was a rose. From the first, Joseph had admired that gentleman's roses. On Sunday morning, before church, he searched the garden for a rose that would be better than the gentleman's, and poked it alongside one of the mother-of-pearl buttons in his jacket. Each Sunday, when standing-up time came, he studied the neighbour's rose to see whose was the better, and usually concluded that he had lost again. Eventually he decided that the black coat set off a rose far better than a light Norfolk jacket could ever do.

When Joseph was sent to boarding school, he liked to take with him some memento of home. For the September term, he took a flower of the lovely Bourbon rose, 'Souvenir de la Malmaison'. He kept it in an empty barley sugar tin where it remained fresh for quite a long time, from which we may deduce that people in those days were better at making tins than at heating schools. At Christmas, he brought his rose home, brown and battered.

Joseph's father was proud of the family home and garden. With one or both of the children, he would inspect and savour the little estate, thereby instilling in them a love for it. When Joseph was about twelve, his father taught him how to propagate a rose by budding, generously attributing the initial failure to a deficiency of sap at the time, although his pupil owned that maladroitness was the more likely reason. Joseph was given a little patch for his own garden, with three red standard roses in it. He went on occasion with his father to the annual Rose Show at the Crystal Palace, the object of the visits being to choose roses for the garden. Young Joseph took care to wear a rose in his button-hole, both to salute the occasion and to conform to Victorian fashion. As an old hand at button-hole competition, he wore the best rose he could find. Adorned with a fragrant flower of 'Marie Baumann', which was a large, light red Hybrid Perpetual, he became aware as they walked across London Bridge that people were looking at his rose. At the Crystal Palace, he searched through the exhibits at the show for a better bloom, but could not find one and was content.

One of the pleasures of life in Victorian England was that companionable servant of mankind, the horse; another was cricket, a game with some of the elements

35 (above left) 'Karen Poulsen' *Floribunda* Svend
Poulsen 1933   36 (left) 'Chinatown' *Floribunda*
Niels Poulsen 1963   37 (below left) 'Pernille
Poulsen' *Floribunda* Niels Poulsen 1965
38 (above) 'Troika' (Royal Dane) *Hybrid Tea* Niels
Poulsen 1972   39 (below) 'Ingrid Bergman' *Hybrid
Tea* Mogens and Pernille Olesen 1983

40 (above left) 'Frühlingsgold' *Shrub* Wilhelm
Kordes II 1937   41 (left) 'Fritz Nobis' *Shrub*
Wilhelm Kordes II 1940   42 (below left) 'Maigold'
Climber Wilhelm Kordes II 1953   43 (above)
'Kordes' Perfecta' *Hybrid Tea* Wilhelm Kordes II
1957   44 (below) 'Iceberg' *Floribunda* Reimer
Kordes 1958

45 (above) 'Lilli Marlene' *Floribunda* Reimer Kordes 1959   46 (below) 'Ernest H. Morse' *Hybrid Tea* Wilhelm Kordes II 1964   47 (above right) 'Peer Gynt' *Hybrid Tea* Reimer Kordes 1968   48 (right) 'Korresia' (Sunsprite) *Floribunda* Reimer Kordes 1974   49 (below right) 'Congratulations' *Hybrid Tea* Reimer Kordes 1978

50 (above left) 'Nevada' *Shrub* Pedro Dot 1927
51 (left) 'Mme Grégoire Staechelin' (Spanish Beauty)
Climber Pedro Dot 1927   52 (below left) 'Perla de
Alcañada' *Miniature* Pedro Dot 1944   53 (above)
'Rosina' (Josephine Wheatcroft) *Miniature* Pedro
Dot 1951   54 (below) 'Simon Dot' *Hybrid Tea*
Simon Dot 1978

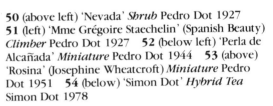

of chess, played with living pieces instead of bits of wood or ivory. Joseph enjoyed both of these delights; he became for a time a breeder of horses. At cricket, he was a left-handed batsman, and played regularly for the village. At some time it was settled that his future career should be the church; but before he embarked upon it, his beloved father died. Joseph was then twenty-one years old, and between brother and sister there was a strong bond of interests and companionship, as they responded to the needs of their bereaved mother and their little realm.

The summer after his father died, that of 1874, Joseph made up his mind to enter some of the family roses in a rose show. With the help of the gardener, he adjusted a borrowed chrysanthemum stand for the purpose. He found twelve blooms good enough, and took them to the show with many misgivings, but no spare blooms in case of accidents. He won second prize, and from that moment, like a Red Indian on the warpath, he was an exhibitor of roses, with his sister as his willing and enthusiastic helper. They had entered a charming and esoteric world of friendly fanciers, few of whom had started their hobby in petticoats at church.

In December 1876, the National Rose Society was formed, and Joseph joined it in 1877, followed by Florence in 1878. On the 4th July 1877, the Society staged its first rose show, in St James's Hall. With three years' experience behind him, Joseph was determined to enter, but he was unprepared for the stringency of the regulations. He had learned that, no matter what the rules stated, show secretaries would never refuse an entry after the advertised closing date, because they wanted roses to furnish their show.

His entry for the show at St James's Hall arrived a day late, and the National Rose Society, to his consternation, refused it.

He went to the Society's offices, then in the Adelphi, to persuade the Secretary to change his mind; but the answer he got was that already a day before the closing date, more entries had been received than could be accommodated. Therefore not only Mr Pemberton's entry but many others had been refused.

Pemberton replied, 'I must show, entry or no entry, and I will take one box instead of the two I entered.'

He arrived at the show, with a box of twelve different roses, two spare blooms stuck amongst them. The show was in an old hall, due to be pulled down, with dim lights and narrow passage ways, a confused turmoil of men and boxes of roses and no room for them all. Pemberton went up and down in the midst of it, until he found the Secretary, the Rev H. Honywood D'ombrain. Would he accept the entry? No! Then might it be staged 'Not for Competition?' Certainly not, there was no room — look!

D'ombrain lifted the green baize, and revealed under the bench a magnificent box of twenty-four 'Mlle Marie Cointet', a pink Hybrid Perpetual raised in France by Guillot.

'Rejected,' he said.

Pemberton went back to the turmoil, and when he found an empty space, he put down his box of twelve. But not for long. D'ombrain spotted it, and made him remove it. He put it in another space, and was obliged to lift it away again. He walked around with it, getting in everybody's way, waiting for another vacant spot, when D'ombrain, perceiving that this insistent exhibitor would be a menace until he was stilled, called him into the office, and gave him an entry card.

'Put them on the floor,' he said, 'and leave them there.'

Joseph went to work on the floor, and observed nearby a distinguished exhibitor in similar abased circumstances, a Mr Smallbones of Chatteris. One look at the Chatteris roses and Joseph's hopes sank, they were much better than his; if these were typical of the exhibits, then his had no chance. He noticed that Mr Small-bones' roses stuck up in a stiff and assertive way; he set to work to raise his own blooms higher. Then time was up, and the exhibitors were ordered out.

He had come without his member's pass, and he had lacked the nerve to ask Mr D'ombrain for an exhibitor's ticket. The admission fee to those without such passes was 10/6d, an exorbitant sum to him, and no wonder, for the equivalent in 1984 is fourteen pounds; but at 5 pm it was reduced to 2/6d, therefore he hung around Regent Street the whole afternoon.

When he obtained admission for half a crown, he found that the boxes had been moved, and in the course of looking for them, he saw affixed to a pillar a list of awards. In the class of twelve different varieties, there had been forty entries, of which Mr Smallbones had been placed first and Mr Pemberton second.

He was overjoyed.

Joseph and Florence were partners at rose shows with great success. They travelled all over the country, won the highest honours, and thoroughly enjoyed themselves. Their vintage year was 1896, when at twelve shows, including such distant ones from Essex as Ulverston and Manchester, they staged forty-nine boxes and won forty-eight prizes, including thirty-two firsts. A photograph of their trophies 'has quite the appearance of a first-rate silversmith's window', reported Mr D'ombrain. At this time they were growing about 4,000 roses.

Joseph was recognized as a first rate authority on roses. His judgement was so good, that to him were entrusted the most difficult judging assignments, and the knotty problems of identification. In those days, when the conditions of entry usually stipulated a number of different varieties, up to seventy-two for the professionals, in one or three blooms of each, there was a temptation, if an exhibitor were short of a variety, to duplicate one already used, and to label it with the name of one similar. It was not easy to get away with that trick if Pemberton were a judge.

He was much admired for his management of his roses. Most exhibitors were at their best for the fortnight when their roses were in full flush. Pemberton persuaded his roses to succeed all through the season. His successes in 1896 began on June 18th, and ended on August 4th. In those days, the rose shows ended then, for want of any later blooms of exhibition type.

He was a cool, ingenious and indefatigable exhibitor. If he arrived early at a show, he would relax while others were fussing and probably spoiling their roses. His advice was to put one's box in the best part of the allotted area, having regard to freedom from draughts and the most mellow light, and then have forty winks. He paid attention to such details as the temperature of the water, which he thought should be about 5°F lower than the afternoon air temperature. If it was too cold, it would make the petals curl over instead of expanding. Before wire supports were used, he made his roses stand upright with the aid of sections of rhubarb stem in the tubes, and little forked twigs.

He was grateful for the advice and encouragement he had from other exhibitors, particularly at the start of his exhibition career from Benjamin Cant of Colchester and George Prince of Oxford. He met these and other great rosarians of the day, including Dean Hole, the President of the National Rose Society, a man of giant stature; Joseph saw Dean Hole as every inch a priest to whom one could take one's troubles, with his loving eyes and winning smile; but a man of the world withal.

Much as he enjoyed his exhibition roses, Joseph was aware of their shortcomings as garden plants, and he dearly loved the remnants of his grandmother's roses in the garden. In 1882, he took some of them to a National Rose Society Show in South Kensington, and asked permission to stage them 'Not for Competition.' This being granted, he showed the family's old favourites, which the gardener had made into nosegays, 'Aimée Vibert', 'De Meaux', 'Tuscany' and others. He labelled his exhibit 'Grandmother's Roses'. The onlookers thronged around it all day, their interest in old-fashioned roses thoroughly awakened.

It is not our purpose to trace Joseph's career in holy orders, but lest it be supposed he did nothing but play with roses, let us say that he was ordained by the Bishop of St Albans in 1881, and was for some years curate at St Edward the Confessor's Church in Romford. In 1886, he became the first Priest in Charge of the newly built Church of the Ascension, at Colliers Row, Romford. From 1891 to 1914, he had the additional duty of Diocesan Inspector for the diocese of St Albans.

He was a fairly tall man, of dignified presence and neat appearance, in clerical dress, with a small pointed beard and a moustache, both neatly trimmed. He kept his hair short. In later life, when he retired from the church, he reverted to his childhood dress of a Norfolk jacket, without the mother-of-pearl buttons this time; and knee breeches.

For some years he had contributed terse and undidactic articles to gardening papers and the *Rose Annual*. In 1908, Longman Green published his book, *Roses, Their History, Development and Cultivation*. It is recognized as an important contribution to rose literature. It was affectionately dedicated to 'The Memory of a Dear Father ... to Whom the Author Owes so Much.' It says much about the Pemberton family, that thirty-four years had passed since that father's death; and that some of the illustrations in the book were from the hand of Florence.

21. The Rev Joseph Pemberton. Originator of the Hybrid Musks.
From the Rosarian's Year-Book 1898, *by permission of the Royal National Rose Society*

She was well known at rose shows as the indispensable partner, without whom the Reverend Joseph could not have exhibited so freely and successfully. This very able and energetic sister received a tribute from Alexander Dickson of Newtownards, who introduced in 1903 a creamy pink Hybrid Tea rose named 'Florence Pemberton'.

Joseph stood at the head of the list of Dean Hole Medallists, being the first to receive that honour, which is the chief one the National Rose Society confers on individuals in recognition of outstanding services to the Society and the rose. The medal was struck after the death of Dean Hole, and the award was made to Joseph in 1909. In July of that year, his mother died at the age of 79.

In 1911, he became President of the National Rose Society, and served for two years, that being the regular presidential term of office. He was a good chairman, and as one might have hoped from his chosen calling, a ready speaker.

By this time, the rose-mad cleric had turned his thoughts towards breeding roses. It cannot be denied that he had enjoyed a sheltered and privileged life, with little sign of the financial difficulties familiar to most of humanity. It is not for us to judge the return he had rendered for his good fortune, through his work for the church and the rose, and in his private life; though we may fairly observe that he is clearly marked as a gentleman and an enthusiast. He was now about to add a significant page to the book of human happiness.

84

It might have been expected that the man who delighted in showing roses would breed exhibition varieties, but such an expectation would ignore his first love among roses. Ever mindful of his family home and the happiness of childhood, he cherished his 'Grandmother's Roses'. He set out to breed such varieties, with the intention that they should outbloom his grandmother's, most of which were finished for the season in July, by flowering as long as the winter allowed, even up to Christmas Day. He wanted roses which would survive and bloom after all around them had perished, rather than those cosseted and nursed through their sickly lives by the showmen.

For the foundation of his breeding line, he chose a rose bred in Germany by Peter Lambert, and introduced in 1904. It is a shrubby rose, with small pale pink flowers, in which is a touch of yellow, its name, after Lambert's home town, being 'Trier'. The parentage, according to Herr Lambert, made it a mixture of Polyantha, Noisette and Hybrid Tea, as enticing to a breeder as a desert mirage to a traveller with an empty water bottle, and just as false, for almost certainly there was no Hybrid Tea in it. Polyantha and Noisette made a good enough mixture, and a more fertile one. Joseph could add the Hybrid Tea element himself.

His ideas about breeding were well ahead of his time, and were based on his simple understanding of roses, and his modest, practical common sense. It would have paid Dickson and McGredy to copy his treatment of seed. He believed in removing it from the hip at once, and either sowing it straight away, or else keeping it in damp fibre or sand until he was ready to sow it. Over half a century after Joseph had published this advice, breeders were keeping their seed in hips over winter, and wondering why germination was minimal. Joseph explains it lucidly in terms of expelling carbon and admitting oxygen, and if he was not scientifically exact, he nevertheless had the heart of the matter.

Breeders had long bemoaned the losses of their young seedlings at the stage of transplanting them from the place where they germinated into small individual pots. Joseph said, sow them thinly, then transplanting will not be necessary unless they all germinate. This excellent advice appears to have been ignored for years, and young Sam McGredy, in the 1950s, had to learn it from Reimer Kordes.

Joseph had his own recipe for dispelling mildew, its main ingredient being Calvert's Carbolic Soft Soap. Take $1\frac{1}{2}$ lbs of it, boil it in $7\frac{1}{2}$ quarts of water, and spray the roses with one pint of that brew mixed with six pints of soft water. Keep on with that, he said, and you will never have mildew.

In 1913, the Rev J. H. Pemberton, Havering-atte-Bower, Romford, became a nurseryman, offering two new roses which were described as Hybrid Teas, although they could scarcely have been more foreign to that class. They were 'Danaë', and 'Moonlight', both shrubby, cluster flowering, and pale yellow to white, the latter being particularly beautiful in its clear, broad blooms. With delight their breeder recorded that flowers of 'Danaë', all cut from the open, and sufficient to furnish six vases, had been placed on the altar of his church on Christmas Day, 1913.

'Moonlight' was his first Gold Medal rose, and in reporting its success, which occurred at the Autumn Show on 9 September, 1913, the *Rose Annual* questioned whether it was a Hybrid Tea, or as some people thought, a Hybrid Multiflora. Joseph continued to advertise his roses as Hybrid Teas, until Courtney Page, secretary of the National Rose Society, reviewing the new roses for 1917, classed 'Pax' as a Hybrid Musk, with these words:

'When I first saw this Rose in the early part of June I immediately recognized an entirely new break, and on referring to my notes made on that occasion I find the following: "A new Hybrid Musk of the first order, very strongly perfumed — real musk —".' He described the colour as pure white, tinted lemon in the bud, with prominent golden anthers, and ended his paragraph, which was written late in 1917, 'May it indeed be a happy omen!' In 1919, Pemberton adopted the term Hybrid Musk.

In 1918 he omitted the word 'Rev' from his advertisements, and became plain J. H. Pemberton, whether from a sense of impropriety at using the title in his business, or in connection with his recent resignation from his curacy.

His Hybrid Musk roses were received with delight by many discerning gardeners, the more so as Floribundas barely existed at that time; even today, most rose catalogues contain some of his roses, of which the best known are the blush 'Penelope' (1924); the pink 'Cornelia' (1925); the gaunt but beautifully pink 'Vanity' (1920); the double white 'Prosperity' (1919); and 'Nur Mahál' (1923).

He was obliged to explain the name of 'Nur Mahál', which was one of the more colourful of his generally pale roses, being described, perhaps generously, as bright crimson. It was first shown under his seedling number, whereupon the name was proposed by a lady who had lived in India a long time. The story was of Nurjahan the Beautiful, Crown Princess of Persia, who met her future husband in her rose garden. He was Jehangir, son of the Emperor of India, but when he succeeded to the throne he was not a successful ruler, and it was his wife who ruled the country as the power behind the throne. Far from objecting to her dominance, her devoted husband gave her the name Nur Mahál, which means The Light of the Palaces, and must confirm our admiration for a more than capable lady. Her life story, said Joseph, may be read in *Mistress of Men*, by Annie Steel.

Interesting discoveries can still emerge from Joseph's breeding line, as are indicated by two of his own introductions. One was 'Sammy', 1912, which he described as thornless; another was 'Pemberton's White Rambler', 1914. One would expect to find some climbers and ramblers among the progeny of 'Trier', and it would perhaps be worth the time of a rose breeder to explore the Hybrid Musks with that end in view.

'Penelope' had a mixed reception; the National Rose Society awarded it a Gold Medal which, according to a commentator, 'came as a great surprise to many, including the raiser, I believe. Somehow it did not strike one as being a Gold Medal Rose.'

The award was no doubt justified, for 'Penelope' has long survived her rivals of that day; but in one respect, the comment was correct. 'Penelope' is the least likely of the Hybrid Musks to produce autumnal flower generously, being unfaithful to the great virtue of the class: to break into shoots during the summer.

When asked how to prune his Hybrid Musks, Joseph said that cutting them back disheartened them, and if pruned severely they would never be seen at their best. He advised that the new basal shoots be shortened by not more than one third of their length; and if needful, the old wood could be thinned out or excised. That advice was reinforced by an account from Cork, of a marvellous plant of 'Pax' which had been untended through being surrounded with barbed wire. 'You can attribute the success,' he replied, 'to the barbed wire.'

He was concerned that some of the early Hybrid Teas had brought their great advantages at the cost of scent, thus, in his view, contradicting a quality so elemental that the impulse to sniff a rose had become one of humanity's hereditary instincts. His own Hybrid Musks were fortunately blessed with a pleasant, refreshing scent, or rather most of them were. He said that in rose blooms there were four basic perfumes: the Musk, which is delicate and refined, suggestive of heather and lime blossom, and the only one of the four to diffuse itself freely into the air; the Damask, heavy, strong and positive; the Tea, not as definite or dominant as the Damask; and the fruit-scented, arrived by way of 'Persian Yellow', subtle, fruity, suggestive in one rose of apricot, in another of pineapple.

He was taken ill in 1926, and could not attend the Summer Golden Jubilee Show on July 2nd. It ill suited him to be confined to bed at the height of the rose season, and he insisted on being propped up so that he could see his plants through the window. He died before July was out.

Florence continued the business after her brother's death, with the help of the two gardeners, J. A. Bentall and R. Spruzen. In 1927 they introduced 'Robin Hood', which in the hands of Kordes was to have an important effect on modern roses, and, incidentally, was the seed parent of 'Iceberg'. 'Robin Hood' is red, more of a Polyantha than a Hybrid Musk.

'Felicia' came out in 1928, a typical Hybrid Musk in pale pink, with a touch of yellow, from a typical Pemberton cross, 'Trier' × 'Ophelia'.

Florence died in 1929, and with her death, the story of the Pembertons of The Round House, Havering-atte-Bower is at an end. It has, however, sequels.

The two gardeners each started a nursery of their own, Bentall at Havering and Spruzen at Stapleford Abbots. Bentall introduced roses on his own account for some years, including 'The Fairy', 1932, and 'Ballerina', 1937, two delightful and successful pink roses of individual character. The Spruzen nursery is still in business.

The little boy who had an eye for roses while still in petticoats, and the old man who demanded to be propped up in bed to see his roses, paid their forfeit to Father Time. They committed to his care their creations, and he has dealt kindly with them; their genes are safe in his pouch for future rose breeders.

8

Poulsen

A few inventors or innovators in human history have made such a mark on their professions as to see their names purloined and attached for a period to their inventions. They may have regretted it, as possibly Dr Guillotin did when he regarded his machine, or as Mr Hoover did when he saw his competitors sweeping up their portions of the reward of his fame. I suppose Mr Plimsoll was pleased with his line, for which many of us might envy him, and I am in no doubt that one Danish family was delighted when the rose world talked of 'Poulsen Roses'.

The Poulsen family was for many generations one of farmers and cattle breeders, no uncommon career in fertile Denmark; but on 29 November, 1850, the birth occurred of the Poulsen who changed that tradition. He was Dorus Theus Poulsen.

After serving an apprenticeship from the age of fourteen, and working for four Danish nurseries, he studied for three years at the Royal Veterinary and Agricultural High School in Copenhagen, from which he graduated in 1872. He found employment as a means of gaining more horticultural experience with E. G. Henderson of London, where he stayed for two years. In 1874 he obtained a post in his old High School, where he worked for four years. He was then able to buy a farm called Maria-Lyst at Roskildevej 78 in Copenhagen. In those days it was in grazing country, about three miles from the centre of Copenhagen.

Thus in 1878 he started his nursery, growing asparagus and strawberries. Before many years he was selling vegetable seed, particularly beet, swedes and cabbages. He sold the seed in Denmark and in Germany. It is natural for a seedsman to become a selector of the better forms nature sometimes gives him, and from that it is a short step to helping nature by becoming a plant breeder. D. T. Poulsen started to breed radishes and cucumbers. Towards the end of the 19th century, he sought to increase his business by growing fruit trees, shrubs, herbaceous plants and roses.

The best way to expand a nursery has often been to breed sons, and in this respect D. T. Poulsen and his wife Johanne were fortunate. They reared three young nurserymen, Dines in 1879, Poul André in 1882 and Svend in 1884. Assessing the progress he had made and hoped to make, in 1907 D. T. Poulsen bought an old farm called Lille Toelt, in Kelleriis, Kvistgaard, well away from Copenhagen, deep in the Danish countryside.

Of the three sons, Svend, the youngest, was kept at home to manage the nursery in Copenhagen: Poul became the business manager of the whole firm; and Dines was put in charge of the new premises at Kvistgaard. Before those appointments were made, the young Poulsens received a horticultural education that was to shape the firm's destiny.

Remembering the value of his own experience in England, D. T. Poulsen had sent his three sons abroad also. Dines, after working in Danish nurseries, went to Trier in Germany, to work for one of the great rose breeders of the era, Peter Lambert, whose name is remembered as the breeder of the famous white rose, 'Frau Karl Druschki'. Dines worked for nearly a year at Lambert's nursery, and then went to England, where he lived in Stanmore, made some experiments in breeding roses, and with his employer's permission brought the seedpods back with him to Denmark in 1907. He was by now an expert horticulturist, especially interested in trees and fruit. In Kelleriis he began to plant an arboretum which would be a plantsman's delight. He was serious in his work, good natured and humorous in his life.

His English seeds grew, and he had the fortune to introduce in 1912 two good varieties. One was a pink Polyantha, which he named 'Ellen Poulsen', and which had darker and harder foliage than most of its type. The second was 'Rödhätte', which is Danish for Red Riding Hood; this is an important rose. It was a cross between a red Polyantha, 'Mme Norbert Levavasseur' and a red

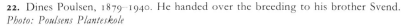

22. Dines Poulsen, 1879–1940. He handed over the breeding to his brother Svend. *Photo: Poulsens Planteskole*

Hybrid Tea, thus showing a clear intention, and indicating that an observant student had attended to Peter Lambert. The result was a semi-double red rose, one of the forerunners of the then unknown Floribunda class. There was some inconsistency about the Hybrid Tea parent, as to whether it was 'Richmond' or 'Liberty'; opinion finally settled on the former, but the fact that the question arose at all tempts one to ask whether the breeder was quite sure.

We should not blame him. Rose breeding was a little sideline to this grower of trees and shrubs and fruit trees. Nevertheless it was plain that, if roses were to be as useful to the Poulsen nursery as were their other crops, then a more useful type of rose was needed. The British could tend and cosset their weakly exhibition roses, the French could prize the rose as a cut flower, but in Northern Europe one needed hardier roses, which could be planted in parks and gardens in the confident expectation of a fine flourish of flowers in return for a minimum of attention.

About the beginning of the First World War, Dines handed over the rose breeding to his youngest brother, Svend. Up to 1917, another eight varieties which Dines had raised were introduced, but they achieved only a moderate reputation or less. In 1918. Svend's first two varieties were offered for sale, one of them a pale yellow Hybrid Tea with the appropriate name 'Luna'.

Svend's wedding to Petra Thomsen had been celebrated in 1916; Grethe, the first of their five children, was born in 1917, followed by their only son, Niels Dines, in 1919. The other three, all girls, were Nina, Ellen and Anne-Mette, the last arriving in 1930, nearly seven years later than Ellen. Young Niels Dines suffered no shortage of sisters, and if he needed more feminine company, his cousins from Uncle Dines' family included Dorrit and Kirsten; and from the family of Uncle Poul, Karen and Else.

In pursuit of his hardy, free-flowering and trouble-free roses, Svend had been mating Polyanthas and Hybrid Teas, in the hope that the qualities he desired from the one and the other would eventually come together in their children. His vision and his faith were justified by the progeny he raised from a pink Poly-antha, 'Orléans Rose' crossed with a semi-double Hybrid Tea of Dutch origin, 'Red Star'. As a result, in 1924 he introduced 'Else Poulsen' and 'Kirsten Poulsen'.

These two roses, particularly 'Else Poulsen', were immediately recognized as a decided breakaway, and perhaps the advance guard of a new race of roses. Roses which flowered in heads or clusters of little flowers were quite familiar; Poulsen now offered such roses with big flowers, and consequently a greater area of colour. Moreover, the former varieties used for bedding were so short in growth as to be called Dwarf Polyanthas. Else and Kirsten grew tall and strong. They marched into beds in gardens and parks where roses had never before appeared, for want of varieties of suitable habit and growth. Their chief fault was an almost complete lack of perfume.

'Else Poulsen' was bright rose pink, semi-double, with large and even heads of flowers carried on top of a tall bush. 'Kirsten Poulsen' was cherry red, single, a better plant than Else, but not so interesting a flower. A proof of their novelty is shown by the confusion they caused. When first shown in England, they were called Dwarf Polyanthas, but that being plainly ridiculous, they became Hybrid Teas, which being no more sensible led to the invention of a new class, Hybrid Polyanthas. During the eight years this point was argued, the world at large called them 'Poulsen Roses', and that name continued as a description of Svend Poulsen's particular type of plant.

The question may well be asked, that if 'Rödhätte' were the forerunner of the type, why didn't Svend breed from that rose? The answer is that it was not fertile; the same stumbling block obstructed quick progress from Else and Kirsten. The reason for this came from the marriage of their parents. The Polyanthas had fourteen chromosomes, and the Hybrid Teas twenty-eight; the embryo therefore took seven from one parent, fourteen from the other, total twenty-one, which as a general rule means an infertile triploid. Fortunately general rules admit of exceptions; but several years passed before those exceptions led to advancement.

In 1925, the year after Svend made rose history by introducing Else and Kirsten, the founder of the firm died at the age of seventy-four. Dorus Theus Poulsen had lived to see his business prosper to an extent he could not have expected at the start of it in 1878. His three sons, Dines, Poul and Svend, jointly took control, keeping their father's name as the title of the firm, D. T. Poulsens Planteskole. We say 'nursery', but the Danes expect their plants to be a stage ahead, and say 'plant school'.

They also commemorated their father by naming a good red Hybrid Polyantha 'D. T. Poulsen'. It was introduced in 1930. The beautiful scarlet 'Karen Poulsen' appeared in 1933, a single rose of great charm, but not as vigorous as a Poulsen rose should be. It won for Poulsens their first Gold Medal of the National Rose Society.

Svend was a quiet man, for a Poulsen, by nature gentle, studious, and with his own innate dignity. There is, to my knowledge, only one recorded instance of his anger, and it occurred in England, when 'Anne-Mette Poulsen' was on show.

Although Svend's roses were putting money in the bank for every rose nursery in Britain, they were earning no pounds for Poulsens, because no copyright or patent could apply to them. A firm from Huntingdon, Wood and Ingram, introduced the roses in England. They had been appointed because they were Poulsen's best customers in England, and imported every year large quantities of flowering trees, shrubs and conifers. As the years went by, the new Poulsen varieties disappeared into England, with no result for the breeder. Svend went to a show in London in 1934, and saw a fine display of the double carmine 'Anne-Mette Poulsen', and Wood and Ingram doing great business with it. He had a strong feeling that justice was not his portion. Many originators knew this experience. Gilbert and Sullivan had fought vigorously for some return from those

23. Svend Poulsen, 1884–1974. The man who made the 'Poulsen Roses'.
Photo: Poulsens Planteskole

who performed their works to their own profit. Jerome K. Jerome had watched helplessly while the Americans sold *Three Men in a Boat* by the tens of thousands, without paying a penny to the author. Svend wanted to tear down his roses at this English show, and take them back to Denmark.

He was stopped by Samuel Davison McGredy, that third Sam McGredy of the short life, and then very near the end of it, who said,

'Don't make a fool of yourself, Mr Poulsen, your roses are too good for that. You'd better come with me, back to Portadown.'

McGredy and Poulsen entered into an agreement, whereby McGredy would introduce the Poulsen roses in Britain, and despite the lack of legal obligation, McGredy would for a period of three years pay royalties to Poulsen on each variety he introduced.

The first fruit of that agreement was a rich and ripe one, in the lean and menaced year of 1938. It was a rose called 'Poulsen's Yellow'; McGredy advertised, 'We are proud of our appointment as sole introducers.'

There had been no yellow Polyanthas, and no yellow Poulsen roses. To raise one, Svend had intelligently rescued from the past a little known rose called 'Gottfried Keller'. It was in some respects a lost fortune of a rose for its breeder, Dr Franz Müller, of Weingarten in Germany. Back in the 1880s, contemporary with Joseph Pernet-Ducher, he had been using 'Persian Yellow' to bring yellow

92

into modern roses. 'Persian Yellow' was a double form of a wild rose from the country of its name, quite foreign to the roses of Europe's gardens, obdurate in flowering briefly in summer, and sulky in yielding pollen or seed. Joseph Pernet-Ducher succeeded, Dr Müller failed, but the genes of his failure were lively, as Svend found when 'Poulsen's Yellow' appeared. Not only did 'Poulsen's Yellow' extend the colour range of Hybrid Polyanthas, but also it admitted into the class the greater variation of habit that a more liberal selection of parents would bring.

The Second World War was no friend to rose growers, and Svend thought it a waste to introduce his roses while it was going on. The priorities for the Poulsens were to produce food, maintain their business, and walk up the street the Germans had just left. In the Danes there is a strange mixture of solidity and impishness; they must have been difficult for an occupying power to rule. You would think they would be too sedate to play tricks, and at the same time they would calmly do something so outrageous that the more volatile would shy at it.

Svend's son, Niels Dines, was twenty years old when the war started. He was tall, six feet three inches when fully grown, and strong. In 1936 he had been to work at M. Jensen's nursery in Holmstrup, where he remained in an atmosphere of trees and shrubs until 1938. He returned home, but was soon called up in the Danish forces, and as quickly disbanded by the Germans. Like his grandfather before him, he attended the Royal Veterinary and Agricultural High School in Copenhagen, from which he emerged with distinction in 1943. He then started his duties at the Kvistgaard nursery of D. T. Poulsens Planteskole. In 1946, he married Inge Andersen.

In 1953, Poulsens sold their now urbanized headquarters in Copenhagen, and following a family re-organization, Svend and his eldest brother's widow, Harriet, took over Kvistgaard.

Svend produced a regular flow of new roses, true to his Hybrid Polyantha pattern, and in many cases bearing the family name, as witness Poulsen's Peach, Bedder, Pearl, Crimson. In 1954, Niels started breeding, working for a time with his father, who had by that time almost forty years' experience. The last of Svend's roses appeared in 1963. The most successful of his later years was 'Rumba', introduced in 1958, a bright red and yellow Floribunda, as by that time Hybrid Polyanthas were termed.

Despite his tally of seventy years, and unworried by the prospect of not surviving to see the results, Svend began to breed cherries and apples, raspberries and lilies, ever dreaming of better plants and fruit to delight the golden boys and girls of the glorious future. In 1958, the Royal Veterinary and Agricultural Foundation conferred a doctorate of honour upon him. He died in 1974, ninety years old and, as Sam McGredy said, 'still dreaming'.

His son, Niels Dines Poulsen, attributed his own early successes to beginner's luck; expert witnesses, however, believe that no statement from Niels should be accepted at face value, but should better be studied with the same care the Foreign

Office accords to a note from a foreign power, to search not for the snags and the menaces, which the diplomats may expect, but for the jokes and the mockery rose breeders expect from Niels.

His first introductions came in 1962, and consisted of a good red climbing rose, 'Copenhagen', which was bred with the aid of pollen from 'Ena Harkness'; and an unusual biscuit white Floribunda, 'Hakuun'.

I first saw 'Hakuun' in Sam McGredy's nursery, and fancied breeding with it. By permission of Niels, I had plants from Sam, but I was not clever enough to raise any good varieties from it. Niels told me of its origin, which I repeat here for two reasons: one, that it has not as far as I know been printed before, and two, that it is a pretty and healthy variety which will please those who like light coloured roses of simplicity and individuality.

Svend had visited Armstrongs in California in 1954, and had seen a white Floribunda seedling, under the nickname 'Dogwood'. Armstrongs allowed him to take some home, and Poulsens began to breed from it in 1957. It had the type of growth he wanted, compact and yet producing a tremendous amount of flowers.

Only one of the seedlings from 'Dogwood' looked promising, one pollinated by a selfed 'Pinocchio' seedling; they knew it to be a triploid, that is one with twenty-one chromosomes. They sent it on trial to Japan, and two years later received a silver medal for it. As the Japanese were the only people to show appreciation of the rose, Poulsens named it 'Hakuun', which in Japanese is White Cloud. Niels said: 'It is in my opinion a lovely rose, but it is creamy-white and the market is very little for that colour.'

The real slice of beginner's luck was 'Chinatown', which was introduced in 1963. This was a wide shrub rose, with large and lustrous leaves and double, yellow flowers. In some degree it is a foretaste of a type of rose that breeders have yet to offer, that is shrubs with whopping great roses on them. Sam McGredy summed it up by saying he wanted to breed roses as effective as the hibiscus one sees in warm countries. Niels won a Gold Medal for 'Chinatown' from the National Rose Society.

Like all breeders, he has his good ones and bad ones. Of the latter, we may mention 'Western Sun', a Hybrid Tea of colours indicated by the name. Sam McGredy teased him about it, and named it 'Mildew Sun'. But Niels was more than a match for that sort of joke. He took Sam to an inn at Humlebaek, where by a strange coincidence was a display of Sam's latest varieties, bearing such misleading names as 'City of Humlebaek' and 'Molly McPoulsen'.

He also arranged for Sam's discomfiture at Copenhagen airport, with the willing help of a gorgeous Danish blonde. As Sam the businessman entered, accompanied by the travelling companion in whom he had been confiding the serious purpose of his journey, the blonde rushed up and greeted him with a great, smacking kiss, redolent of anything but respectable commerce. Enter Niels and companion, like two Roman censors, apart from some difficulty in subduing laughter.

24. Niels Dines Poulsen, born 1919. Followed his father, Svend.
Photo: Poulsens Planteskole

Niels' companion on that occasion was the husband of his cousin Dorrit, by
name Knud Sorensen. He was a popular member both of the family and of the
firm. Unhappily he was killed at the age of fifty-three in a car crash, which occurred
as a result of another vehicle emerging unexpectedly from a side road. Two years
later, in 1963, the three Sorensen children and Niels were made partners in the
business. By this time, the three daughters of Niels were growing up; they
were Pernille, born in 1949, Ulla in 1951 and Lise in 1955. A fine pink
Floribunda, early in flower, was named after the eldest 'Pernille Poulsen'.

The Danish government made Plant Breeders' Rights the law of the land in
1962. In order to operate those rights, the breeders formed an organization called
Nord-Rose. Niels was President, and the man in charge of the operation was
Reider Hagard. Nord-Rose took the whole of Scandinavia as its area of respon-
sibility, and saw to the licensing and contracts between the plant breeders, of
whom Poulsen was by far the most important, and over 200 members, who were
in effect the licensees.

The maintenance of such rights has two facets: good relations with those who
accept the justice of paying the breeder for his work, and firmness with those
who try to avoid paying. Reider Hagard was good in either case. He would put
on a peaked cap, such as a yachtsman might wear, and announce to the co-operative

licensees that he was the inspector; make a joke of it, remove the cap, and get down to business in good Danish humour. When he had reason to believe that undisclosed roses were being grown in a remote area, he hired a helicopter, located them from the air, and brought the law down upon the offender.

'Chinatown' was the first rose to be granted Danish Plant Breeders' Rights, but even more valuable was a red rose, 'Nordia'. Little known in Britain, because it was grown chiefly on the continent for the cut flower trade, 'Nordia' came out, fortunately for Niels, in 1967, just when the growers of cut roses were looking for a good red variety.

Niels decided to celebrate his fiftieth birthday with a party his friends would remember. A glass-house was cleared, and two hundred guests came, many of them foreign. Naturally Sam McGredy was among them.

That evening, the Order of the Blue Nose was instituted. It was a serious joke, typical of Niels Poulsen. It mocked the pompous, and bound close companions still closer. As far as I have been able to observe, the opening of bottles is an important part of the Order's work; and Sam McGredy is on record as saying that the only rule he recalls is that which obligates a member 'never knowingly to refuse a drink.' The members add the impressive letters OBN to their names. I have a visiting card of Niels, showing him to be President of the Order, and incorporating such unconventional information as height 190 cm; weight 105 kg (naked); Loyal Taxpayer — so far; ROSE BREEDER — still better than SAM McGREDY.

And after Niels' jokes, if you walk with him among the trees his Uncle Dines planted around Kelleriis, you might be with a priest in a chapel, as he lovingly indicates the beauty and the rarity of one specimen after another. He knows them better than some men know their own sons and daughters. Time means nothing to him in that secret glade; I call it secret, because a stranger would be hard put to find it among the lanes and folds of that quiet Danish scene. When the sun goes down, Niels regretfully leaves his trees for the night, goes into the house, puts decanters on the table, and tells his guests that the rule of the house is to help themselves.

'Troika' was introduced in 1972. It is an excellent bronzy orange red Hybrid Tea, strong in growth, and it deserves greater popularity than it achieved. Niels' original name for it is 'Royal Dane'.

Following a time of illness, Niels agreed to changes in the business in 1976. The eldest of his three daughters, Pernille, and her husband, Mogens N. Olesen, took control, with Mogens as managing director and Pernille as rose breeder. The company became a limited one (ApS in Denmark), with Pernille and Mogens holding two thirds of the shares.

They celebrated their centenary in the pouring rain in June 1978, with a grand gathering of rose breeders from France, Germany, Holland, Belgium, New Zealand and Britain. The local girl guides, beautifully attired and complete with band, marched nobly up and down the squelchy grass. Speeches were made, with the

55 (left) 'Prima Ballerina' *Hybrid Tea* Tantau 1957
56 (below) 'Super Star' (Tropicana) *Hybrid Tea*
Tantau 1960   57 (above) 'Fragrant Cloud'
(Duftwolke) *Hybrid Tea* Tantau 1963

58 (left) 'Blue Moon' *Hybrid Tea* Tantau 1964
59 (below left) 'Whisky Mac' *Hybrid Tea* Tantau
1967   60 (above) 'Sunblest' (Landora) *Hybrid Tea*
Tantau 1970   61 (below) 'Polar Star' *Hybrid Tea*
Tantau 1982

62 (above left) 'Peace' (Mme A. Meilland) *Hybrid Tea* Francis Meilland 1942   63 (left) 'Michèle Meilland' *Hybrid Tea* Francis Meilland 1945 64 (above) 'Baccara' *Hybrid Tea* Francis Meilland 1954   65 (below) 'Starina' *Miniature* Louisette Meilland 1965

66 (above left) 'Darling Flame' *Miniature* Alain
Meilland 1971   67 (left) 'Sweet Promise' (Sonia
Meilland) *Hybrid Tea* Alain Meilland 1973
68 (above) 'Swany' *Shrub for ground cover*
Louisette Meilland 1978   69 (below) 'Colibri 79'
Miniature Alain Meilland 1979

25. Mogens and Pernille Olesen. The young generation in the Poulsen firm. Pernille is the daughter of Niels Dines Poulsen.
Photo: Poulsens Planteskole

unfair distinction that the speakers were sheltered and the audience wetter by the word; but such was the good will, the sense of importance of the occasion, and the confidence in the forthcoming refreshments, that the rain was endured without a murmur.

That night, Niels gave a dinner to the rose breeders, and presented the Gold Medal of Nord-Rose to me; a handsome act, I thought, on an occasion which was their party and in their honour rather than mine.

Pernille and Mogens are still running the firm, and although they had some difficulties in 1982–83, they appear to have overcome them. Bright varieties of their breeding are to be seen in the Royal National Rose Society's trials; like all rose breeders, they seek a red Hybrid Tea, and introduced 'Ingrid Bergman' in 1983; they have an interesting set of roses with small flowers and leaves, extremely dense in their low, shrubby growth; they are 'Pink Bells', 'Red Bells' and 'White Bells'.

Niels takes a philosophic view of rose breeding. He says,

'All raisers should calm down a little and think twice before they introduce "the best rose ever seen".'

9

Kordes

Wilhelm Kordes was born in 1865 in Holstein, at a time when his homeland was becoming the property of Prussia. The Schleswig-Holstein question, for many years troublesome to European politicians, was being solved by force. The former rulers, the Danes, were obliged to yield; yet now, over a century later, their influence remains in the landscape, and in the character and the memory of many Schleswig-Holsteiners.

The territory lies northward from Hamburg up to the Danish border. To the west is the North Sea, to the east the Baltic, and between the two seas are miles of fertile soil. In the summer it is hot, and in the winter very cold.

Wilhelm Kordes' career was decided for him: he should go to sea. He preferred the land, braved the misgivings of his mentors, and in 1887, when no more than twenty-two years of age, he started a nursery in Elmshorn. He described it in a strange style as an 'art and trade nursery'. After several years, he abandoned most of the plants he grew in favour of roses, which eventually became his only crop.

He had two sons who joined him in his business, Wilhelm, born in 1891, and Hermann. In their hands the firm was destined for such success as their father cannot have dreamed of; the credit for guiding them belongs to him.

The best rose in the world, he told them, was the pink 'Caroline Testout'. But the Queen of Roses, if only one had it, would be that same 'Caroline Testout', coloured not pink, but rich, deep red.

Such talk led young Wilhelm to think about breeding roses. At the age of fourteen, he learned the mechanics of hybridizing, and realized that man's intelligence, through the means of pollen and seed, could explore the hidden mysteries of nature. He felt in his hand a key to one of the great wonders of life.

Promptly he began to fertilize 'Caroline Testout' with the pollen of red roses, especially the famous 'Général Jacqueminot'. Caroline declined to give birth to red children. That was disappointing. It merely proved there was more to learn.

He discovered the work of Gregor Mendel, an Austrian monk, who had in 1865 propounded a theory of heredity, based on his observations of the behaviour of peas. Mendel's work had been filed away and forgotten, until in 1902 the British biologist, William Bateson, pointed out its originality and importance. As young Wilhelm Kordes studied Mendel, he felt once more the key of life in his hand.

The tradition in nursery families is to send sons away, to labour at the dirty

26. Wilhelm Kordes I, 1865–1935. Founder of the Kordes nursery in 1887.
Photo: W. Kordes Söhne

27. Wilhelm Kordes II, 1891–1976. 'Possibly the greatest rose man of all time'.
Photo: W. Kordes Söhne

jobs they can all too easily avoid at home, to learn from other growers, to make friends within their profession. Wilhelm went as apprentice to a large German nursery; he worked in Switzerland; the year 1911 he spent in Orléans, working for the well known rose grower, Léon Chenault.

Whenever opportunity offered, he visited the great rose breeders, men who had travelled far down the road he longed to travel. At Lyon, he called upon Joseph Pernet-Ducher; the 'Grand Master', he called him.

Wilhelm landed in England in 1912, to work at the nursery of S. Bide & Sons Ltd, of Farnham, Surrey. There he found a link with another of the names holy to him, that of Henry Bennett. Bennett's youngest son, Edmund, had been working for Bide until he left in 1911 to live in Australia. He had been breeding roses, his plants were still in one of the glass-houses. To Wilhelm, this was a direct link with the Father of the Hybrid Teas; he studied the roses intently, assessing the designs and purposes which lay behind the selection of each one.

The following thoughts went through young Wilhelm's mind: the nursery at home was in the good hands of his father and Hermann. He was happy in England. He had a close friend, another German student of horticulture, named Max Krause, whose ambition was to be a rose nurseryman. It might even be easier to earn a living in England than in Germany.

The two young Germans, Max and Wilhelm, opened a nursery in Witley, Surrey, in the year 1913. The very next year, Kordes W. and Krause M. were interned in the Isle of Man as enemy aliens. They stayed there, in Knockaloe Camp, for the next four and a half years.

Many years afterwards, Alec Cocker asked Wilhelm whether he felt bitter at being interned. The reply was, 'It was a chance for me to learn the King's English.'

It was also a chance to learn more about roses and breeding them. By that time, Wilhelm was familiar with many varieties. He spent much of his time in the Isle of Man reading rose books, from which he extracted every record of parentage. He then analyzed the characteristics which each parent had transmitted, trying to equate his findings with those of Mendel. He considered not only the obvious, such as colour and scent, but also many other features of the flowers, leaves and stems. He identified some dominant characteristics, which were firmly and immediately stamped upon the progeny. Other features disappeared for a generation or more, to reappear later. He called them 'go and comes'. Some of the reported parentages were 'very peculiar'; he probably knew that he could not rely implicitly on the printed records.

He carried in his head for evermore a working knowledge of heredity in roses. Outside, leading a busy life, he might never have attained that knowledge. He later described his studies in internment with masterly restraint: 'During the war I found time to look at the Rose breeding business from the theoretic side.'

In matters of rose breeding, he took for his guide a German saying, 'The soup ladle will only bring out what is in the tureen.'

Another guest of the British government in the Isle of Man was Karl Herbst, the son of a German fern grower. In 1919, they were released, described, to their hurt, as undesirable aliens, and shipped back to Germany. Max Krause went home to start a nursery in Hasloh, Holstein; after success as a rose grower and breeder, he died in 1937. Karl Herbst sold his father's nursery and joined the firm of Kordes, for whom he worked for over forty years, selling their roses. Wilhelm went home to his father and brother Hermann.

Hermann was a mountainous man, over six and a half feet tall, and generously broad. He was solid and reassuring. Searching for words to communicate his character, I stick at one delightful parallel to the confidence that came from him. When Popeye the sailorman swallowed his spinach, all doubt was set at rest, a favourable outcome was ensured. So it was with Hermann, without the painful necessity of spinach.

In 1919, the Kordes family bought a farm at Sparrieshoop, and moved the nursery there from Elmshorn. Wilhelm senior handed over the direction to his two capable sons, the firm being known henceforth as W. Kordes Söhne.

Although Hermann had dabbled in rose breeding, and had introduced 'Adolf Koschel' and 'Adolf Kärger' in 1918, he agreed that Wilhelm should pursue that activity. Accordingly, serious rose breeding started in Sparrieshoop in 1920, some fifteen years after Wilhelm's first hopeful try. Before he had anything to show from breeding his roses, he married. His wife, known to the family as Ama, gave birth to a son, who was christened Reimer.

Given a weighty tome of some thousand pages or so, one might do justice to Wilhelm Kordes the rose breeder. What follows is quite similar to condensing the works of Shakespeare in a nutshell, a difficult task, even if one had the presence of mind to stipulate a coconut.

He returned to his red 'Caroline Testout'. He knew already that he could not breed it directly. It was an example of his 'go and comes'. On studying the descendants of Caroline, he thought he detected the entry he wanted in a pink rose called 'Superb', introduced by Evans of Brighton in 1924. He crossed 'Superb' with 'Sensation', a red rose introduced in 1922 by Joseph H. Hill Co. of Richmond, Indiana. Most of the seedlings were pink, but one was ruby red, giving him the break he had sought. He named it 'Cathrine Kordes' and introduced it in 1929.

The next task was to make it redder still. One rose, he knew, could give him all the qualities he wanted, but it was scentless. It was 'W. E. Chaplin', introduced by Chaplin Brothers in England in 1929. He did not know its parentage, but hoped that scent would be a 'go and come' in it, for 'Cathrine Kordes' had little fragrance to offer. She accepted Mr Chaplin's pollen, with the result of 'Crimson Glory', dark red, very fragrant, soon grown everywhere as the best red rose in the world. It was introduced in 1935. In the same year, his father died.

Wilhelm Kordes was one of the first breeders to see the potential in 'Charles P. Kilham', which even its breeder, Sam McGredy, had apparently undervalued, for he passed it on to Beckwith of Hoddesdon to introduce in 1926. In the

28. Hermann Kordes. Brother of Wilhelm Kordes II.
Photo: W. Kordes Söhne

future, Meilland would employ it on the way to 'Peace'. From 'Charles P. Kilham', Kordes introduced two fine roses in orange shades that would have done justice to that specialist in flamboyant colours, Pedro Dot. They were 'Heinrich Wendland', 1930, and 'Hinrich Gaede', 1931. His other great Hybrid Teas we will pass with brief mention; 'Geheimrat Duisberg', 1933, known in the USA as Golden Rapture, was one of the best yellow roses of its decade; coming to more recent times, we record 'Karl Herbst', a red rose for his old friend, in 1950; 'Kordes' Perfecta', creamy pink, in 1957; and 'Ernest H. Morse', red, in 1964. In 'Karl Herbst' he had given rose breeders a valuable and productive parent.

Floribundas were in great demand in Germany, and Kordes produced many of them, one of his earliest being 'Fortschritt', which means Progress, in 1933. It was creamy pink, with a touch of yellow, bushy, free flowering, and a good cross, between a yellow Hybrid Tea and an orange red Polyantha. In 1936 came 'Rosenelfe', pink, an important variety, because it was the first of its class to show that Floribundas need not be confined to single or semi-double flowers, but could in form imitate Hybrid Teas. 'Minna Kordes', red, came out in 1938, and under the name World's Fair made a fortune for its American distributor at that festival in New York in 1939. 'Rosenmärchen', with double light pink flowers, touched yellow, was introduced in 1940, and named Pinocchio in America. The scarlet 'Korona', 1955, achieved much popularity in Britain. As in the case of Hybrid Teas, Kordes gave a wonderful breeding Floribunda to his competitors, especially Boerner, who made hay with 'Rosenmärchen'.

Wilhelm Kordes studied many aspects of the rose with the same thorough scholarship he had applied in the Isle of Man to the problems of parentage. The cold winters of Schleswig-Holstein directed his attention to frozen roses in Kordes' field and in their customers' gardens. He tried to breed hardier roses, taking as his sources two varieties of the Scotch rose that grew wild near the borders of Siberia; and the Sweet Briar, which had survived ten thousand European winters. The Scotch line gave him some lovely shrub roses, among them 'Frühlingsgold', primrose, 1937, and 'Frühlingsmorgen', pink and cream, 1941; and a fine orange climber, 'Maigold', 1953. Other breeders went further with 'Frühlingsmorgen', especially Sam McGredy, who founded his 'hand-painted' roses upon it.

The Sweet Briar he chose was 'Magnifica'. Introduced by Hesse of Ems in 1916, it was a seedling of Lord Penzance's 'Lucy Ashton'. At first sight it is only a deep rose pink briar, more at home in a hedgerow than in a garden, an unlikely candidate for the hybridizing house.

From it, Kordes obtained three notable results, a most beautiful pink shrub rose, 'Fritz Nobis'; several hardy Floribundas, from one of which I raised 'Margaret Merril'; and, most remarkable of all, yellow roses which in vigour and hardiness excelled those previously existing. He mixed his Sweet Briar hybrids with 'Peace' to obtain the yellow line, culminating after some generations in 'Cläre Grammerstorf' in 1957. Cläre is a rough looking character, coarse in leaf and growth, existing in gardens not so much in her own person, as in her yellow descendants, of which some are Reimer Kordes' 'Honeymoon', 1959; Niels Poulsen's 'Chinatown', 1963; and Sam McGredy's 'Arthur Bell', 1965.

It is a feature of Wilhelm Kordes' breeding, that his vision was constructive, opening up long routes with destinations foreseen by him, but by nobody else. The benefits he conferred on the rose breeding fraternity were rich indeed. The greatest achievements of many breeders would not have existed, had there not been a Kordes variety to breed from.

Wilhelm was fascinated by the characteristics of 'Château de Clos Vougeot', a red Hybrid Tea of 1908 vintage from Pernet-Ducher. It had a long lasting deep red colour as a virtue; for the rest it abandoned itself to vices, such as sprawling growth and small leaves with mildew on them. The colour was an example of the 'go and come' characteristics. It had come into a rose called 'Ami Quinard', a grandchild of 'Château de Clos Vougeot', introduced by a clever French breeder, Charles Mallerin, in 1929.

For vigour and hardiness, Kordes mated 'Ami Quinard' with a rose called 'Eva', which he had bred from Pemberton's 'Robin Hood'. In doing so, he got more than the two qualities he sought, because 'Robin Hood' came from the Polyanthas, and carried within itself a colour pigment, pelargonidum, recently manifested in them. The pollen of his 'Eva' × 'Ami Quinard' seedling was applied to a red Hybrid Tea from Cants, 'Aroma'. The result was a plain, red rose which Kordes named 'Baby Château', and introduced in 1936, knowing nothing of the new colour latent within it. From 'Baby Château' issued 'Independence' in 1943, the first rose of Floribunda or Hybrid Tea type in those flaming orange scarlet colours which set rose gardens ablaze in the 1950s and 1960s, much to the regret of the fastidious. 'Baby Château' was not a great rose, but Wilhelm said, 'as it is with mankind, a good soul may rest in the heart of even a loser.' As for 'Independence', it was so different from any predecessor that the German name was 'Kordes' Sondermeldung', or 'Special Announcement'.

One more example of this great rose breeder's work will suffice. In 1919, James H. Bowditch, of Pomfret Center, Connecticut, introduced a trailing rose he had discovered in a garden in America. It had pink flowers in summer, and covered the ground effectively with creeping growth. The habit and foliage suggested it was a hybrid of R. *wichuraiana* and R. *rugosa*, two species notable for health and hardiness.

Mr Bowditch named it 'Max Graf'. Some years later, Gordon Rowley pointed out a likeness to 'Lady Duncan'; and Norman Young said it was almost certainly that rose, raised by Jackson Dawson of the Arnold Arboretum from the two parents postulated for 'Max Graf', and introduced in 1900.

'Max Graf' was declared to produce no seeds; but its interesting parentage persuaded Wilhelm to obtain a plant, in the hope of using its pollen. He planted it on a south facing wall, obliging it to climb rather than creep, for the sake of tidiness. He soon discovered the pollen was of no use, but he left 'Max Graf' on the wall for many years, even though it did not pay for the six square yards it occupied.

Of the thousands of flowers on that plant over the years, most behaved according to specification by producing no fruit. Exceptions, however, occur in nature. From time to time Wilhelm noticed a hip or two, the seed of which he sowed. In the spring of 1941, two seedlings germinated, the one taking after its grandparent R. *wichuraiana*, the second showing signs of the other grandparent, R. *rugosa*. The latter died during the following winter, but the former lived.

That chance seedling from 'Max Graf' was deep rose pink, with semi-double flowers; it was quite a pleasant shrub rose, but flowered only in the summer. Wilhelm Kordes was more interested in its breeding capabilities than in its worth to gardeners, and he soon discovered that it was fertile, and more than that, it was compatible with modern garden roses. Nature had given him an astounding gift, by doubling the fourteen chromosomes of 'Max Graf' to twenty-eight in the seedling.

The rose was considered a new species, and was named by the botanist, Wulff, R. *kordesii*. Wilhelm raised many climbing and shrub roses from it, including 'Hamburger Phoenix', 'Dortmund' and 'Leverkusen', all introduced in the 1950s. Later Alec Cocker used the strain when breeding 'Silver Jubilee'.

Wilhelm described R. *kordesii* as 'a rose not of my work, but a lucky chance.'

The Second World War depressed him greatly. He and Hermann kept the nursery going, in spite of two disastrous winters, which killed half their plants and wiped out some irreplaceable varieties. Their staff went into the forces, to be replaced with unskilled workers. Sparrieshoop was bombed, but luckily Kordes' glass-house survived, the worst damage being from an air fight, when half the panes were smashed by bullets. Wilhelm kept on breeding, but in a small way for him, at the rate of about 4,000 seedlings a year, until the Allied occupation.

Hermann was arrested by the British, who considered him unsympathetic. They locked him up, but did not reckon with the Schleswig-Holsteiners. When the news of the big man's arrest was known, farmers and nurserymen for miles around put down their tools until such time as Hermann was released. The British let him out.

Hermann's son, Werner, served in the German army on the Russian front; when he came home, he had only one leg. Ten of the nurserymen who had formerly grown roses for Kordes either never returned from the war, or were too crippled to resume their careers.

The war ended with Germany in ruins, and her former enemies in occupation. The winter of 1946–47 laid a savage lash on those already hurt. It killed 90 per cent of the roses budded to be sold in 1947, and nearly all those new varieties which Wilhelm had raised during the war.

He wrote, in despair, 'We are slowly realizing in Germany that we have become the poorest devils on earth.' On rebuilding he added, 'We shall have to do so from the lowest bottom possible.'

29. Werner Kordes. Son of Hermann Kordes.
Photo: W. Kordes Söhne

Their remarkable recovery is in the history books, or if one wishes to see it in terms of roses, a journey to Sparrieshoop is all that is necessary. W. Kordes Söhne is one of the largest, most successful and forward looking rose nurseries in the world.

Wilhelm taught his son, Reimer, the business of breeding roses, with results most creditable to teacher and pupil. Reimer's first introductions came in 1956. In 1958, he sent out 'Iceberg', the white Floribunda to be seen in gardens all over Britain, and in many other countries. It was named 'Schneewittchen' in Germany. Near to it in countless gardens, one may often see 'Lilli Marlene', 1959, a red Floribunda; Sam McGredy suggested the name, after a sing-song at Reimer's table, on which stood the unnamed red rose and a bowl of wine cup, both subjects of much interest to the rose breeders present.

Wilhelm retired in 1964, his trim and spare figure a contrast to the massive frames of his brother Hermann and his son Reimer. He had a good sense of humour, but no time for frivolity. With his small goatee beard, well disciplined moustache, upright stance and miss-nothing eyes, he looked what he was, a German country gentleman, not to be trifled with. He made a retreat for himself in the wooded heathland near Hamburg, surrounded it with rhododendrons and his seedlings from rose species, and often disappeared there to study plants and wild life in solitude and peace.

30. Reimer Kordes. Son of Wilhelm Kordes II.
Photo: W. Kordes Söhne

He died at home in Sparrieshoop in November 1976, at the age of eight-five. With prescience, the Australian rosarian, Dr A. S. Thomas, had summed up his career over thirty years earlier:

'One of the greatest rose men who has ever lived, possibly the greatest rose man of all time.'

His son, Reimer, calm and courteous, follows the road signposted Success. He appears to need no signpost, his steps are so inevitably in the right direction that one could keep the Success markers in store, and set them up later, in Reimer's tracks. W. Kordes Söhne made a lot of money out of Reimer's 'Mercedes', an orange red Floribunda introduced in 1974. The money came from its sale not to gardens, but to the growers of roses as cut flowers. Among his other roses are 'Peer Gynt', 'Marlena', 'Korresia', 'Korpean' and 'Congratulations', the last being known as Sylvia in Germany. But if asked which means most to him, I think Reimer would reply with his normal modesty and good humour that it was 'Colour Wonder'. He named it, with an echo of his grandfather's words, 'Königin der Rosen' — Queen of Roses. It is a fine coral orange colour, bred from 'Kordes' Perfecta' × 'Super Star'.

Reimer, his cousins Hermann and Werner and his son Wilhelm, are now in charge of a great rose nursery. Werner, the most ebullient of the family, is a man of energy, laughter and forceful decision.

Werner has two daughters, of whom Margarita became friendly with my daughter, Elizabeth. They are both married, with families now. Some years ago I took them to London, where we paid the obligatory visit to the Tower. It is a disappointing place for a rose grower; I could find only one bed of roses there. It was 'Orange Triumph', which Wilhelm Kordes had introduced in 1937.

'There,' I said to Margarita, 'look at that. The only rose in this famous place is a rose of Kordes.'

She smiled politely, as much as to say, 'But of course.'

I had to agree with her.

10

Dot

The work of Pedro Dot is a lively justification of the familiar text: 'Ask, and it shall be given you; seek, and ye shall find; knock, and it shall be opened unto you.'

Those words could very well be written on the heart of every rose breeder.

Pedro Dot was born in 1885, the child of three of the proudest and most independent provinces in Spain; his mother was of Basque and Asturian descent, his father Catalan. His native town was San Filieu de Llobregat, near Barcelona, and in that Mediterranean paradise he lived nearly all his long life.

His father was a gardener, at one time in the employment of the Marques de Monistrol, on whose estate was a notable collection of roses, and a *grande dame* in the person of the nobleman's mother, the Condesa de Sástago. Eventually Señor Dot departed, in 1899, to become a general nurseryman on his own account.

Pedro Dot attended the local elementary school, and left at the age of fourteen to be apprenticed to the Establecimento de Successores de Joaquin Aldrufeu. It will be observed by those who follow the careers of rose breeders in this book, that most of them are out of school and into nurseries as fast as they can go, with a blind disregard for those academic qualifications considered so necessary for a successful career in our own times.

Joaquin Aldrufeu was something of a pioneer, being the only rose breeder of note in Spain before the turn of the century. He introduced a few roses during the 1890s, but died, without any great successes, before Pedro Dot joined the firm.

After his apprenticeship, Pedro spent a few years gaining experience in France and Belgium; in Paris he learned the valuable lesson of how to hybridize roses, working at the Bagatelle gardens, where the world's first trial ground for roses had recently been opened. There, under the supervision of J. C. N. Forrestier, the distinguished Superintendent of Parks, he had the opportunity to appreciate the importance of such trials, to see the forthcoming varieties of many breeders, and to identify eminent rosarians on their visits.

He returned to his father's nursery in San Filieu at the beginning of the First World War; in 1915 he made his own first, tentative experiments in breeding roses.

San Filieu de Llobregat is a place to challenge one's conception of a dry and dusty Spain. It has been described as one of the finest rose growing areas of the world. The Mediterranean on the one side and the mountains on another temper the brilliant sun. The soil is rich and fertile. Pedro Dot declared that roses, grown on land which had previously been used for apples, grew luxuriantly, more like trees than bushes. The district is like a huge, natural glass-house.

Pedro took advantage of his climate, by conducting out of doors many operations which in France and Britain would require the protection of glass. He mated his chosen parents in the open, under his own 'automatic system' of pollination.

The system derived from the problem that the seed bearing parent, the mother, must be emasculated before her pollen was ripe, otherwise she would fertilize herself; but when the pollen was unripe, her stigmas were also unready, and while they were maturing, it was likely that pollen would be deposited on them by the wind or by insects. Therefore a chastity belt was necessary, and a simple one was provided in the form of a paper cone, slipped over the de-petalled and emasculated flower head, and tied to the stem beneath it. This had been practised by Pernet-Ducher.

Pedro's idea was to break off the head of the chosen pollen parent, the father; to remove its petals and sepals, and to stuff it, inverted, at the top of the paper cone. Then he had no need to undo his cones, nor to return to his mothers. They were automatically receiving a steady fall of pollen within their paper harems, to a more thorough extent and for a longer period than if they had been manually pollinated.

'Ask, and it shall be given you.' In Hybrid Teas, Spanish rose growers asked for bright, gipsy colours, blazing with red and yellow. The pale roses of the north, with their subtle touches of colour, lost their charm under Spanish skies, turned from beautiful to anaemic. Irish roses were treasured for their beautiful form, which even in Britain was an evanescent quality, and in Spain more quickly so. 'Open your petals wide,' the Spaniards told their roses, 'and show us gorgeous colours.' Droopy necks could be tolerated in Britain, for the sake of a wonderful bloom, but in Spanish sun those necks sank with dismal haste, at the bud stage rather than when the blooms were heavy and full. Spanish rosarians demanded strong flower stalks.

Pedro Dot set about satisfying those desires. The first rose he introduced was 'Francisco Curbera', in 1923; it was salmon pink and yellow, a foretaste of what he had in store for Spain.

His roses were not only for Spain. Other countries have Spanish climates, including parts of the United States. Robert Pyle, an energetic rose nurseryman from Pennsylvania, scented good business in Spanish roses, and from the late 1920s, he introduced Pedro Dot's roses in America.

The United States was the first country to pass a law giving plant breeders some rights in their originations, similar to those due, by general consent, to inventors and other creative persons. The rights were given in the form of Plant Patents, the first of which was granted to the American rose 'New Dawn' in 1930.

31. Pedro Dot, 1885–1976. Spain's greatest rose breeder.
From Modern Roses 6, *by permission of the American Rose Society*

To obtain a Plant Patent was a complicated business, involving specifications, photographs and the assistance of a lawyer or patent agent. One of the requirements was that the variety concerned should not have been offered for sale longer than a year before the patent application was filed. Pedro Dot was already selling his varieties in Spain when Robert Pyle first obtained them to test in America; therefore those roses failed to qualify for Plant Patents. In such cases it was Pyle's custom to pay a royalty to the breeder for three years. By 1934, the times of introduction in Spain and of application in America had been adjusted. Pedro Dot thereafter enjoyed the benefit of US Plant Patents, which held good for seventeen years. The dollars from America were more than welcome. At least six of his new Spanish roses were successful in other countries, but not with any corresponding flow of pounds or marks or francs.

Fifty years and more have passed since those brilliant roses were presented to mankind, and though time has undone them, the first sight of them remains a memory to quicken the pulse of more elderly rosarians. In 1929, Pedro introduced the coppery orange 'Federico Casas', and the orange salmon 'Duquesa de Peñaranda'. The following year came 'Condesa de Sástago', a strong plant, bearing flowers coloured red one side of the petal and yellow the other. It had been entered in the new rose trials at Rome, and had the distinction of winning the first Gold Medal awarded there, in 1933. The most vivid of all was 'Catalonia', 1931, a wide and petal-stuffed bloom in orange red, with touches of yellow; no other rose at that time was as bright. Two beauties came in 1932, 'Luis Brinas', rosy orange, and 'Angels Mateu', rosy salmon; the latter, perhaps the best of them all, is gratefully remembered for the silky look of its delightfully coloured blooms.

Pedro Dot had obtained the Hybrid Teas he had asked for.

'Seek, and ye shall find.' Where to seek? The rose breeder has the whole of the genus Rosa open to him, with the knowledge that of its hundred or more species, only a handful have been explored. Infinity applies to little things like roses, as to the mysteries of space.

In 1926, Pedro Dot had introduced a pink rose, which he had hoped would be large and orange to judge from the parents, the white 'Frau Karl Druschki' and the flame 'Mme Edouard Herriot'. Its name was 'La Giralda'. He fertilized it with the pollen of wild or nearly wild roses of eastern origin. Among the progeny was a shrub rose with large white flowers, semi-double, but beautiful. He discovered, on growing his new shrub rose, a plant of extraordinary beauty. It was nothing like a Hybrid Tea, more like a wild rose, with great stems smothered in white in the summer, so that the leaves disappeared from view. He thought of snowy hills, and called it 'Nevada'. He introduced it in 1927, and it has outlasted all his flamboyant Spanish Hybrid Teas.

He said that the pollen parent was R. *moyesii*, but experts doubted whether that were possible, owing to the difference in chromosome count between the forty-two of that rose, and the twenty-eight of 'La Giralda'. The two might have mated, but could scarcely give birth to a child with twenty-eight chromosomes, as 'Nevada' was. The censorious critics said that Pedro Dot's parentage records were wrong, and the sympathetic pointed out that there was a form of R. *moyesii* with twenty-eight chromosomes, which no doubt was the rose Señor Dot had used.

I resolved this problem to my own satisfaction by a long familiarity with the beautiful 'Nevada'. It is not a fertile rose, but I raised some seedlings as a result of applying its pollen to the Floribunda 'Pink Parfait'. One of them was like a spindly wild rose; at first I thought it could resemble R. *moyesii*, and perhaps Pedro Dot had been right; but I afterwards realized that one could imagine in it likenesses to many other wild roses. A feature of 'Nevada' is its black hips, nearly always empty of seed, except for the odd one or two, none of which I have succeeded in germinating. Black hips are a feature of one section of roses, the *Pimpinellifoliae*, to which the Scotch roses belong. This suggests to me that 'Nevada' must seek her father in that section. After some years, 'Nevada' produced a pink form, 'Marguerite Hilling', the marbled colour of which is also typical of Scotch roses. Therefore my guess, and it can be no more, is that the pollen parent of 'Nevada' was a type of Scotch rose, most likely R. *spinosissima altaica* or possibly R. *spinosissima hispida*. I am sorry to disbelieve a greater man than I. Pedro Dot certainly found something wonderful, whether he sought where he said or not.

He produced another beautiful rose in 1927, the pink climber, 'Mme Grégoire

Staechelin'. The name, pronounced 'stahklin', was promptly changed by Robert Pyle to 'Spanish Beauty'. It is, to this day, one of the best climbing roses in the world, even though its period in bloom closes firmly after one summer showing. The flowers are large and wide, with a slight frill to the petals, warmly and richly rose pink, scented, and so abundant as to coat the plant like pink icing covers a cake.

If left to itself, 'Mme Grégoire Staechelin' atones for its absence of autumn flower by an abundance of fat, green hips. Some experts declare that the hips should be sacrificed in the interests of next year's bloom, by spurring back the laterals as soon as they have flowered. I have never had the heart to do it, myself.

This rose was bred from two famous parents, 'Frau Karl Druschki' and 'Château de Clos Vougeot'; it won the Gold Medal from Pedro Dot's old Parisian training ground, Bagatelle, in 1927.

A strange little rose was introduced by Henri Correvon of Geneva. It was 'Rouletii', whose story is told with that of Ralph S. Moore in Chapter 13. We should immediately recognize it as a Miniature; but as the rosarians of that time knew little or nothing about Miniatures, to them it was unique.

Was there not the possibility of breeding some fairy-like roses from 'Rouletii'? At least two rose breeders thought so. One was Jan de Vink, of Boskoop, Holland. To keep the progeny short, he crossed 'Rouletii' with dwarf Polyanthas, and raised a series of Miniatures which Robert Pyle introduced in America under such names as 'Cinderella', and 'Tom Thumb'.

Pedro Dot had a different conception. Suppose one crossed Hybrid Teas with the tiny 'Rouletii', might one obtain Hybrid Teas in miniature?

'Knock, and it shall be opened unto you.' He began knocking on this particular door in the 1930s. By this time, European nurserymen had at last come to him, seeking to introduce his roses. He received a hairy visitor from England, the flamboyant Harry Wheatcroft; a business-like Frenchman, Francis Meilland; and he supplied them with stock of his early Miniatures.

This promising business suffered long delays, thanks to the Spanish Civil War which lasted from July 1936 to March 1939, and to the Second World War which began a bare six months afterwards. When the war started, Wheatcroft had begun to introduce Dot's Hybrid Teas, which were a poor lot at that time, but had not yet raised sufficient stock of the Miniatures.

The Hybrid Tea which Pedro had chosen to marry to the miniature 'Rouletii' was a yellow seedling of his own, 'Eduardo Toda'. It was bred from two famous roses, 'Ophelia' and 'Julien Potin'. Although he had used it in his breeding since about 1935, he did not introduce it until 1947, when the world was again more or less at peace.

Robert Pyle introduced 'Baby Gold Star' in America in 1940; this rose, named in Spain 'Estrellita de Oro', was bred from 'Eduardo Toda' × 'Rouletii'. It is a good clear yellow, the flowers rather big for a Miniature, the plant not too healthy. Nevertheless it is still being grown for sale.

70 (above left) 'Magic Carrousel' *Miniature* Moore
1972   71 (below left) 'Dresden Doll' *Miniature
Moss* Moore 1975   72 (above right) 'Stars 'n' Stripes
Miniature Moore 1975   73 (below right)
'Rise 'n' Shine' *Miniature* Moore 1977

74 (above) 'Allgold' *Floribunda* LeGrice 1956
75 (below) 'My Choice' *Hybrid Tea* LeGrice
1958   76 (right) 'Vesper' *Floribunda* LeGrice 1967
77 (below right) 'News' *Floribunda* LeGrice 1969

78 (above left) 'Olympic Torch' *Hybrid Tea* Seizo
Suzuki 1966   **79** (below left) 'Eikou' *Hybrid Tea*
Seizo Suzuki 1978   **80** (above right) 'Kam-Pai'
Hybrid Tea Seizo Suzuki 1983

81 (below left) 'Nozomi' *Climbing Miniature* Toru
Onodera 1968   **82** (above) 'Suma' *Shrub* Toru
Onodera, date of introduction unknown

32. The Dot Family. Simon Dot, with his son Albert (right), his son Jordi and Jordi's wife (left), and his daughter Pilar seated in front.
Photo: Simon Dot

Francis Meilland brought out 'Perla de Alcañada' in France in 1944; this bushy plant was more Polyantha than anything else, an exception to Pedro's usual breeding line. It is rosy carmine, with small, neat blooms on a short, wide bush. When Wheatcroft introduced it in Britain, he named it 'Wheatcroft's Baby Crimson'.

One of the best of all Miniatures is the creamy white 'Pour Toi', introduced by Meilland in 1946. Dot's name for it was 'Para Ti'. The blooms have kept a charming Hybrid Tea shape, while shrinking, like Alice, to diminutive proportions. 'Eduardo Toda' provided the seed.

In 1951, Meilland introduced 'Rosina', a yellow Hybrid Tea in miniature; this little beauty needed only a few more petals to be perfect. The parents were the same as for 'Baby Gold Star'. It was introduced in Britain as 'Josephine Wheatcroft'.

For some years, Pedro had been helped in his work by his two sons, Simon and Marino. His nursery was known far beyond San Filieu; to many Spaniards, the words Dot and Roses were joined by the bond of authority; the roses he had bred ensured his international reputation.

When the time came for him to retire, he employed himself peacefully in his garden; he was a man who loved his home, his own place; and there he received most of the globe-trotting rosarians, with modest pleasure that they should seek him out. A number of them travelled to Spain for his 90th birthday party, which according to Harry Wheatcroft was a 'festive occasion'.

He died on the twelfth of November, 1976, in the town where he had been born ninety-one years before. His son, Simon, and his grandsons, Jordi and Albert, are still growing and breeding roses, at Villafranca del Panadés, a few miles away from the home that Pedro loved so much. They favour brilliant Hybrid Teas, as their father did, such as the red and yellow 'Simon Dot', introduced in 1978. Although their roses have not been grown internationally to the extent that Pedro's were, who can tell what may yet come out of Spain?

11

Tantau

To breed roses, one needs patience and perseverance; but to sell the roses one has bred, publicity and aggression are required. Most rose breeders, therefore, are all too ready to caper before the camera, and to confide their inner hopes and dreams, inventing them as they go along, to charming young journalists called Susan or Tessa, who are not quite sure of the difference between a seedling and a sucker.

I advise Susan and Tessa not to make the journey to Uetersen, a few miles north west of Hamburg, just north of the river Elbe. There lives the most private and reserved of rose breeders, Mathias Tantau. He is tall, handsome, with silver hair, commanding brow, uncompromising gaze, and no time at all for nonsense. Susan and Tessa would come away with their note books stuffed with the genetics of rose breeding, details of the latest Tantau varieties, statistics about Tantau's four million rose trees, and no pretty little fables at all. If either should reveal her ignorance about seedlings and suckers, she would get a look that might well blast her into the Elbe. As far as Mathias Tantau is concerned, the subject for publicity should be not himself but his roses.

The first Mathias Tantau, father of the present one, was born in 1882; after his years as a student were over, he started a nursery at Uetersen in 1906. His first interest was in trees for forestry, always an alluring prospect for a nurseryman, on the theory that if one can find a customer, he will need an awful lot of plants to make a forest.

In such a nursery, one raises a great many plants from seed, until it becomes almost an instinct for the nurseryman, upon seeing a seed, to sow it. He has usually prepared a spare seed bed or two, preferring a possible waste of ground to a waste of seed; and when his sowing is done, the temptation to fill the spare space is apt to lead to experiments. Mathias began to sow the seed of Polyantha roses, which caught his interest, because whereas the seeds of his trees grew true to their species, those of the roses were all different.

By 1918, Mathias Tantau declared himself a specialist in rose growing and breeding. He introduced the first two varieties of his own origination in 1919. They were both seedlings of the Polyantha 'Orléans Rose': 'Schöne von Holstein', pink; and 'Stadtrat Meyn', red. They were not particularly successful.

The 1920s were difficult years in Germany. The mark became almost worthless, but gradually the business community began to make the wheels of civilization turn. Mathias Tantau made his living with some difficulty, compounded by the

33. Mathias Tantau, 1882–1953. 'Faithful, hopeful and unlucky'.
Photo: Mathias Tantau

most destructive hailstorm he ever saw. It occurred in 1925, when it destroyed a large part of his crop.

In 1928 he introduced a successful rose, 'Johanna Tantau', which he called a Polyantha, although we should see it as a Floribunda. It was a cross between 'Dorothy Perkins' and 'Ophelia', white with some pink and yellow at the centre, the flowers borne in clusters. I well remember his 'Heros', which came out in 1933, a dark red Hybrid Tea, with rather small flowers and spindly growth, but a wonderful deep colour. It was from 'Johanniszauber' and 'Etoile de Hollande', the former being a Tantau variety of 1926, bred from 'Château de Clos Vougeot.'

During the 1930s, in spite of continuing economic difficulty, the future of the business was ensured by the presence and the interest of a son. Born in 1912, and also named Mathias, the young Tantau was carefully taught by his father. The lessons given had their emphasis not so much on business, but on the wonderful secrets of nature it was the privilege of father and son to explore.

The business outlook was discouraging. Continental Europeans, some of whom saw the produce of the land as their only way of making money, worked so hard and so long and so productively as to harvest more plants than could ever be sold. Down went the prices, off went the plants for export, to countries whose own producers protested against what they termed 'dumping', to such effect that governments raised tariffs against the imports. The Continentals grew fewer plants, but even so Mathias Tantau celebrated each Christmas with a heart made heavy by the number of plants standing in his field unsold. In May, when it was too late to sell any more, he made a huge bonfire of the surplus, sometimes nearly half of the crop he had so hopefully and laboriously grown.

Then he turned to the new season's hybridizing, and lost himself in the secrets of nature, breeding roses which, due to the long time needed for the work, would not earn him a pfennig until another seven lean years had passed. His faith in the future seems to have been unaffected by the hardships of the present.

He was a faithful, hopeful and unlucky man, but at least he established a good nursery. In 1937, he became interested in breeding with a wild rose from China, a rose with small, dainty leaves and clouds of little pink flowers, called R. *multibracteata*. He knew, for all rose breeders know it, that for such a project one should allow at least twenty years; in fact it was twenty-three years before his son reaped the reward of that initiative.

His breeding was soundly based, for he owed a lot, as he owned, to his rose growing neighbour Wilhelm Kordes, some twenty miles away in Sparrieshoop. By mixing the Kordes varieties 'Baby Château', 'Hamburg' and 'Eva' with his own strains, Mathias Tantau produced at last some of the finest and hardiest Floribundas in the world, just in time to lose most of the benefit from them by the coincidental outbreak of the Second World War.

One of these Floribundas was 'Käthe Duvigneau', 1942, a fine red with a white mark on its petals; by the time it emerged from Germany, an English variety named 'Frensham' had usurped its place.

Another was 'Floradora', bred from 'Baby Château'. It showed some of the orange geranium colour of 'Kordes' Sondermeldung', but not quite enough. However it proved valuable to Dr Lammerts in America; he bred 'Queen Elizabeth' with its help.

These roses had a touch of quality and hardness about them which other breeders were ready to recognize. 'Fanal', 1946, was a rose-red Floribunda, widely grown in Europe. 'Garnette' was a marvellous discovery by Mathias Tantau, a red rose with hard petals; it came out in Germany in 1947, and in 1951 was introduced by the Jackson & Perkins Co in America. A most successful cut flower on account of its durability, it was a Kordes-Tantau mixture, being ('Rosenelfe' × 'Eva') × 'Heros'.

Quite a cult arose around 'Garnette', once people had bought a bunch of it, seen the close clusters of small red flowers open in their homes, and found them lasting longer than anyone expected of a rose. The growers of cut roses planted glass-houses full of it, and began to discover mutations, of which 'Pink Garnette', from Boerner in 1951, and 'Carol Amling', from Amling & Beltran in 1953, were fairly similar in deep pink. Some nurseries began to offer 'Garnette Roses' in other colours, but apart from having small flowers, most of these had little affinity to the original. People who planted 'Garnette' in their gardens in Britain experienced some disappointment because in their climate its proper environment is under glass and in a vase. 'Garnette' taught other breeders what to look for in a cut rose: 'petals of tin', Reimer Kordes said.

Mathias Tantau died in 1953; the year before his death, his son introduced 'Red Favourite', a Floribunda which was an international success. Originally its name was 'Schweizer Gruss'; it was also known as 'Holländerin'. In England Wheatcroft introduced Tantau's coral Floribunda 'Anna Wheatcroft' in 1958 and scarlet shrub 'Dorothy Wheatcroft' in 1960.

Before those events, the young Mathias Tantau had been to war, spent some time as a prisoner, and returned to real life to find the nursery in a poor way. In 1946, he took over from his father who, we may suppose, was considerably relieved. After much trouble and difficulty in post-war Germany, young Mathias decided that he must start again from 'zero', which he did in 1948. One may wonder, from the difficulties of his career up to that time, that he had returned to nursery work at all. The reasons, I think, were that he had been well trained to love plants, that he had a strong sense of duty and of love for his father.

If you are a nurseryman, you can appreciate Mathias Tantau from a visit to his nursery. You need only see it — the incredible order, tidiness, method and discipline — to know that a master is in complete control. It is almost soldierly, in the best tradition of the Brigade of Guards. Any other nursery in comparison is untidy, many are slovenly. Most nurserymen don't like to try so hard. We get along, we tell ourselves, with our own easy ways and occasional inspirations.

I can almost hear Mathias Tantau saying, 'Inspirations are not occasional, you must have them every day. I will show you.' He did so for twenty years to the following schedule, as amazing a succession of winners as ever a rose breeder produced:

    1955   Konrad Adenauer
    1956   Baby Masquerade and Olala
    1957   Prima Ballerina
    1958   Paprika and Stella
    1959   Golden Jewel
    1960   Super Star
    1963   Fragrant Cloud and Tip Top
    1964   Blue Moon
    1967   Whisky Mac
    1968   Duke of Windsor and Eroica
    1970   Fountain, Miss Harp and Sunblest
    1971   Belinda
    1972   Topsi

The most famous of these was 'Super Star', a Hybrid Tea of rosy vermilion

34. Mathias Tantau, born 1912. He bred an amazing succession of winners.
Photo: Mathias Tantau

colour, the like of which had never been seen before. This was the rose which came from the complicated *R. multibracteata* line started by Mathias senior in 1937. It has been the promise of many a rose breeder to his wife, that his finest rose shall bear her name; but as perfection is always in the future, a long wait is her normal lot. Mathias proposed to honour his wife by naming his wonderful rose 'Ilse Tantau'. Eugene Boerner, who was preparing to introduce it in America, pleaded for a name the whole world could remember, and suggested 'Super Star', a proposition of such sound business sense that Mathias reluctantly agreed. Alas for Gene Boerner's brainwave! The name was considered an infringement of that used by another American company, 'Star Roses', and in America the rose became 'Tropicana'.

Fragrance is a notable feature of Tantau's roses, and most of his rivals would give a lot to know how he gets it. The pink 'Prima Ballerina', the scarlet 'Fragrant Cloud' ('Duftwolke' in Germany), the lilac 'Blue Moon' ('Mainzer Fastnacht' in Germany) and the vermilion 'Duke of Windsor' are all strongly scented.

'Belinda', an orange Floribunda, has been one of the most widely grown roses for the cut flower trade. The light orange 'Whisky Mac', although not a great grower, is beautiful in colour, form and scent. It has been for several years the most popular of all the roses to which plant breeders' rights apply in Britain.

Genealogy of the Rose 'SUPER STAR' (Tantau 1960)

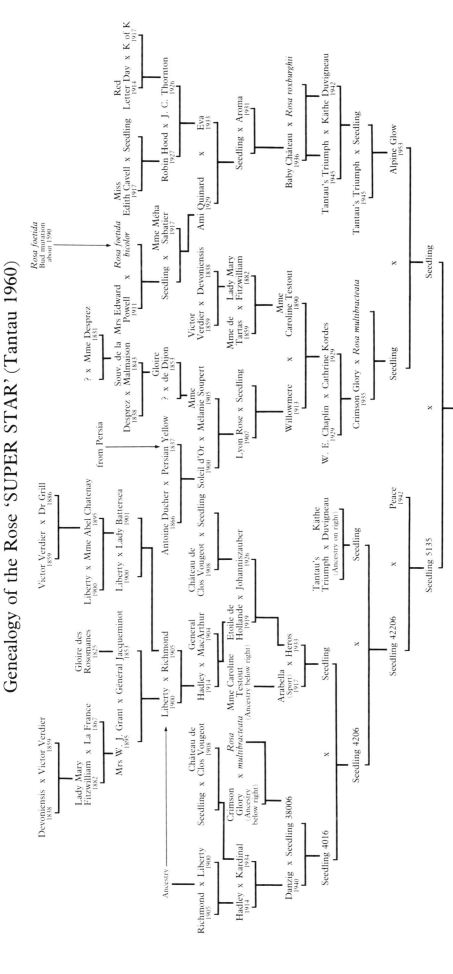

35. Genealogy of the Rose 'Super Star' (Tantau 1960).
Reproduced by permission of Mathias Tantau

Medals and awards are almost superfluous when one has such a catalogue of glorious roses. The Royal National Rose Society's highest award, the President's International Trophy, has been given to 'Super Star', 'Fragrant Cloud', 'Fountain' and 'Topsi'. 'Fountain' is a red shrub rose, and 'Topsi' a bright orange scarlet dwarf Floribunda.

'Miss Harp', a yellow Hybrid Tea, collected a number of names. It began as 'Anneliese Rothenberger' in Germany, became 'Oregold' in America and 'Silhouette' in France; and under the influence of Guinness, 'Miss Harp' in Britain. I think the rose world owes an apology to the original nominee, who surely deserved a rose of her own in return for the pleasure her artful voice has brought to the world.

Occasionally our German friends appear insensitive, as when Kordes named a rose of explosive colour, 'Atombombe'. In the sex-crazed sixties, when northern Europe embarked on a programme of permissiveness which would have won respect and envy from the wilder citizens of Sodom and Gomorrah, a red rose came from Tantau with the name 'Erotika'. Some aesthetic person changed it to 'Eroica'.

Rose growers in Britain have voted Tantau's white Hybrid Tea, 'Polar Star', Rose of the Year 1985. It was introduced in Germany in 1982; in the same year, came a fine pink Hybrid Tea, 'Wimi'.

There is a mystery about Tantau. A retiring, gentle and charming student of nature, he has managed his affairs with such efficiency and effect as is achieved more usually by the ruthless. He is uncompromising, a man to whom the right way is the only way. In his business he has stood firmly for his rights as a breeder to receive royalties for his roses, and through his staff he has exercised strict control of those rights. His representative in Britain is Christopher Wheatcroft, a son of the famous Harry, who introduces the roses of Tantau with considerable success.

The business of Tantau is almost entirely wholesale. They grow, or employ others to grow, about four million roses a year. Their catalogue is a lavish production, designed to sell a few thousand roses per wholesale customer, with page after page of glossy paper and ink, every variety looking so perfect that after a while one feels like an over indulgent eater, looking at the twentieth chocolate éclair, and wondering whether it is wise. Surfeit, I suppose, is a shorter way of putting it. But the catalogue is not meant for the likes of me; it is perfectly aimed at the market it serves.

Mathias Tantau has created a great nursery, he has given the world some of its favourite roses, and as for himself, he spends more and more time in his home in the country, where there is enough wild life to keep him engrossed in studying the secrets of nature, as his father once taught him to do.

12

Meilland

To praise, justify and thank the Meilland family, only four words are needed: 'They gave us "Peace".' Behind those four words lies a tale of toil and enterprise, one which owes its telling to the sturdy figure of Antoine Meilland.

He was born in June 1884, in the village of Chamboeuf, about thirty miles from Lyon. He was one of four children, the family being kept by hard-working parents on the proceeds of their smallholding. His father had experienced the horrors of war in Paris during the siege by the Prussians in 1870. His mother, Jeanne, always known as Jenny, kept her family clean, fed and well brought up on the minimum of money, and in spite of the disability of having lost a hand. She had instead an iron hook.

His career at the village school was successful, in that his education came to its climax at the age of twelve with a certificate to show for it, to his mother's pride. Another influence had already entered his life, through Mme Mivière, the widow of a schoolmaster. Antoine often visited her, admiring her garden, especially her roses. She directed his attention to nature in a friendly and companionable way, and taught him, among other things, how to bud a rose. He counted up every sou he had managed to save, and on the next visit into town with his mother he invested his entire fortune of thirty sous in a budding knife. At the age of twelve, he informed his parents that he had made up his mind to be a rose grower.

His father tried to dissuade him, explaining that people would always buy food; therefore a sensible man would produce a necessity of life in preference to a luxury, which in times of hardship might not be wanted at all. These arguments did not change the boy's mind.

Antoine wrote, asking for a job, to a rose grower of Lyon, Francis Dubreuil, whose address he had from Mme Mivière. The reply advised him to work on a nursery nearer home, and to apply again when he was sixteen. Accordingly, with some disappointment, he went to a nursery which grew trees in nearby St Galmier, and worked there for four years. Then he wrote to Monsieur Dubreuil again.

Francis Dubreuil was a tailor, who had been tempted away from his trade by roses. For this, his father-in-law was responsible. Francis had married Marie, daughter of Joseph Rambaux, who was a gardener at the Parc de la Tête d'Or, where he spent most of his life training fruit trees to a degree of perfection only possible if the cost of human labour were entirely discounted in favour of artistry. In his spare time, this fruit tree expert grew roses in his garden, augmenting

36. Antoine Meilland, 1884–1971. 'Papa Meilland'.
Photo: G. Meunier Doc. Meilland

his gardener's income by selling them. He made experiments of breeding roses, and had ten new varieties of his own, but never introduced them for want of time and resources. After marrying Joseph's daughter, the new son-in-law dropped into the way of helping Joseph on his little plot in the evenings; they bought an adjoining plot, extended their operations, and Francis Dubreuil said goodbye to tailoring with a light heart, and became a nurseryman. In due course Joseph died. In continuing the enterprise, Francis was ably assisted by his young daughter Claudia, who acted as secretary, florist and market trader according to need. Francis Dubreuil introduced old Joseph's new roses, one of which was the enchanting little 'Perle d'Or', a China rose with light pink and yellow blooms on a miniature scale. Francis made a name for himself as a grower and breeder of roses; in short he was the sort of person to whom a would-be rose grower such as Antoine Meilland might well address himself.

On his second application Antoine was accepted, and took up his duties for Francis Dubreuil. He was a handsome, well built youth, with a broad and open face, the result of work in the open air around him, and a good, orderly home behind him. After nine years with Dubreuil, during which he fell in love with Claudia, he sought his employer's permission to marry his daughter. The wedding took place on the fourth of December, 1909. A son, Francis Meilland, was born in 1912, and was not very old when Antoine was called up to fight the Germans in 1914.

Claudia Meilland, then in her twenties, was thus left with four responsibilities: an elderly father, a small son, a home, and a business. The business changed from roses to vegetables; the small son went to market with her, their transport being a hand cart. The war years went slowly and painfully by; Claudia's father, the former tailor, died. And at last Antoine came back from the army in 1919, and they could resume their real lives, grow roses again.

With great difficulty they got twenty thousand root-stocks, planted and budded them, only to see the crop wiped out by a plague of root eating maybugs. Had it not been for a stock of fruit trees which they were able to sell, they were out of business. Antoine, having no time for any crop that was not promptly ready for sale, gave up the rose breeding which his father-in-law had done. He grew another crop of roses, and pulled himself back into business.

Their nursery in Lyon was plainly too small to allow expansion and was indeed surrounded by a great amount of city. They sold Claudia's old home, moved outside the city to Tassin-la-Demi-Lune, and from that point began to achieve a modest measure of success.

Francis, who had been at his mother's heels during the war, learning that if something grew one sold it, was a bright and intelligent boy with a burning ambition to get out of school. He succeeded in that aim, to his mother's regret, at the age of fourteen, when he began to go every day with his father to work on the Meilland rose nursery.

There lived at that time in the small town of Varce, near Grenoble, a remarkable man named Charles Mallerin. He had done well in his profession as an engineer, in central heating, rising to a high position in his firm at Grenoble. His heart was not in that business, but in roses; and as soon as he had the money and the excuse, which was his health, he left others to heat France centrally, retired to his little property at Varce, and applied himself to growing and breeding roses. Not only was he a successful breeder, but a missionary of the craft, developing theories he longed to impart to others for the advancement and benefit of the rose.

In 1929, Charles Mallerin decided to invite French rose growers to see his new roses, especially a yellow Hybrid Tea; that was good business, to which he added to his invitations his missionary zeal, by telling his guests to bring their sons. Antoine and Francis therefore went to Varce.

The yellow rose proved a success in France and America under the name 'Mrs Pierre S. du Pont'. The impression made on one of the sons who went to Varce that day is made evident by Francis Meilland, who began breeding roses the same summer. It was, after all, in his blood. Claudia had told him of his grandfather, Francis Dubreuil, and his great-grandfather, Joseph Rambaux.

Francis found little in rose breeding during his first few years except dashed hopes. He went further than that, to dug up hopes, when the family dog, Caddy, decided to bury a bone in the middle of the newly planted seedlings, and unearthed all but one of them. Claudia encouraged Francis when he might easily have given up. Knowing where knowledge rested, he persistently turned to Charles Mallerin for information and advice.

Charles Mallerin wrote to Francis, whom he called 'My Student', that an American rose grower from the Conard-Pyle Company was coming to France, one Robert Pyle. He proposed to bring Mr Pyle to Tassin to see the student's roses. In truth there was not much to show, but if the Meilland roses were not carrying conviction, the Meilland family, backed with Mallerin's recommendation, persuaded the shrewd American of future business. He made a contract to introduce the roses of Francis Meilland, when they should materialize, in the United States.

Before that contract was consummated, Antoine and Francis suffered the shattering loss of the light of their home. The admirable Claudia died, only in her early forties. Grand'mère Jenny, with her iron hook for a hand, came to take charge of the household. Her first act was to send Antoine and Francis away for a holiday; as rose growers, such a proceeding had scarcely entered their heads.

They went to the south of France, and put up in a hotel in Antibes. After a while it occurred to them that holiday making in a mood of mourning and loss was a poor pastime, which would best be alleviated by visiting local rose nurseries. They knew of one rose nurseryman in Antibes, because they supplied roses to him. His name was F. Paolino. They went to call upon this customer and stranger.

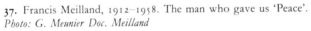

37. Francis Meilland, 1912–1958. The man who gave us 'Peace'.
Photo: G. Meunier Doc. Meilland

Francesco Giacomo Paolino was an Italian immigrant, a member of a large family which had left the hunger and poverty of Calabria in 1892 to seek better times in France. He was one of seven children, but the contingent consisted of quite a tribe of Paolinos in addition to his immediate family. They came to Antibes, where they addressed themselves to the transition from poverty to well-being as a family unit, accepting with tireless industry every task that offered, and saving every sou. Francesco had for a brief time been assistant to a bootmaker, and showed such talent as to set up in business on his own account at the age of sixteen. Unfortunately he was too young and too kind to make his customers pay, which led to a speedy end in bankruptcy, to the consternation of the Paolino tribe. His mother subsequently spent some years in collecting the money he ought to have received, and in discharging the debts he ought to have paid.

Between home and the bootmaker's shop lay the market. It had been Francesco's custom to leave home early, in order to linger in the market on the way to work. Of all the beautiful things to be seen there, he thought the most perfect, the most supremely desirable and right were the bunches of fresh roses. When the family debated his future after the bankruptcy, he settled the matter himself. He should be a rose grower. He rented a small patch of ground, accessible with some difficulty in the middle of the overgrown, uncultivated wilderness which was then Cap d'Antibes. The rent was minimal for so useless a site. He cleared the ground, grew vegetables, flowers and roses, and made a success of it. Seeing what he had done, the Paolino family pooled their savings, borrowed some money and invested in land on the Cap before others should realize its potential. The illiterate Italian immigrants had acquired a share in one of the prime sites in Europe through their industry and intelligence.

There are, I have long believed, three essentials which must march together if any human enterprise is to succeed; two of them are not enough, a project falls in the absence of any one of the three. The afore mentioned industry and intelligence are two of them, and the third is good will.

When Antoine and Francis Meilland presented themselves at the nursery of F. Paolino, good will was overflowing. The serious Frenchmen and the effervescent little Italian found themselves fellow spirits among Paolino's roses. Francesco, like Francis, had started breeding. Their tongues were loosened by roses, confidences were exchanged. When Francesco's wife, Marie-Elisabeth, heard their story, she had Antoine and Francis out of their hotel and into her house in no time at all. There Francis met the daughter of the house, a little girl of thirteen, Louisette Paolino. About seven years later, she would be his bride.

Thanks to the Paolinos, the holiday was a blessing. Antoine and Francis returned to Tassin, to Grand'mère Jenny and their nursery, to find that the bleakness of life without Claudia had lifted a little.

Francis formed the opinion that there was something parochial about rose growing in France, and in the Meilland operations. He determined to visit that El Dorado, the United States of America, and to see for himself what was happening

38. Francesco Paolino. Father of Louisette Meilland.
Photo: G. Meunier Doc. Meilland

in the wide, progressive world. After counting the cost and comparing it with his savings, he announced his intention to his stunned relatives, and departed in 1935. His father and grandmother thought it an extravagance. He saw it as an investment.

The cheapest way to see America, in his opinion, was to buy a second hand car when he arrived, and to sell it before his return. He found a Studebaker, was amazed at its cheapness, and drove it about 12,000 miles around North America. He returned home with several lessons imprinted in his mind: to sell roses, one needed a good catalogue with colour; to grow them, one must employ machinery; to keep them in good condition for sale, cool storage was essential; and for the breeder, some protection of his copyright was just and right. He spent the rest of his life putting those maxims into effect. Meilland's catalogue was in colour the very next year, a procedure by no means the habit of French rose nurseries.

His first successful variety was introduced in America by the Conard-Pyle Company in 1937. The name was left for Robert Pyle to choose; that astute operator tied the yellow rose to the International Exhibition in San Francisco, under the name 'Golden State'. When the royalties arrived, Francis promptly spent them on a cool store.

The fortunes of the Meilland family turned on one strong hinge, if one may so describe the rose eventually known to the English-speaking parts of the world as 'Peace'. Its story is as familiar to rosarians as Cinderella to children, from which I suppose it will be sufficient to recount it briefly. According to Francis Meilland, the pollination was done on 15 June, 1935; he was less precise about the parentage, of which three different versions have appeared, indicating that it is a wise rose that knows its own mother and father.

The original plant of 'Peace' was a weak seedling, but they budded a few eyes from it in 1936, and in October of that year saw that one of them had shot away sooner than normal, and was already in flower. From that point, the character of the plant became obvious, especially its vigour, its fine dark foliage and its wonderfully large flowers in delicate yellow and pink. It was, without doubt, the most beautiful Hybrid Tea the world had ever seen.

On 14 January, 1939, there was a wedding in Antibes between Francis Meilland and Louisette Paolino. During the ensuing summer, Francis sent eyes of 'Peace' to the United States, Germany and Italy; in September, France was at war with Germany, for the third time in Grand'mère Jenny's life. Francis failed to satisfy the medical board that he should be a soldier, and turned to the sorry business of growing vegetables instead of roses. He and Louisette had two children, Michèle and Alain; the latter was born on 25 May, 1940.

A friend in the United States Consulate in Lyon telephoned to say that the Consul was leaving by air for the United States, and would take a small package with him. Within two hours the packet was delivered. It consisted of propagating wood of 'Peace', addressed to Robert Pyle, just in case the previous consignment, of which Francis had heard nothing, had gone astray.

Antoine and Francis introduced that rose in France in 1942, and with one accord named it 'Mme A. Meilland' in memory of Claudia. The Germans brought it out as 'Gloria Dei', the Italians as 'Gioia'. In 1943, Grand'mère Jenny died at the age of 87.

After the war, the Conard-Pyle Company quickly informed Francis that his rose was to be 'Peace' in America, and had so been named at a ceremony which had taken place, by a stroke of luck, on the very day Berlin fell. They introduced it in 1945, and shortly afterwards started to send dollars to Tassin in extraordinary numbers, as a result of the enormous popularity of 'Peace' in the United States. Francis compared this windfall with the lack of income from other countries, and came to two decisions. He would henceforth give up growing rose bushes for sale, and earn his living from breeding roses alone. Thus he would be purely an originator, and no longer in competition with those producers who should sell his new roses. On the other hand, he would see to it that other countries copied the entirely just and admirable provisions that existed in America.

The Meillands therefore offered to sell their nursery at Tassin to a competitor and friend, Francisque Richardier. He studied their accounts, listened to their proposals, and said that in their place, he would have thought it prudent to retain half the interest in the business. It was accordingly agreed. In 1946, the establishment became Meilland-Richardier under the management of the latter. The Meillands bought land on the Cap d'Antibes, with Mr Pyle's dollars and M. Richardier's francs. In 1948, they set up a large breeding centre, with extensive glass-houses, close to the Paolinos, much to Louisette's delight.

Francis became lawyer, businessman and breeder. In the latter role, he was much influenced by his Italian father-in-law, to whom the prime virtue of a rose was its use as a cut flower. As a result he introduced in 1954 a rose which must have stood on the shelves of every flower shop in the world, the long stemmed, bright red 'Baccara'. His garden roses are remembered by everyone who grew roses in the twenty years after war: 'Michèle Meilland', 'Eden Rose', 'Belle Blonde', 'Bettina', 'Moulin Rouge', 'Grand'mère Jenny' and 'Charles Mallerin' are just a few of the familiar names.

Francis the lawyer disciplined himself to study the intricacies of the French patent law, and in 1951 obtained from the Ministry of Industry and Energy a *Brevet d'Invention* for his new rose 'Rouge Meilland'. This was a red variety for cutting, introduced in America as Happiness.

The French rose nurserymen were shocked at this innovation. The prospect of paying royalties was not to their taste at all. Francis suddenly found himself the most unpopular man in the trade.

He delved into the mysteries of trade marks, and through his British agents, Wheatcroft Brothers, applied for UK trade marks on several roses. The application was opposed by the Wisbech Plant Co. Ltd; backed by the National Rose Society and most of the British nurserymen. After an expensive court hearing, the judge ruled that varieties of roses were not proper subjects of trade marks. Francis resigned from the National Rose Society, and withdrew his roses from its trials, not out of pique, he said, but to protect the validity of his continental trade marks. He made this clear to a British visitor to Antibes, saying, 'To love roses is sufficient to make you welcome here.'

By his persistence in studying the laws of several states, and by his burning sense of justice in his cause, he did more than any other person to create a favourable opinion of plant breeders' rights, which have gradually been adopted by many countries.

In business, he sought an international network of agents who would simultaneously introduce his varieties all over the world. He called it Universal Rose Selection. The prospective varieties for the future were sent to each member; after everyone had the opportunity to assess the roses at home, a June meeting was held annually at Antibes, to determine which should be introduced. The weakness of the plan was that the participants occasionally found themselves obliged to introduce a rose which was not successful in their particular climate. The strength of it lay in the catalogues. They were beautifully printed in France, and so designed that each participant would provide his own text. The pictures of the roses were exquisite, such as could not be afforded by an individual nursery.

83 (above left) 'Morning Jewel' *Climber* Cocker
1968   **84** (left) 'Alec's Red' *Hybrid Tea* Cocker
1970   **85** (above) 'Anne Cocker' *Floribunda*
Cocker 1971

86 (left) 'Rob Roy' *Floribunda* Cocker 1971
87 (below left) 'Glenfiddich' *Floribunda* Cocker
1976   88 (below) 'Silver Jubilee' *Hybrid Tea*
Cocker 1978

(opposite) 89 (right) 'Escapade' *Floribunda*
Harkness 1967   90 (below right) 'Alexander'
Hybrid Tea Harkness 1972   91 (far right)
'Yesterday' *Polyantha* Harkness 1974   92 (centre
right) 'Margaret Merril' *Floribunda* Harkness 1977
93 (below far right) 'Anne Harkness' *Floribunda*
Harkness 1980

94 (above) 'Greensleeves' *Floribunda* Harkness
1980   95 (below) 'Mountbatten' *Floribunda*
Harkness 1982   96 (above right) 'Amber Queen
Floribunda Harkness 1984   97 (right) 'Cosette'
Floribunda Harkness 1984   98 (below right)
R. persica seedling Harkness, not introduced

Francis appeared to have the single-minded energy of at least three people; any one of his three projects, his breeding, his business and his legal studies, would have been more than enough for an ordinary person. He was in haste to succeed, as though he knew his time was short. The rôle of Antoine Meilland is of interest. If, with his simple upbringing, he had stood aside in puzzlement as his son let loose the tide of change, one could have understood his feelings perfectly; but on the contrary, Papa Meilland, as he was always called, was a rock, a central figure in the fast growing empire. He was a man to depend on, calm, simple and constructive. Francis was no less fortunate in Louisette, a rose grower born and bred, and a willing worker in the breeding houses. As for young Alain, a short, tough, resilient youngster, with dark curly hair and a deep voice, surely sprung from Italy, he made the nursery his province.

Francis left his beloved family prematurely, by dying of cancer in 1958, at the early age of forty-six; but if one family dynamo had been stilled, another was ready to start up.

Alain continued and developed his father's policies, with the active help of his mother and grandfather. 'Papa Meilland', a deep red rose introduced in 1963, was named for Antoine. A good flower of it is indeed a glory of dark colour and fragrance, but in Britain such blooms are not produced often, the plants being small and prone to mildew. It looks better in some warmer climates, and must have given pleasure to Papa Meilland in his last years. He died on the ninth of February, 1971, in his eighty-seventh year.

The Meilland organization has prospered under the direction of Alain and his mother, and is now a large, international business. To that prosperity, roses for the cut flower trade have been the main contributors, especially the rosy salmon 'Sonia Meilland', known as Sweet Promise in Britain, and introduced in 1973. Sonia is Alain's daughter.

Cut flowers can easily be transported by air, a fact which enabled growers to dodge the high costs in Europe of fuel and wages, by growing crops in far-off countries, such as Kenya, Mexico, Colombia and Israel. Those and other countries needed foreign business and money, and welcomed such enterprises. In so doing, they greatly complicated the breeder's task in maintaining his rights over his origin-ations. Alain was obliged, like his father, to travel, to study legislation and to fight for his rights. He did so with vigour and bounce, backed by a ruthless French logic in following a principle. In consequence he was not the most popular person in the industry. The bitter-sweet nickname attached to him was Napoleon.

He is fluent and emphatic in speech, can out-English most Britons in the grace and expression he puts into their language, and is remarkably open and frank in stating his position and policies. He established trial nurseries for cut roses in France and Holland, and production nurseries to supply the plants which glass-house growers need, in Spain and other countries. Meilland's area of glass for research and trials is about 100 acres, more that twice the size of the entire cut rose industry in England.

39. Louisette Meilland. Widow of Francis, mother of Alain.
Photo: G. Meunier Doc. Meilland

When he sees an unfulfilled need, he directs the Meilland research establishment to supply it. When people began to talk of patio roses, that is small plants for little gardens, out from Antibes came a whole range of them, linked by the name 'Sunblaze'. To the demand for Miniatures, Meillands responded with some excellent varieties, the orange red 'Starina', the bright bicolour 'Darling Flame' and the charming pink and yellow 'Colibri 79'. Ground cover roses and hedge roses were similarly produced, 'Swany', white, being their main variety for ground cover.

I often think that working in the Meilland organization must be like camping on a volcano; one would never know what its volatile leader would require tomorrow. His nature, like the skill of John McEnroe, is to return shots faster than they arrive.

Then one sees him, kindly, solicitous, hospitable and charming, wearing the loving and jolly character of his little Italian grandfather, as if there were no empire to sustain, no battles to fight, nothing in the world but roses and friends — and Peace.

40. Alain Meilland, born 1940. The present head of Universal Rose Selection—Meilland.
Photo: G. Meunier Doc. Meilland

13

Moore

Ralph S. Moore was born in Visalia, California, on 14 January, 1907. His father was Orlando Moore, a grower of vegetables by trade. His mother, before her marriage, had been Muriel Witherell. Had Gregor Mendel inspected the Moore family, he would at once have concluded that, in Ralph's case, the Witherell strain was dominant.

For further evidence of this, we need only accompany little Ralph on one of his visits to his Witherell grandparents, Willard and Della. They lived in a little timber-clad house in Visalia. Willard grew roses in the small yard around his home, and spent many an hour among them. There Ralph would find him, and once received a lesson from the old, stooping man, on how to take cuttings from roses. Put sixty years on the boy, and the two might have been twins: the same balding domes; grey hair remaining at the sides and back; the same large ears, though grandfather's stuck out more; the same benign expression; Ralph's face is fuller, perhaps because the old man's teeth were scanty; and the same long, strong, forceful fingers.

The old man gave more to Ralph than physical resemblance. From his father's market garden and from his grandfather's roses, plants were Ralph's environment. Between the two, his choice was roses; the mystery of making cuttings was like an initiation into one of life's secrets. He never forgot it; it was only a simple lesson, but the grandfather could have given the child no greater gift.

Ralph attended the Visalia Junior College, and then the University of California at Davis. During his schooldays, it occurred to him that his father's vegetables were grown from seed, therefore it might be interesting to sow rose seed.

He collected hips from 'Crimson Rambler', from a large, rambling plant of 'Climbing Cécile Brunner', and from various other roses. Eventually, in 1929, he named three of the seedlings. 'Baby Mine' was a light yellow bush from the seed of 'Cécile Brunner'; 'Shelby Wallace' was a light pink climber from the same source. From 'Crimson Rambler', he obtained a somewhat similar variety, which he called 'Gypsy Queen'. Ralph Moore had produced his own roses at an early age. He began to cross Hybrid Teas.

At this stage of his life, he had three threads to weave into his future; one was to marry the right girl; the second to make a good career; and the third to continue in the Christian faith of his local Presbyterian Church. The career and the woman and the faith were interwoven in his resolve, which he described, simply, as a desire to do something worth while.

41. (left) Willard and Della Witherell. Grandparents of Ralph Moore. 42. (right) Ralph Moore,
aged 3, on left.
Photo: Ralph Moore

The girl he wanted to marry was Ann Newberg; he persuaded her to become
Ann Moore, and they were married in 1931. It was to be a long and happy marriage;
they celebrated their golden wedding a few years ago.

Ralph's experience with 'Cécile Brunner' had given him a liking for small roses.
In 1935, he saw the smallest rose in the world. It grew only a few inches high,
with the leaves and stems and pink flowers scaled down in proportion. Here,
truly, was a miniature rose. Its name was 'Rouletii'.

It was so named after Colonel Roulet, a medical officer in the Swiss Army;
he obtained it in the Jura, from the village of Mauborget, where the villagers
grew it in pots on their window ledges. It seems to have been a local speciality,
preserved in that place and discarded by the rest of the world. According to the
villagers, it had been in one family for 150 years, an estimate in which we may
suspect exaggeration. About its origin, there are theories, but no certainty, except
that it is a miniature China rose.

In 1917 Colonel Roulet had given some stems to a friend of his in Geneva,
a plantsman named Henri Correvon. Correvon was able to supply plants from
1920, and he named it 'Rouletii'. Fifteen years later, Ralph Moore first saw the
wonderful little rose, and held his future reputation in his hands.

By reading and by practice, he had slowly learned how to breed roses. His
Hybrid Teas were such stuff as one would expect of a beginner. Two of them,

133

'Lois Crouse' and 'Rochelle Hudson' were introduced in 1937 by Brooks & Son, of Modesto.

The same firm had in the previous year introduced a far more important variety, Ralph Moore's 'Sierra Snowstorm'. It was more important to Ralph, genetically, than to Brooks commercially, being a cross between 'Gloire des Rosomanes' and 'Dorothy Perkins'. The flowers were small and white, the growth shrubby.

Armed with 800 dollars, a few hundred rose bushes, and the idea of breeding Miniatures, Ralph went into the nursery business on his own account in 1937. He called his establishment the Sequoia Nursery, and began with a general range of plants, in which roses predominated.

As we have seen, Ralph was not the first to think of breeding from 'Rouletii'. The Dutchman, Jan de Vink, had already started. His red variety, 'Peon', was introduced in Europe in 1935; de Vink had fertilized 'Rouletii' with the pollen of 'Gloria Mundi', or at least he was fairly confident of the pollen's identity. 'Peon' was introduced in the United States by the Conard-Pyle Co in 1936, under the name Tom Thumb. Ralph Moore made haste to obtain it.

Miniature roses were not new; they were being re-discovered; a period of popularity in the nineteenth century had been succeeded by a total and unexplained oblivion. One survivor, found in England by C. R. Bloom, in a garden near Cambridge, was 'Oakington Ruby'. Its flowers were red, each petal white at the base; it was introduced in 1933. Ralph Moore added it to his collection.

A rose breeder needs his own strain; it is all very well to take existing varieties, such as 'Peon', 'Oakington Ruby' and 'Rouletii', and breed them together; it is much better to add in the special ingredient, the extra something. Ralph had it: 'Sierra Snowstorm'. He put its pollen on a coppery Polyantha, 'Etoile Luisante', and raised as a result a pink, five-petalled rambler, which he named 'Carolyn Dean', and introduced in 1941. Then he went to De Vink's 'Peon' for pollen. Mated with 'Carolyn Dean', it produced a vigorous, thorn-free, pink rambler called 'Zee'. Ralph did not put 'Zee' on the market. He kept it for breeding, rambler though it was. He had discovered that when tiny Miniatures were crossed with vigorous climbers, some of the progeny would be miniature. More than that, a rambler such as 'Zee', which was conceived by a union of shrub and Miniature, could be mated with another rose of climbing habit, and yield among the seedlings a proportion of Miniatures.

His first conspicuous successes came from crosses of that nature; he used two climbing roses, 'Copper Glow' and 'Golden Glow', which had been raised by Dr and Mrs Walter D. Brownell, of Little Compton, Rhode Island. 'Golden Glow' × 'Zee' gave him the straw yellow Miniature 'Jackie', introduced 1955; 'Copper Glow' × 'Zee' produced the bright yellow 'Bit o' Sunshine', 1956.

Those who breed Miniatures discover that it is fiddly work, because the flower parts are small. Many Miniatures are extremely mean with their seed, producing either none at all, or if in lavish mood perhaps two or three seeds in a hip. By applying the pollen of Miniatures to fertile mothers with large flowers, Ralph reduced tedium and increased production. After throwing away the useless climbers and shrubs, he had more Miniature seedlings left than he would have obtained from a similar number of crosses directly between Miniatures. He also had better strains, from the qualities that entered his seedlings from sources other than the Miniatures.

Ralph applied for a US plant patent, and received it, for his wine red Miniature 'Centennial Miss', introduced in 1952. It was difficult at first to sell Miniature roses; mainly as a result of his persistence, they became more and more acceptable to gardeners and exhibitors. He became quite expert at filing patent applications. During his career he took out patents on over a hundred of his varieties.

The name Moore became to rosarians a synonym for Miniature roses during the 1950s and 1960s. In 1957, the Sequoia Nursery abandoned virtually every other plant in order to concentrate on Miniature roses. Unlike most rose nurseries, which line out root-stocks in a field, and then bud them, the Sequoia Nursery grew its roses from cuttings. In Visalia, one can root cuttings for very nearly twelve months of the year. The cuttings are grown both under cover, from soft shoots kept moist by fine mist expelled from thermostatically controlled jets; and in the open, from hard shoots on raised beds or trays. They are never planted in the field, but stand in pots until they are sold.

Much the same process applies to the new roses. Ralph Moore sows his seed in boxes in an unheated glass-house in January. When the seedlings begin to flower, those which show any promise are marked by a short stick, and in due time are potted on when the rest are discarded. The assessment of pot plants continues, a practice contrary to that of most breeders, who examine their plants in the fields. The method certainly teaches Ralph which seedlings grow in pots and are beautiful. It is less efficient in weeding out varieties prone to disease. As to hardiness, Visalia is no place for testing it.

Given the splendid range of Miniatures bred by Ralph Moore, who at one time seemed to sustain the whole class like Atlas the heavens, it is fair to say that there are some which do not thrive. Some of the best are 'Rise 'n' Shine', yellow, 1977; 'New Penny', light coral, 1962; 'Magic Carrousel', red and white, 1972; 'Easter Morning', cream white, 1960; 'Little Flirt', orange pink, 1961; 'Little Buckaroo', red, 1956; 'Orange Honey', 1979; 'Baby Darling', orange red, 1964; 'Mr Bluebird', purple, 1960; 'Stacey Sue', pink, 1976; 'Sheri Anne', orange red, 1973; and the red and white striped 'Stars 'n Stripes', 1975.

Breeders are born to see visions, but not always to touch them. An apparently attainable aim, from the mixture of Miniatures and ramblers in Ralph Moore's breeding house, was a climber in miniature. One may imagine it, a pretty plant tied to a cane, growing demurely to head height, neatly covering itself with little leaves and flowers, a slender column of colour in summer and autumn.

Ralph found a few, the best of them 'Pink Cameo', which he introduced in 1954. It was neither sufficiently repetitive in bloom, nor gentle in colour. Here is a prospect of great delight for some breeder to travel towards.

43. Ralph Moore. Aged 76, and still working among his Miniature Roses.
Photo: Ralph Moore

Another vision was to transfer the beauty of old fashioned Moss roses to modern varieties. How charming, he thought, to see his Miniatures adorned with mossy green tendrils upon their sepals and seed pods. He set himself the task of breeding the moss into modern roses in 1948.

At first sight, it was one of those tasks which might be accomplished in fifty years or so. The Moss roses are almost as sterile as mules. They flower briefly, in summer, and spend much of their time moping with mildew. They are gaunt and shrubby.

The first step was to grow some breeding stock, by finding what little pollen the Moss roses might occasionally offer, and fertilizing modern roses with it.

Ralph took an orange Hybrid Tea, 'Président Chaussé', raised by Mallerin, and known in America as Mark Sullivan. He found some pollen on 'Golden Moss', which had come from Pedro Dot of Spain in 1932. The cross yielded a number of seedlings which flowered only in early summer, and grew eight to ten feet or even more. Only one had any moss worth speaking of; it had leaves of modern rather than moss rose type, and orange yellow flowers. It bore no seeds, but had good pollen. Ralph called it OM, short for Orange Moss.

He crossed it back on to modern roses, to make it have children to flower in autumn as well as summer. The children lost practically all the moss. He tried again, wondering how many more rose generations must pass. The children were all tall and summer flowering, but some were mossy. Pollen from one of them was applied to 'Rumba', and at last, in 1972, after twenty-four years at work, he introduced a modern Moss rose, which he called 'Goldmoss'.

In the same year, he introduced 'Rougemoss'. This had arisen from similar experiments, involving Wilhelm Kordes' 'Rosenmärchen'; an old purple Moss, 'William Lobb'; a red Floribunda from Kordes' friend, Max Krause, called 'Willi Maass', but known as Red Ripples in America; and Ralph's OM. The last stage, as in the case of 'Goldmoss', was to make 'Rumba' the seed parent.

The first of his Miniatures to show signs of moss was the deep pink 'Fairy Moss', which he introduced in 1969. It came from a cross 'New Penny' × ('Rosenmärchen' × 'William Lobb'). Fertile both in pollen and seed, it opened the path to better varieties, being seed parent of 'Dresden Doll', 1975, 'Lemon Delight', 1978 and 'Mood Music', 1977.

It is difficult to breed and select roses for climates other than one's own. Those which are thrown away due to their miserable appearance in California might be beauties in Britain; those which thrive there may not do so here. Few breeders appear to have followed Ralph's work with moss roses, perhaps because they think he has too great a lead, or perhaps because the prospect does not hold commercial appeal. When breeders in Europe overcome their inhibitions, they may surprise themselves and the rose world by their discoveries.

If Ralph Moore could pluck mossy buds from the past, then by similar persistence and intelligence rose breeders should be able to ransack all the treasures of the genus Rosa: the sharp apple tang of sweet briar leaves, the long, shining flasks of R. *moyesii* hips, the thornlessness of Banksia, the rich scent of olden days, the perfect shrubby habit of many wild roses, the health of the rugosas.

His career has brought him honours and renown; his marriage, life-long content; he kept to his faith, teaching in the Sunday School of the Presbyterian Church of which he is now an Elder.

He is a man of peace, not of political peace, but the real peace, which he describes as 'something of the spirit which can and will not wish or cause harm or loss to another.'

14

LeGrice

On 5 July, 1976, rosarians from nearly every country one can think of were congregated in Sir Christopher Wren's beautiful Sheldonian Theatre at Oxford. The occasion was intended to be memorable. The Royal National Rose Society, in its hundredth year, was acting as host to the world's rosarians.

It was the most glorious summer in living memory, a hot un-British summer. Delegates from five continents were housed in Oxford colleges; having heard of the ancient lawns, and the prescription for achieving them, by cutting and rolling for two hundred years, they were greatly disappointed by the brown and withered quadrangles the weather had produced.

They awaited the opening of the conference, decorating the rows of the circular Sheldonian by wearing their lightest clothes. The sun filtered through the windows upon a sparkling array of roses and people. The Reverend Vice-Chancellor, Sir John Habbakuk, welcomed all present to Oxford. And then came the inaugural lecture, indeed an ordeal for the man who should deliver it.

With all the talent in the world at their disposal, the organizers had selected a quiet, shy, Norfolk rose breeder, one whose health had frequently failed, one who was seventy-three years old and, had anyone known it, was due to die in eleven months time.

Edward LeGrice came forward to speak. His hair was becoming silvery, his movements slow but purposeful; his dark eyes were as ever alert, in a pale, peaceful face. His address had been prepared in a scholarly manner. He delivered it calmly and with humour, discussing the brief he had been given, namely the highlights of the Society's first hundred years. That little history he put in perspective with the larger history of human society, and of the evolution of the rose. It was a brilliant address, a masterpiece of sincerity without showmanship. The International Conference was already a success before the inaugural lecture was finished.

Edward Burton LeGrice was born at North Walsham on 10 December, 1902, the newest member of a family that had lived around Harleston in the south of Norfolk for hundreds of years. His father had moved to North Walsham where he kept two shops, a grocery and a general store, into one of which it was vaguely expected young Edward should go, but two factors barred him from the counter. One was his mother, who enjoyed the roses in her garden so much that she passed on her enthusiasm to her son; the other was the Paston Grammar School in North Walsham.

That school, situated in a farming county, included in its syllabus, along with history and French, a subject likely to be of practical use to the pupils, namely agricultural science. Edward, rather a bookish boy, did well at school. In those days, in Norfolk, schoolchildren took the Cambridge Senior Certificate; Edward passed it with honours, gaining a distinction in agricultural science. He told his parents that the shop was not for him, he wanted to live in the open air, and to grow plants. He wished to be apprenticed to a nursery.

The LeGrice family knew nothing of nurseries, except for buying plants from them occasionally; they set about finding one which would train Edward. They soon discovered that nurseries had no objection to employing boys as labourers, but no time to waste in teaching them. The answer to their first inquiry was: 'He needs no teacher; let him keep his mouth shut and his eyes open and he'll learn.'

Somebody suggested they should try Henry Morse & Sons, of Norwich, and from that firm they got a more favourable reply. In 1918, in his sixteenth year, Edward was bound apprentice, on the terms that his father should pay thirty shillings a week to Morse during the first year; in the second year, Morse would pay that money back at the same rate to Edward; and in the third year, when he would presumably be of some use, the firm would for the first time dip into its own pocket, and pay him a wage. It is not recorded how he was expected to get through the first year.

This unpromising contract proved so successful that, over half a century later, Edward described himself 'a close friend and grateful pupil' of the Morse family.

It was a large, vigorous and cheerful family. Henry Morse was one of four brothers, all of whom had started nurseries. He had begun his own in 1902; when Edward joined it, three young Morses were already helping their father. They were Ernest, William and Fred.

Work started at 7.30 each morning, except on Sundays; it was hard. The only machines employed were the muscles of men and horses; the tools were forks and spades and hoes and knives, with one brilliant, labour-saving device, a one-wheeled Planet hoe. Attached to it was a rope, by which a boy pulled it along the rows, while a man walked behind to guide it.

Edward learned to bud roses and fruit trees, but he was slow at it, and was teased by the others. He found a sense of companionship, working under the clean Norfolk sky, with the talk, serious or jesting, rattling along in Norfolk style.

The Morse brothers were a remarkable trio, more amicable to one another than any brothers I ever met. The world was a simple and sunny place to them, all its men and women lovable and trustworthy; the meaning of life was clearly explained by the Bible; the process of living was a short prelude to the eternal joys of heaven, made possible by faith in our Lord and Saviour, Jesus Christ. Of the three, Ernest was the most committed Christian; all three followed St Paul's advice to think of those things which are true, honest, just, pure, lovely and of good report. They were truly simple men.

They might be accused of naïvety, but if so, in extenuation they could plead mountains of sunny confidence, happiness and laughter. Edward LeGrice was in no danger of falling into bad company; he had Morses and roses.

The question of his future arose. His father was not in favour of Edward doing nursery work, but was persuaded to invest a tax rebate received after the end of the war in ten acres of land. The Morse family, with generous disregard of any fears of future competition, encouraged him to start business as a rose grower on his own account. They advised and assisted him, so that in 1920, the third and final year of his apprenticeship, he was able to buy, plant and bud his first root-stocks. His first crop of roses was therefore ready for sale in 1921. Edward was then on his own.

He found life lonely, and hard. The successful rose nurseries of the day were in nearly every case run by the second or third generations of the families who owned them. It seemed to be the fate of the first generation to toil at the foundations; succeeding generations had the inestimable advantage of assimilating knowledge from early childhood, and of then applying it to build from the point their fathers had reached. He had at least been lucky in having a father who could buy land, and from that start he must labour.

The Morses, although not rose breeders, were keenly interested in new roses, and were friendly with the Sam McGredy of their time. Edward had seen McGredy at the first rose show he attended, as an employee of Morse, at Norwich in July 1919, when the new pink rose 'Mrs Henry Morse' won a Gold Medal. He wanted to breed roses himself, but having no accommodation for it on his ten acres, he started with some roses in pots in the vinery at home.

He became an employer, a sign of progress, even though the staff was only one boy, at ten shillings a week. He erected his first building, a small wooden hut. He took his roses to shows, where he saw Joseph Pemberton and other rosarians of note.

During the 1930s, he introduced the first roses which he himself had bred, starting with a cherry red Hybrid Tea in 1933, 'Mrs F. J. Jackson'. The most successful was 'Dainty Maid', in 1937, a beautiful rose of the type he liked best, that is single, with five petals only. It was clear rose pink, the stamens showing yellow at the centre, the flowers neither crowded nor distant in the clusters, but so spaced that each one paraded its beauty to the advantage of itself and the others.

Less successful, but more important, had been 'Yellowcrest' in 1935. The brilliant yellow roses of that time, such as 'Golden Emblem' and 'Mabel Morse', left much to be desired in the way of growth and hardiness. Edward took as his objective a hardy, golden rose; he set out to obtain a breeding strain which, once established, should yield a good number of golden roses in its progeny. His starting point was the rose 'Mrs Beckwith', raised by Joseph Pernet-Ducher and introduced in 1922, a yellow rose which like many of the era opened the season with its first flowers almost white.

When 'Yellowcrest' appeared, he thought he had gained his object, for here was a golden yellow rose with every appearance of vigour, even though the flowers were small for a Hybrid Tea. An unpleasant surprise was to come. When the first flowers shattered and fell in late July, the leaves, perhaps out of sympathy, followed suit. They grew again to accompany the September flowers, only to fall off in similar fashion again. It was a bad fault, which would render the strain useless unless it could be corrected.

He thought the cure might lie in 'Mrs Beatty', a creamy yellow rose introduced by B. R. Cant in 1926. This choice was made by the almost intuitive eye he now had for roses. He used 'Mrs Beatty' as seed parent, 'Yellowcrest' for pollen, and waited eagerly to see the seedlings. *Modern Roses* quotes 'Lilian' in place of 'Mrs Beatty', but Edward told me that 'Mrs Beatty' was the rose he used.

His seedlings were very small, because he grew them in the old-fashioned way, by potting them in small pots soon after germination. They grew a few inches high, showed a small bloom on a thin stem, and at that stage he would propagate those in which he saw promise. The propagating wood was no thicker than a thin knitting needle. One golden yellow seedling from 'Mrs Beatty' × 'Yellowcrest' afforded him three fiddling eyes, which he budded in his painstaking way.

The war then interrupted his work; he suffered the directions of the local War Agricultural Executive Committee, who had been charged to obtain the greatest amount of food, and had power to enforce their will.

Edward received what he afterwards termed 'short sighted orders'. He had for some years been breeding with a Musk rose, a project requiring many years of experiment, without any certainty of success. That stock, with most of his other work, was consigned to the flames. While digging up roses to make way for food, he came across the three plants of 'Mrs Beatty' × 'Yellowcrest', grown from those three spindly eyes. One yellow flower was out; it was good; he kept the plants.

During the war, his duties were to grow food, and to go to the rescue of the crews of such aeroplanes as crashed or slithered into Norfolk, usually in the course of their journeys to Germany and back.

He was a member of the local Baptist Church, which he served for many years in the offices of scout master and lay preacher. He was married in 1944, fairly late in life, for he was then forty-one.

The six years of the war, tedious and interminable, were six golden summers struck out of the careers of British rose breeders. In truth it was a little suffering to set beside much greater ones, a little waste among many more wanton. Edward strongly believed that a nucleus of the work should have been retained, that a corner of his glass-house could have been spared from tomatoes. After the war, he soon discovered that of all the combatants, Britain appeared to be the only one that had closed the rose breeders down completely. He gave up his long term projects, such as the Musk rose. He had neither the time nor the money to pursue them. In fact he was painfully short of both, especially the money needed to re-establish his nursery after the war.

He had two seedlings from happier days to introduce, a dark red Floribunda, 'Dusky Maiden', which appeared in 1947, and won his first Gold Medal from the National Rose Society in 1948; and the yellow rose, so nearly lost, which appeared in 1949 bearing the name of his wife, 'Ellinor LeGrice'. Jackson & Perkins introduced 'Ellinor' in America in 1950, sending cheques for royalties sufficient to tide Edward over a difficult time.

The quest for a golden rose was not ended with Ellinor. She had the colour, she held her leaves, but her flowers were too globular, her petals were scalloped too much. Among the new roses that came to Britain after the war was an American Floribunda, 'Goldilocks'. It was light butter yellow, with small but shapely blooms, short but bushy growth. Its main fault was to hold its petals until they withered, a dismal sight. Despite that fault, Edward decided to breed with it, especially as its alleged descent could be traced to *R. setigera*, an American wild rose, known as the Prairie Rose.

His practice was to make a few crosses, raise the few seeds they gave him, and if the progeny pointed in the desired direction, to repeat the cross in quantity the following year. The results from his trial of 'Goldilocks' × 'Ellinor LeGrice' were promising. The following year he fertilized a few hundred blooms of 'Goldilocks' with Ellinor's pollen. The number of seeds he obtained has been put at various quantities, from one to eight thousand; I think it unlikely that anybody counted them. Among them was the justification of his faith in his yellow strain in the form of the golden rose that was to be 'Allgold'.

'Allgold' is truly a yellow rose, its petals, stamens, stigmas and pollen all the same colour. The dark leaves, low, bushy growth, elegant flower form and good health are a few of the qualities that make it famous. It won a Gold Medal in 1956, the year of its introduction. It was in close competition with another yellow Floribunda, 'Faust', for the highest award, the President's International Trophy. The judges preferred 'Faust', a bad decision, because within a short time it was seen that 'Faust' had sold his soul to the devil Mildew. Edward was unlucky; but having won Gold Medals for 'Charming Maid' in 1953, and 'Bonnie Maid' in 1954, neither of them obvious candidates for the honour, he was due for some bad luck.

Hundreds of thousands of 'Allgold' were grown for sale in Britain each year, with no financial benefit to its originator, other than what he could get from the few plants he grew on his own, small nursery. Edward had known for years that his hybridizing was not profitable. 'Only a fool would be a hybridist,' he often remarked. He enjoyed the work; he knew that against the losses should be set such imponderables as reputation; but having taken all into consideration, he concluded: 'If one is to consider this matter in the cold light of finance then few if any breeders would remain.'

He had proposed to the Horticultural Trades Association, at a meeting in Chester in 1953, that some form of protection was essential if plant breeding were to prosper in Britain, and that the Association should support it. He failed to get

44. Edward LeGrice, 1902–1977. 'A quiet, shy, Norfolk rose breeder'.
Photo: E. B. LeGrice (Hybridizers) Ltd.

a seconder, but in the following year, the resolution was passed. The government
had set up the Committee on Transactions in Seeds in July 1954, and when the
studies had advanced to a serious consideration of plant breeders' rights, Edward
LeGrice was appointed a member. He served from 18 April, 1957 for three years,
after which came the report upon which legislation was to be founded. He was
the only professional rose grower on the Committee, although Alexander Dickson
was called in for consultation.

The Plant Varieties and Seeds Act 1964 was finally given the Royal Assent,
but it was not of much benefit to Edward. His most popular roses, 'Allgold'
and the pink and cream Hybrid Tea, 'My Choice', were already in commerce,
and not eligible for rights. He had turned his attention to purple, blue and brown
roses, which although more exciting for the breeder are of less attraction to
gardeners.

The basic principle of breeding roses should be, in his consistent view, to build
up a strain. One should not at the start aim to produce a winner, although it
might arrive by luck; but rather to produce those parents which could be expected
to bear the new rose preconceived by the breeder.

He had followed this policy when breeding 'Dusky Maiden' and 'Allgold'. He
now applied it to the more difficult task of purple, grey and brown roses.

His interest in such exotic colours stemmed from an American Floribunda,

'Lavender Pinocchio', from which he raised 'Lilac Charm'. It was indeed charming, if somewhat pale to be compared with lilac, a single Floribunda after his favourite style, down to pretty yellow stamens. It was introduced, with a well merited Gold Medal, in 1961.

After some years of characteristically careful work, his book *Rose Growing Complete* was published by Faber in 1965. Like all rose books, it needs revision from time to time, because the varieties it extols go out of date. It is one of the best rose books written since the war.

The nursery was by now well established, with a good reputation for supplying plants of quality. The firm had come a long way in one generation; and the presence of two sons, Jim and Bill, promised a second.

Edward suffered a severe coronary thrombosis, and thought, as he struggled back to health, that his working life was over. He expected to be an invalid for the rest of his days. He was distressed to discover that after washing his face and hands, he had to sit down in order to find the strength to dry them. After six months, he was able to walk a hundred yards, and eventually he recovered, and declared himself completely fit. His advice to others so afflicted was to be patient with themselves, to regard the enforced rest as a source of energy for the future; he said the most difficult part was 'putting up with myself'. From that time, his wife, Ellinor, was his chauffeur, despite her considerable disability from arthritis.

The name of LeGrice became attached to strange roses: the brownish 'Vesper', 1967; the purple 'News', 1969, and 'Purple Splendour', 1976; the red and grey 'Victoriana', 1976, and 'Grey Dawn', 1975. Edward was able to show them to good effect at Chelsea Show for which, because of the date, it is necessary to grow the flowers under glass. The best of them for the garden is 'News'; it was raised from the seed of 'Lilac Charm', fertilized in exploratory fashion by the pollen of an old Gallica rose, 'Tuscany Superb', a strange result if it were indeed a direct cross.

Such roses were of interest to breeders and flower arrangers. A market so limited returned a like reward. Edward's royalties in Britain were paltry; his hybridizing enterprise was paid for by royalties from abroad, from countries where the breeder had been able to secure rights in the days of 'Allgold' and 'My Choice'.

He wrote to me on that subject on 14 October, 1976, adding, 'anything I may produce now is more likely to be for my wreath than my crown!'

He died on June the third, 1977, and was buried in the churchyard of his beloved Baptist Church, deep in the Norfolk countryside, near North Walsham. It was a perfect summer day, with the new season of roses starting.

As Secretary of the British Association of Rose Breeders, I had been taking the notes at the last meeting Edward attended, on 21 April that year. He said something which impressed me. I immediately wrote it down:

'People have to play for safety if they want to make a living; and that is quite the wrong way for a hybridist.'

15

Japan

One sunny Saturday morning in 1968, I strolled back to the house after spending an absorbing few hours among my rose seedlings. Betty and I lived at The Orchard then, a house standing alone on a part of the nursery, the perfect place for a peaceful weekend, and the roses blooming all around it.

Betty greeted me with the news that Harry Wheatcroft had telephoned, to ask if we could accept a Japanese rose grower. She had replied that we could, rose growing guests being a normal part of her housewifely experience; and Harry had said, 'Good, I will drive him over straight away.'

We looked at each other, as much as to say, 'Oh well, bang goes our quiet weekend.' I began to think of the Japanese.

Up to that time, my transactions with them had been of an explosive nature, uncomfortably so, especially when I dived to the ground on hearing the flight of one of their shells, and suffered the indignity of receiving a portion of it in my backside. I remembered many things, including dead comrades, but the most relevant occurred towards the end of my service. When I found two of their soldiers ill and helpless by the track, I did all I could to save them, a natural instinct one might think, except that we had to keep moving, and nobody had much time or sympathy for the enemy. I hope the arrangements I made saved at least one life, but I heard no more about those two.

When we took over Singapore, I saw the Japanese prisoners not as monsters but as human beings, and treated them accordingly. Their commander expressed himself by forming up his men to accord me a ceremonial bow, a compliment I accepted with some surprise and a salute in return, wondering what on earth the Brigadier would say if he heard of it. It had all happened in a different world; but I was not entirely comfortable about entertaining a Japanese.

Harry Wheatcroft drove up in a Rolls-Royce no less, brushing the shrub roses that grew on each side of our drive. He stopped near the venerable Citroën, recently acquired by our two elder children for the princely sum of forty pounds. The two cars were as dissimilar as the two people who emerged from the Rolls. Harry was long, lean, whiskery, flamboyant. The Japanese was shorter, thick set, clean shaven, apologetic. His name was Seizo Suzuki.

We went into the house to refresh our guests, and to make Seizo feel at home. While we were talking, our elder son, Robert, who was just seventeen, came into the room, and politely asked if Mr Wheatcroft would mind moving his car, so that he and his sister could drive their Citroën out. Harry made as if to rise, looked at Robert, sat back again, and lobbed the car keys into his hands. I knew he had thought the boy would be thrilled to handle a Rolls, if only for a few yards, and had summed him up as capable. Excited voices sounded from the hallway, as Robert and Elizabeth retreated. I liked Harry, and always got on well with him. In company, he gave off sparks, on his own he was modest and pleasant. Eventually he departed, with the air of one who had done good deeds and got a free weekend into the bargain.

I forget how long Seizo stayed on that first visit, a couple of nights probably, but before he left, and in spite of his halting English, he had become a friend. He was breeding roses somewhere near Tokyo, at the Keisei Rose Research Institute. His description of himself is: 'I am not great rose breeder, only poor rose breeder in Orient,' a disarming approach apt to extract the maximum of information. He has a profound love and knowledge of roses. I asked him some years later to write an article for the *Rose Annual* on roses in Japan, and here are some of the interesting things he related:

Cherry blossom and chrysanthemums are the greatly loved flowers of the Japanese, but that is not to say that the rose has been neglected there. The China rose arrived in Europe only in the eighteenth century; but by reason of propinquity the Japanese knew it a thousand years sooner, for there is a reference to it in a poem by Kino Tsurayuki in the year 905. Seizo Suzuki refers to a succession of Japanese publications during the seventeenth, eighteenth and nineteenth centuries, in which various garden and wild roses were illustrated and described. These roses were forms or seedlings of oriental wild roses, except for the interesting intrusion of 'Hachiyo-bara', which means 'Rose from the far-away island.' This appears to be R. *gallica*, which had somehow travelled to Japan many years ago. The Japanese words for rose are 'bara' and 'ibara'.

The Japanese became interested in modern roses during the 1930s, due to their admiration of the Hybrid Teas they imported from Europe and America. The war, naturally, diverted their attention from roses, but was followed by an intense longing on their part for the pursuits of peace. Roses might have regained their modest pre-war place in Japanese hearts, but in fact did much better, on account of the wonderful French variety 'Peace'. The delicacy of its yellow and pink shading, combined with the wide expanse of its open petals, were in complete accord with Japanese ideas of beauty. 'Peace' was a missionary among roses, converting Japan to its cause.

Its advent was followed by the establishment of some rose nurseries from 1949, and by the formation of the Japan Rose Society, (Nippon-Bara-Kai) which arose from merging the societies of Tokyo and Osaka. The Imperial Family became members, and the Prime Minister, S. Yoshidu, was president. The Society instituted trials for new roses, and ran them in such a way as to command the respect of the international rose breeding fraternity.

Despite his claim to be 'only poor rose breeder', Seizo Suzuki has a first class breeding station, a fine rose nursery and a notable collection of roses. Sam McGredy

45. Seizo Suzuki and colleagues. Seizo is on the right.
Photo: Seizo Suzuki

had visited Japan some years before I first met Seizo, and on his return predicted that it was only a matter of time before Japanese rose breeders would be showing the rest of us the way home.

That forecast has not yet come true. The success Japanese roses have enjoyed has been regional rather than international. This of course is a common experience for rose breeders. Their roses are most likely to succeed in the climate wherein they have been selected; roses which flourish in many different climates are comparatively rare. I have tried several of Seizo's roses in Britain, with the active wish to introduce one for my Japanese friend, but so far have regretfully concluded that I could not find one suitable for English skies. I hope it will yet arrive. It is fair to add that except for 'Princess Chichibu', he has had a parallel experience with mine.

He has been more fortunate elsewhere. His 'Olympic Torch' was introduced in the United States in 1966. It is a Hybrid Tea, yellow and rose red, the yellow on the outer side of the petals, and to the base of the inner side. The Japanese name for it is Sei-ka.

I thought at one time I might introduce 'Eikou', a yellow Hybrid Tea with bold red marking at the petal rims; but in the end I had to admit that, although the good flowers were spectacular, there were not enough of them. The spelling seems to vary between 'Ei-koh', 'Eikō' and 'Eikou'; Seizo introduced it in Japan in 1978. He won a Gold Medal in Rome with 'Kam-pai', a bright red Hybrid Tea, introduced in 1983, and now tells me he has high hopes of a shrubby ground cover variety. In Japan it is 'Hanami-gawa', which means 'looking at cherry blossoms by the riverside'. Seizo tells me that Alain Meilland hopes to introduce it in Europe soon, under the rather more terse title of 'Ferdy'.

One of the more splendid rose books of modern times has arrived from Japan, *Roses in Colour*, published by Heibonsha of Tokyo in 1983. The text, by Seizo Suzuki and Yasuichi Momiyama, escapes my criticism through being in Japanese, but I take it on trust from my respect for the knowledge and ability of one of the authors. The colour illustrations are superb, more so of the species and old garden roses than of the modern roses. They are painted by Yoshio Futakuchi, and are superbly reproduced, more life-like and identifiable than photographs. Some of them, I venture to say, are the best since Redouté. We count ourselves among the fortunate to have received a copy inscribed by brush:

'Dear Jack and Betty, I am very honored to present you this rose book written by me to the memory of your hearty friendship. Seizo.'

Leaving Seizo Suzuki to continue in his amiable and admirable ways, we now turn to the lean and upright figure of Toru F. Onodera. He is an amateur, or to use his words, 'only a passionate amateur rose lover', but it may well turn out that he will have a profound influence on the future of the rose.

I own to a foolish act. In the 1960s, there were six little Miniature bushes in the Royal National Rose Society's trial ground at St Albans. Tiny leaves, polished dark green, and little single white flowers charmed me to such an extent that I discovered the name of the raiser, and wrote to Japan to ask whether I could introduce it for him. Mr Onodera wrote in return to give his consent.

As the season progressed, it was clear that no more flowers would be borne that season; it flowered once, and that was that; the growth began to creep to such an extent that the Society's gardeners put in canes to support it. The trim bushes, which I had so much admired in the summer, were obviously not the true growth of the variety. It was turning out to be a summer flowering creeper, and my affection for it cooled considerably.

At that juncture Walter Gregory told me that he also had written to Japan, and had learned that I had got in before him. Walter was an old friend, managing director of the famous rose nursery at Chilwell, Nottingham. He said that if I changed my mind about introducing the rose, would I let him know? I told

46. Toru F. Onodera, Doctor of Science, surrounded by his beautiful 'Nozomi'.
Photo: T. F. Onodera

him he could have it, and thus gave away the rose known as 'Nozomi', which I understand means 'Hope'.

'Nozomi' has become very popular, despite flowering only in the summer. More than that, Pat Dickson has bred from it a number of most attractive varieties, due to be introduced in the next few years. They may be described as compact Floribundas with very small and utterly charming blooms of Hybrid Tea type; it seems to me they will take the rose world by storm. One catches a hint of a lovely new class in the offing. That is why I say that Onodera's influence on roses may be profound.

As an amateur, Toru Onodera tried to separate his hobby from his profession by using the pen name of Susumu S. Onodera for his rose activities. He occasionally visits European rose trials, and like Seizo he has been to see us in Hitchin. I like his description of what a breeder needs in selecting his seedlings: 'Strict eyes to discriminate.' That is perfectly true.

Although his English is adequate for most needs, involved discussions place a strain on it. Nevertheless I have understood that he is an idealist. Behind his hobby lies the conviction that roses speak louder than statesmen in spreading the love of peace and beauty between nations. I think it fortunate that he broke away from Hybrid Teas, which all the world breeds, and gave us something with a Japanese flavour in the shape of 'Nozomi'. He has an interesting rose red variety of some character in 'Suma'.

After starting these personal recollections, I drifted into some memories of the war, not without purpose as I shall now show, because among our Japanese visitors was a soldier from the other side.

He is Dr Tomin Harada. He came with his wife to Hitchin, while in England to deliver an address. He wanted to buy some roses for his garden. We found a lot to talk about, and this is what he told me.

He had been in the Japanese Army before the war, in China, and of course had served during the war. He was born and bred in Hiroshima. After the war he resolved to devote the remainder of his life to caring for the people of his native city. It was as if he had chosen to do penance.

He told me of his return to that shattered place, his years of building makeshift treatment centres, of the patients he still has almost forty years later, of the helpful discoveries that have been made in treatment, of the suffering that had come to his gentle hands.

All this was explained with a matter-of-fact serenity; he had spent most of his life patiently trying to repair the outrageous damage that had been done by man to man. He obviously did it with love, not just for his patients and his city, but for all that moved and lived in this great, wide world. Some of the world had been broken, and he was doing what little he could to mend it, an example, a reminder and a rebuke to any who might break it again.

Thus after many years I met in the roses a Japanese soldier, and found him as near a saint as ever I saw.

16

Cocker

The roses in Aberdeen grow luxuriantly, giving flowers of great size and rich colour. For all that, Aberdeen is about the last place I would choose for a rose nursery. The spring is cold and wet, the summer cool and wet, the autumn chilly and wet, with the result that most nursery operations take place after many post-ponements, in circumstances of discomfort, and with shocked eyes on the calendar. To man Scotland's rose nurseries, sturdy and independent characters are needed. The Cocker family provide good examples of them.

The Cocker nursery began in 1841, as a result of a sturdy and independent head gardener presenting an ultimatum to the laird. James Cocker was the gardener, Castle Fraser the estate, the sanctity of the Sabbath the subject of the argument. James Cocker refused point blank to pick fruit on Sunday. He would do it on Saturday, up to any hour, but as for Sunday, he would obey the Lord rather than the laird, to which the response was, in effect, 'Then you can go and serve Him instead of me.'

The year 1840 was wearing on when James Cocker lost his job. He had been born on 6 October, 1807, had married Elizabeth Goudie, shared with her the joy of their son James, born 15 November, 1832, and the sorrow of losing another boy, Alexander, in infancy. As the months passed, it became clear that Elizabeth was pregnant again, with Patrick, who arrived on 10 November, 1841. By that time, James had started a small nursery in the Sunnypark district of Aberdeen, where he grew trees, shrubs and pansies.

The business prospered, especially as young James grew up and took part in it, and despite the prices they charged. The Cocker catalogue for 1880 offered larch seedlings at two shillings a thousand, strawberry plants for half a crown a hundred.

By the time James the founder died, on 22 October, 1880, his firm had taken on more ground nearby at Morningfield, and had leased a shop as a seed warehouse at 82 Union Street, the city's main shopping street.

The second James Cocker was aged forty-seven when his father died. His wife, Margaret Robb, had borne three sons, William, a third James, and Alexander. All three were brought into the business, Alexander after an apprenticeship with the famous nursery of Turner at Slough; the firm became in 1882 James Cocker & Sons.

About this time they developed their strain of 'Bon Accord' double primroses, flowers which were much fancied in those days; and they began to take more

47. James Cocker, 1832–1897.
Photo: James Cocker & Sons

interest in roses. The second James died on 15 September, 1897, leaving his three
sons to carry on. Of them, the third James was the seedsman; he was the father
of several children, but his wife, to the scandal of Aberdeen, preferred another
man, and deserted her family for her new love. William died in 1915, and Alexander,
having survived his two brothers in the business, eventually became the sole
proprietor. He was a staunch Free Churchman, an elder of St Paul's church.

The early Cockers were not notable rose breeders. Their first varieties, brought
out in 1892, were two chance sports from Hybrid Perpetuals. One was a deeper
coloured flower found among their stock of the carmine 'Etienne Levet', and
introduced as 'Duke of Fife'; a pale variation among the pink 'Countess of Rose-
berry' became 'Duchess of Fife'; thereafter, one supposes, the Ducal order was
safe for a few years to come. In 1897 they turned their attention to the Royal
family, with the salmon pink 'Duchess of York'.

The example set by Henry Bennett and followed by Dickson of Newtownards
apparently had some influence in the far north, for one of the three Cocker brothers
crossed two roses closely associated with Henry Bennett, 'Mrs John Laing' and
'Mabel Morrison'. The result was a soft pink rose, good enough to win a Gold
Medal in 1898, and far too good to waste on mere Dukes and Duchesses. They
named it 'Mrs Cocker', after Margaret, their recently widowed mother, and introduced it in 1899.

'Mrs Cocker' set a precedent for the future. Excellent exhibitors though the Cockers were, they were virtually excluded from the important rose shows in England by the climate of Aberdeen. Their roses were not yet in bloom by the time those shows were held. Therefore they entrusted 'Mrs Cocker' to Benjamin R. Cant of Colchester, Essex. He was one of the most highly respected rose growers in the kingdom, and he played his part in making 'Mrs Cocker' well known.

Cockers won another Gold Medal in 1912 for 'Mrs Andrew Carnegie', introduced in 1913. It was white, a weak grower with papery petals, opening with difficulty in England; how the flowers managed to open at all in Aberdeen is a wonder. They also introduced a salmon pink sport of 'Dorothy Perkins' in 1909, under the name 'Christian Curle'.

During this time, in consequence of the pressure of the city around it, the nursery established itself at Springhill on the outskirts, and gave up first Sunnypark, and later Morningfield. It was at the granite house at Springhill that Alexander died in 1920, after a short illness following upon a chill, at the age of sixty. He left a daughter, Margaret, and a son, Alexander Morison, who was then aged thirteen.

The trustees appointed to attend to the children's affairs continued to run the nursery, but not successfully, for in 1923 they closed it, much to the disgust of young Alec.

Alec Cocker was a vigorous young man, with black hair and brown eyes; he was sturdy, stocky, quick in movement and thought. His capacity for enjoyment

48. Alexander Cocker, 1860–1920. The identity of the child is uncertain; most probably Alec Cocker or his sister Margaret.
Photo: James Cocker & Sons

was virtually unlimited, his memory remarkably adhesive, and his resolve to restore the family nursery and pride was like iron. Between his terrorist tactics on the rugby field and on his motor-cycle, he studied horticulture. When a fact entered his mind, it stayed there.

His life was nearly lost on that motor-cycle. A mad ride with friends resulted in a crash that was fatal to one of them during 1931. Alec was appalled, shattered both psychologically and physically. His right leg was broken in seven places. He emerged from hospital fifteen months later, the one leg three inches shorter than the other. He was obliged to limp for the rest of his life.

He rented a field at Springhill in 1936, and started to grow such plants as chrysanthemums and polyanthas. When the war came in 1939, he with his limp was of no use to the services, but proved excellent at growing vegetables, a craft which in his hands was raised to an art, such was the quality of his produce. He began to plot the future with careful thought, with a resolution to build, and then to hold what he might build for himself and his family. He was unmarried, coming up to forty years of age, with a wraith of a business; but he intended to establish a nursery to hand on to a new generation.

He became engaged to Anne Gowans Rennie, a local girl, slightly built, shrewd and intelligent. The pair of them followed Alec's plan with prudence and patience. They agreed to postpone their marriage until the business was safely established, and they both worked hard in the nursery until they judged that first objective was reached, some eight years later. They were married in 1952.

Alec was then in his forty-fifth year, Anne in her thirty-second, time for most people desirous of having children to set aside reasons for delay. The Cockers, however, are not to be hurried. To bring a child into the world before they had the certain means of caring for it, would to them be an act of feckless irresponsibility.

They had decided that the best course for the business was to specialize in roses. As with most things Alec Cocker did, the enterprise was carefully studied and thoroughly planned, with the object of producing plants of the highest quality possible. Quality was almost a religious belief with him. If you took infinite care to do things the right way, disdaining all short cuts and shoddiness, then you produced an article of quality, whether it was a rose tree, a dish of potatoes, a bowl of strawberries, a pair of shoes, or anything else mankind could grow or make. He believed that in a well ordered society all its people could eat, drink, wear and use nothing but the best, if only they put their minds and their will into so providing for themselves. Under the Cocker theory of economics, the throw-away philosophy would itself be thrown away. The antique trade would be ruined, because hardly anything would ever wear out.

He could never understand why distillers wasted time making ordinary whisky, instead of turning to the nobler, worthier business of distilling malt.

James Cocker & Sons entered the rose world at a favourable time, when prosperity beamed upon its worthy practitioners as never before or since. That rosy era lasted for about twenty years, from 1948 to 1968. During the 1950s, Alec Cocker made his own indelible mark in his chosen world. He did it by ensuring that he would be remembered by those he met.

Therefore he would talk by the hour, to everyone from the door porter to the hotel manager, the steward to the station master, the apprentice to the managing director, to people he knew and those he had never met before, to Lords and Labourers, Dustmen and Dukes. He could entertain the lot of them, tell them which variety of strawberry or potato they should be growing. His memory made him appear expert in many subjects apart from horticulture — in whisky, music, fish, Scotland; it retained also dozens of rude Scottish jokes, which he told with the skill of a professional actor; he knew by heart reams of Robert Burns, and most of the songs of Gilbert and Sullivan. Best of all, he remembered the casual acquaintances made at rose shows or on his travels, and greeted them on subsequent encounters as friends, although possibly with some of the same stories. No wonder people liked him; he clearly enjoyed meeting them.

At the shows, it was a mystery to me that Alec and Anne got any work done at all. They had time for everyone and every extraneous little detail, when in their place I should have turned my back until my exhibit was complete. Yet they always finished theirs in time by some kind of miracle. They brought their enormous flowers to the later English shows, and were so successful as to win the top prize at the National Rose Society's Autumn Show six years in succession.

As an example of Alec's provoking deliberation, and the good he got from it, I remember him coming into my room at a hotel, and saying, 'Jack, I think I should give Mildred Hobbs a ring.' Mildred, a good friend, was press officer for the Royal Horticultural Society. I told him to help himself to the telephone.

He put on his glasses, and looked suspiciously at the London telephone directories. After some time thumbing through the Es, Fs and Gs, he eventually gave a triumphant grunt, 'Ah, H, here we are.' The minutes ticked by as he went up and down all the Halls and Hills; I could have found the blessed number in a tenth of the time, but I knew it was impossible to hurry Alec, much as I longed to. Another grunt announced his belated arrival at HO. Down each column he went, until at last he raised his head, looked over his glasses at me, and said,

'Oh my God, Jack, there's an awful lot of Hoares in London.'

In 1959, it was plain that the business had outgrown its home in Springhill; at that time seventy acres of ground came on the market at Whitemyres, about a quarter of a mile down the road, just outside the city boundary. A derelict Queen Anne house stood on the property. The Cockers debated long and anxiously whether they could risk £7,000 to buy it, with the help of their bank. They accepted that risk, fortunately for them because in the future the city would extend its boundary, making their land valuable.

They now had a good rose business, and new land for the future. As Anne was in her fortieth year, they decided the time was ripe to attend to the next generation. Accordingly, on 2 July, 1960, Alexander James Cocker came into the world. Most people, I suppose, would either have done it sooner, or thought it too late; but with the Cockers there was always time to do things in what they saw to be the proper order.

The family lived in a cramped flat in Aberdeen, investing their earnings in the business for the future, rather than spending on themselves. The next investment was in glass-houses. After that, perhaps, they could do something to the ruins of the old house at Whitemyres.

Alec decided to start breeding roses, a project he confided to Sam McGredy, who replied, 'What! At your age, Alec?' The enterprise was thoroughly planned, researched and equipped. Alec needed benches in his glass-house in which to sow and grow the seed, but none of the structures normally used for this purpose were good enough to satisfy him. He therefore designed his own, to be made of the finest, smoothest concrete; the moulds for them were made in the nursery workshop, and in due course the seedling house was equipped with benches fit to see out the rest of the century with ease. At the age of fifty-six, well knowing that he would be in his sixties before the new enterprise earned a penny, Alec was ready to start his career as a rose breeder.

I had started a similar project in Hitchin a year previously. By this time, Alec and I were close friends. We enjoyed trying to beat one another at the shows, we searched and shared each other's knowledge of roses, we were 'happy to meet, sorry to part'. We agreed that if we were to catch up with the long established rose breeders of the world, we should have a better chance if we pooled our knowledge.

This decision was like a seed from the Tree of Delight. What was learned by one was passed to the other. We grew one another's seedlings, stayed at each other's nurseries, exchanged breeding stock and ideas, expressed opinions openly and honestly with no fear of offence. We spent days together among the seedlings, we laughed and were happy.

The rose nurserymen of Britain were in the habit of holding a conference in London each February. Our trade is remarkable for the friendliness and helpfulness of one rival to another, also for the conviviality of its reunions. I was roused after one merry night by the telephone in my hotel bedroom ringing disagreeably early in the morning. It was Alec, asking for help in a whisper.

He had suffered a serious heart attack. I went with him in the ambulance to the Middlesex Hospital, where he was barely off the pavement before they were at work on him. Anne flew down from Aberdeen, and we spent some anxious days while he was in danger. I remember as we walked from the hotel to the hospital, that a church was enlightening the district with Isobel Bailey singing, 'I know that my Redeemer liveth'. I don't like hospitals. Alec was connected to a machine with a light pulsing across it, and I was terrified of the light going out.

Alec made a recovery and a whole host of new friends in hospital. He was especially concerned about an Italian, who had lost his legs by jumping in the path of an underground train, because his girl had ended their love affair. Alec spent a lot of time and thought, helping him out of his troubles. A few years later, I learned that the Italian had done the same thing again, for the same reason, this time losing his life. I never told Alec about it.

Alec made himself an expert on hearts and how to live with them, with the interested manner of a student of natural history; and resumed his life.

His first new roses appeared in 1968: two pink climbers, 'Morning Jewel' and 'Rosy Mantle'. Both were seedlings of the famous 'New Dawn'. He introduced several varieties in 1969, of which the red and yellow 'Gay Gordons' was widely grown, although it was not sufficiently vigorous. His first big success was 'Alec's Red', a cherry red Hybrid Tea with large blooms and rich fragrance. It won the Royal National Rose Society's highest award for a new rose, the President's International Trophy, in 1970, the year of its introduction.

The name was given by his friends in the rose trade to whom he had sent stock, in the hope they would be sufficiently impressed to grow it and pay him royalties. They all referred to it as 'Alec's Red', and Cliff Pawsey of Cants of Colchester told Alec he had better stick to that name.

'Anne Cocker' was introduced in 1971, a tall Floribunda with bright little, tight little, vermilion flowers, very long lasting when cut and put in a vase. Thereafter, year by year, new roses came from Aberdeen, some very good, others not so good. One of the successes was 'Glenfiddich' in 1976, named after Alec's favourite whisky. All the while, Alec Cocker was scheming for the future.

He slowly cleared the fallen masonry from the Queen Anne house at Whitemyres, and began rebuilding it, supervising local craftsmen himself. Some of his rose growing friends, myself included, had advised him to 'knock down that old ruin', and to start afresh. Not him. He spent several years on that house, for right down to the nails all the materials had to be of the best quality; from which it followed that year by year he could afford only to do so much. Whitemyres House eventually emerged resplendent, and I am happy to say that the Harkness family were the first guests in it, before the last workmen had departed.

The canny plans of Alec and Anne had been fulfilled, and as if to put the seal on their success, in 1975 Her Majesty Queen Elizabeth granted a royal warrant to James Cocker & Sons as suppliers of her roses. Whether she knew it or not, the new warrant holders were two of the most devoted royalists in her realm.

Alec thought deeply about his breeding. Of the many different wild roses to be found in the world, comparatively few have been employed by rose breeders; and it is an undeniable fact that all the beautiful roses of our gardens took their origin from wild roses.

Some wild roses have a quality which is uniquely their own, for example the scent of the Sweet Briar's leaves. There is one, and only one, which has a deep red eye at the centre of its yellow flowers. It is R. *persica*, but it is difficult to grow and to mate with other roses. The botanists eventually took it out of the genus Rosa altogether, and renamed it *Hulthemia persica*.

Only one hybrid between *R. persica* and another rose had ever been known. It was raised in the Luxembourg Gardens in 1836, and was called 'Hardii'. It also has yellow flowers, paler but larger than those of *R. persica*, and it exhibits a fine red eye.

Alec had about fifty plants of 'Hardii' growing in pots in his glass-house. He determined to raise a new race of roses from it, but after a few years he discovered that 'Hardii' was incapable of setting seed, infertile in pollen, utterly sterile. The answer, he decided, was to forget 'Hardii', and obtain the species which had borne it, *R. persica*.

He searched for it in likely gardens, even travelling to one in Sussex, where he saw only the place where it had been before it died. He eventually got seed of it by means of a botanist who was travelling to Persia, its chief native habitat. He was then in possession of a plant which lived in semi-desert regions, and it dawned on him that Aberdeen would be a bit of a shock to it.

So he shared the seed with me. It liked our glass-house in Hitchin, where I did a lot of interesting work with it, raising the first recorded hybrids from it since 1836.

Alec and I were asked to report on our work with *R. persica* at the International Rose Conference held in Oxford in 1976, by which time we had nine years' experience of it, and possessed fifty-three hybrids I had raised. We were in the fortunate position of being the only people in the world with such knowledge. A large and eager audience attended.

Alec explained the reasons for the project and its possibilities, and I told what we had done, and what interesting things we had seen. When we finished, to my surprise we received from that distinguished audience a standing ovation. It was a great moment in my life to be beside my old friend on that occasion. Little did we think that our partnership was almost at its end.

Alec had raised a great rose. It had started years previously, when he had the idea of bringing *R. kordesii* into Hybrid Teas, for vigour, hardiness and health. He chose one of its descendants, the red climber 'Parkdirektor Riggers', and crossed it with Hybrid Teas. Most of the progeny were climbers, which he did not seek. All he wanted was a bush, with double flowers, flowering twice or oftener in the season. The pollen of 'Piccadilly' provided it, a dull, dark red, crimped thing, fit for the bonfire without a second thought, except for the genes within it.

He used its pollen on another seedling, 'Highlight' × 'Colour Wonder' this time, and obtained a semi-double shrubby rose of glistening leaves and bright orange red colour. This, being more capable of bearing seed, was obliged to do so, and yielding to the charms of 'Mischief' it produced the kind of rose Alec had been seeking.

On my next visit to Aberdeen, he said he had something to show me, and limped to a few plants of a long petalled, peach and creamy pink Hybrid Tea. I looked it up and down, taking in the points which had become second nature, the type of leaves, the look of the shoots at their base, all those pointers of future

49. Anne and Alec Cocker (right) being greeted by Mr Philip Spink, the then Chairman of Spink & Son Ltd., on the occasion of the striking of a Silver Jubilee medal. Designed by Leslie Durbin, the medal showed on one side Alec's 'Silver Jubilee' rose. Taken in the last year of Alec's life.

Photo: Photo Source — Keystone.

trouble and weakness. The flowers were superb. Would the plant let them down? I could see no dangers.

'Alec,' I said, 'that's the best rose you've ever raised. Better than Alec's Red.'

It was, as all rose growing readers are most certainly by now aware, 'Silver Jubilee'. It won for him his second President's International Trophy.

At Chelsea Show in 1977, my friend worried me a great deal. He stood before his blooms of 'Silver Jubilee', talking by the hour to crowds of admiring visitors, taking orders, laughing, in his element, and looking desperately tired at the end of each day.

On 2 November, 1977, Anne went out to her Scottish dancing class, leaving young Alexander, Alec, and Gleam the labrador at home. They watched the television, became sleepy, and about ten o'clock Alec got up. He put the outside lights on for Anne, and went into the kitchen to make a cup of tea.

When she came home, the pot was warmed, but Alec was lying dead on the kitchen floor. He used to say that when his time came he would go out like a light, and so he did.

17

Harkness

It is only at the insistence of my publishers that I write about myself.

My family started a nursery in Bedale, Yorkshire in 1879, and made a name for themselves as growers and exhibitors of roses. But none of them showed an interest in breeding roses, therefore their story, which is not without interest, achievement and amusement, is scarcely relevant, and may well be saved for another occasion.

I was brought up in Thornton Heath, Surrey, a suburb far from the earthy smell of nurseries, my father having chosen a career in the civil service. He turned his back on horticulture so firmly as to neglect his own garden. I grew up knowing nothing about plants, but was conscious of the family tradition. When I was fifteen, I had two desires, one to get out of school, the other to keep out of such banks and offices as my parents had in mind for me. A life in the open air appealed to me. These motives can scarcely be described as a sense of vocation, but they were all I had. Inwardly I longed to be a writer, but saw no prospect of doing it, and confided that desire to nobody.

In September 1934, at the age of sixteen, I reported for duty as the new apprentice at the Slieve Donard Nursery in Newcastle, County Down. That nursery was chosen because its proprietor, Willie Slinger, had in his time been an apprentice at Harkness & Sons in Yorkshire. I repaid the compliment, but I will guarantee he was a more likely lad than I was.

I enjoyed my three years in Newcastle so much that for years afterwards I was homesick for that place, its beauty, its people, and the sea, which lifted up my heart. The nursery had a marvellous stock of plants, especially of choice shrubs. Their collection of Japanese irises was probably the best in the country. They grew about thirty thousand roses, as well as alpine and herbaceous plants; and as if those were not enough, they had daffodils, over four hundred varieties of them. My wages were £1 2s 6d per week, of which I paid my landlady a pound, and I cannot remember feeling hard up.

It took me three weeks to understand what the men were saying, their accent and vocabulary being quite different from those my mother had taught me. After a while I felt at home with them, and learned a valuable lesson as to the worth of every human being. Some say that all men are equal, but to me it seems that all men are different. I have never met a human being bereft of all sparks from the source of life; all therefore are worthy of respect and consideration. The Ulster nursery workers taught me that; I should have known it, but as a boy in Thornton

Heath I did not. After I had been there a while, a tall lean man called Eddie Rooney said, during a game of pitch and toss in the dinner hour, when I was picking up my winnings,

'When we heard you were coming, we thought to see some soft, rich fellow. Well, we've seen the softness all right, but devil a sight of the bloody money.'

On Friday afternoons I went up a track to a cottage above the town, to visit Geoffrey Livens. That was my education. He taught me botany and German. He had been studying botany in a German university in 1913, and during the war had been gassed. He ought to have had a brilliant academic career, but lived instead on a smallholding — very small — in a happy, pensioned state of little money, delicate health, the Mountains of Mourne around him, and the sea spread beneath him.

I went back to England in 1937, knowing more about shrubs and daffodils than roses, but at least hardened to working on the land. I joined R. Harkness & Co at Hitchin, Hertfordshire. The firm was owned by William Ernest Harkness, first cousin of my father. His roses opened my eyes. They stood straight and thick in the rows, making the Irish roses poor indeed in comparison. I began to realize the difference between a general and a specialist nursery. I also learned that I had enlisted under the command of both a brilliant rose grower, and of a wise, intelligent and compassionate man.

Bill Harkness was resourceful, too. His father's nursery was on its last legs during the 1914–1918 war, the family home sold, and little prospect for him there. Bill had served in the tanks in their early days, but the only tales of the war I ever heard from him revolved upon his ability to brew up tea at unexpected times. He had, I suspect, not much sympathy for military life. When the war ended demobilization was delayed, an exasperating proof of military inefficiency.

He did not wait. He discovered a small crop of roses which stood unsold, and undertook to buy them. He found customers for them, fetched the plants to the stables where he was stationed, and with the help of his fellow soldiers, sorted and packed them.

After the army finally brought itself to dispensing with his services, he became landlord of the Raven, a village pub at Hexton, near Hitchin. His purpose was to grow roses by day and earn some money from beer by night, until such time as he could start his own nursery. He wanted only two things from his father's nursery, although the holder of its effects counted on selling him more. Bill bought the name and the list of customers, and never went back for anything else. From those industrious beginnings he made his successful way.

Bill taught and guided me, played cricket with me, that game being holy to both of us, and treated me like a son. I became a rose grower, and I have only one regret about my training, that I never became a good budder. Both in Ireland and in Hitchin I was always wanted to do something else at budding time. I never budded more than a few hundred roses.

I proposed to Bill in 1938 that the firm should start breeding roses, and that

I would do it. He built a small lean-to glass-house by the packing shed. After much thought, I selected my breeding stock, including several new varieties which we bought from Meilland in France and Max Krause in Germany. They did not grow very well, and I knew little about the task, but in 1939 I duly made my first crosses. It was a bad year to choose.

After six and a quarter years in the army, I returned to Hitchin in June 1946. The first thing I saw was 'Ena Harkness' and the second 'Frensham', two wonderful new roses raised by an amateur, Albert Norman, and entrusted to Bill to introduce.

We had a few years of intensive work to re-establish the nursery, and nothing was further from Bill's mind than that I should resume breeding. It did not appeal to his business sense. The returns were small; and if others like Norman, were prepared to raise the roses, then let them do it. Bill was happy to introduce their varieties. I contented myself with a few plants in a frame in my garden at home, a feeble effort which got the reward it deserved. I had neither the time nor the money to do more than that, being away ten hours a day at five pounds a week.

The years went by, as we grew a new crop of roses every year, and sold it the next, until in 1958 we noticed a sad decline in Bill's health. Our wonderful leader, under whom the company had won the National Rose Society's Championship twenty-one times, was failing, and the last year was painful. He battled against weakness, we fought to disbelieve it. Running the business under those circumstances was difficult. He died in December 1959.

The family trusted me to manage the nursery, and my thoughts soon returned to breeding. We had no glass-houses and next to no experience; I decided to borrow the former until we had gained the latter. Six miles away, in Henlow, a friendly nurseryman named Ken Osborn agreed to lend us a house. I then wrote to Pat Dickson and Sam McGredy, asking if I could see their premises, in order to start up in competition against them.

True to the rose trade's normal comradeship, they invited me to come and stay with them as long as I liked, and to see everything I wished. There followed a riotous week in Ireland, learning about breeding roses by day, and emptying glasses by night. I here and now express my debt to Pat and Sam. Had it not been for them, I should have made a right mess of the job. I did my best in return by telling them some of the ideas tucked away in my mind for the future, two of which Sam used before I did, and he was welcome.

I now realize, as a result of writing this book, that in choosing my first parent plants I followed the same course as the Dicksons had taken some seventy years before me; and for them it had proved a failure. It was simple enough. I planted the best existing varieties, with the intentions of crossing them with one another, and of being guided by what their progeny revealed. In one respect, perhaps, my choice was different from the Dickson precedent, in that I set great store by health. It seemed to me that whatever strain I might discover would be all the better for being founded on health.

In Hitchin I had the right man to entrust with the day to day care of the new enterprise. He had come south from Durham, where at the coal face in his youth he had been rescued from an accident; he never wanted to go down a mine again. Although an employee of the nursery he had spent most of his time in Bill's garden, which proved him a meticulous worker. His hobby was breeding rabbits, suggesting at least some insight into the work at hand. He was a thoroughly good and trustworthy man, not over confident, and I liked him. His name was Matthew Ernest Richards, always known to us as Ernie. He accepted his new appointment, in which I had to instruct him in every detail, and I believe it enriched the last years of his life.

The plants grew well, and in May 1962 we began our careers as hybridists. One has quite an easy introduction to the task before the rush, because for a week or two there are only a few blooms per day. They must be shorn of their petals and stamens before the latter bear pollen. If there is uncertainty as to when that stage is reached, it is soon resolved by trial and error. We quickly learned that some varieties had to be caught young, and others could wait longer, a general guide being to pinch the bud gently to see whether it felt hard or hollow, and to operate in the latter case. A label was hung over the emasculated flower head, to mark it as a recipient of pollen during the next one, two or three days, according to the weather.

The immature stamens were saved as sources of pollen, when it should ripen on them. We found Jeyes' toilet tissue handy for collecting them. One wrote the name of the variety and the date on the tissue, which could be screwed up and thrown away after the pollen was used. To apply the pollen we used childrens' cheap paint brushes, and sterilized them afterwards in alcohol. Another method is to snap off blooms which are not wanted for seed, and to brush their stamens on to the seed parent's stigmas. I would not countenance fingers for this work, because the pollen would certainly be mixed, thus nullifying the observations we might subsequently make on the influence of the parents.

I soon realized how important it is to know one's roses well, because when mating two varieties I found a sort of ready-reckoner clicking in my mind. It warned me not to put the same two weaknesses together, especially as regards weak flower stems, short petals, papery petals, insufficient petals, scentlessness, disease, pale foliage, dubious growth. This subconscious store of knowledge included the parents of some of the varieties we were using, and I am certain it was the vital factor that made our first efforts successful.

It was in 1964 that we saw the results in the open air, and began to select our first introductions. The best was 'Escapade', a semi-double Floribunda from 'Pink Parfait' × 'Baby Faurax', with wide lilac pink blooms, white to the centre. The most popular, because more conventional, were helped by a fortunate thought in naming them in association with one another: 'King Arthur', 'Guinevere', 'Sir Lancelot' and 'Merlin'. We introduced them in 1967, five years from the time of pollination, and so entered the new rose business. Five years was fast going. We usually spend seven or more on testing and propagating.

More important than the roses we introduced were those we kept to build with. They are not recognized as easily as are the obvious introductions, yet without them the breeder is marking time year by year. Two seedlings from that first year's work were to give me some fine roses in the future; one was 'Anne Elizabeth' × 'Allgold'; the other 'Orange Sensation' × 'Allgold'. They were never introduced, because they were not in their own right marketable varieties. I called them 'half-way houses'. The influence of both is well marked in our breeding to this day.

Time to a rose breeder is like elastic, stretching out far to the future one moment, looking back into the past the next, and coming to a snap to startle him into catching the present opportunity. In telling of my 1962 pollination, I have jumped to 1967 and beyond, and had now better put the calendar back.

After a few years under borrowed glass, we built our own on the experience gained. I wish I could express the sheer happiness of working there. The absorbed interest when pollinating, the satisfaction and hope when sowing the seed, the excitement when the little seedlings bloomed in May and June. One could feel that these emotions were shared by those of our staff called in to help out.

To my grief, Ernie Richards died of cancer. For some time the breeding staff had been increased to three, for in addition to breeding we had begun to grow plants under glass to provide both flowers for Chelsea Show and propagating wood for the nursery. Percy Edward Deards succeeded Ernie; he had been gardener to the local squire, who made the great mistake of giving him the sack, much to our benefit as I realized shortly after we took him on. Looking back through my life, I have occasionally asked myself who was the most pleasant fellow I ever met, and the answer is Ted Deards. His sunny nature, his decency, his happy, honest face, his skill with plants and devotion to them, his modesty and unselfishness made him a joy to work with.

His only drawback was his age, but I had provided for that in Ernie's day by adding a youngster to the strength. If he grew up under Ernie and Ted, he should, I thought, make a first rate rose breeder for the future. Meanwhile we had Ted for five or six years before he was due to retire.

The account of our breeding would be incomplete without mention of Alec Cocker; but as this has been explained in the preceding chapter, I need not repeat it here, except to reiterate the pleasure and advantage we each had of the other.

Soon after Alec and I had started, he liked to say that the two of us put together formed the largest rose breeding enterprise in the country. In fact he, with his thoroughness, always raised more seedlings than I did. After a few years it occurred to me that it was no great advertisement of skill to raise an enormous number of seedlings, only to throw all of them away except for the few one might eventually introduce or keep for future breeding. Much cleverer, thought I, to obtain one's introductions from the minimum possible number.

Accordingly I reduced the numbers by careful selection of parents, until we

50. Jack Harkness in Dublin, July 1984. Standing (l. to r.): Leslie Mitchell, President Clontarf Horticultural Society; the Lord Mayor of Dublin; Dick Balfour, President World Federation of Rose Societies. Seated (l. to r.): Pat Dickson, Jack Harkness, John Mattock. The occasion was the presentation of the prizes at the city of Dublin International Rose Trials.
Photo: Dublin Corporation Parks Department

sowed an average of 20,000 seeds per year. It gave me the greatest pleasure to be visited by breeders whose operations were counted in six figures, to find them bewildered that we could obtain so much from so little. In the various international trials we have collected over 250 awards, which is gratifying for a beginner. On occasions we have practically 'swept the board' in various countries.

The trips to trials and agents abroad have been great fun. Sometimes Alec and I would go together, and on one occasion at Heathrow, I was at the passport control while he was some yards behind, in broad Scots conversation with somebody he had just met. His voice gave rise to a happy thought, and with the co-operation of the official concerned I ushered him through the Foreign passport control, on the strength of being Scots, much to his indignation and my amusement.

He got his own back in Aberdeen, by taking me to his Rotary Club, and informing me as he stopped the car that I was the speaker for the day. It was necessary to do something about that, and by the time I had to speak, I was ready to present as fact a story I had only just invented, concerning my rose 'Alexander' and a female admirer of Alexander Cocker, who said to me (in my best Aberdonian):

'Oh, Mr Harkness, you surely named "Alexander" after Mr Cocker?'

'No,' I replied, 'it was named after Field-Marshal Alexander.'

'Do you tell me that now? And I never knew Mr Cocker was a Field-Marshal.'

The Rotary Club loved that one, rightly reckoning Alec's chances of military promotion; and so did Alec, for he often repeated it to other people.

165

To recount each season's work would sorely try the reader's patience. Suffice it to say that the business has been modestly profitable, and that the varieties have been well received. It is not a business to grow rich by. The income attainable predetermines a small business, and the expenditure must therefore be kept down. There are the exceptions, like Meilland and Kordes, but one cannot budget to be an exception.

Among my varieties some of the best known are 'Alexander', 'Compassion', 'Mountbatten', 'Yesterday', 'Elizabeth Harkness', 'Southampton' and 'Amber Queen'. Some of these, and others, are depicted in this book. I refrain from giving a sort of catalogue of them here. Perhaps you will grow them, and see them for yourself.

We followed some intricate breeding lines, and I usually had about three dozen projects in hand. One of these resulted in the strange colour of 'Greensleeves'; another in the unusual petal formation of 'Cosette', which has been introduced on the Continent, but not in Britain. Some projects failed to yield a satisfactory variety, but we came very near to brown roses. The most interesting project was *Rosa persica*, a difficult species, of which I probably held the largest stock ever grown outside its native regions. The object here was to raise a fertile hybrid, but although we got in the end over a hundred, some very beautiful, and notable as the first recorded since 1836, they were all sterile and bloomed only in the summer. Their beauty lay in a dark red eye at the centre of the bloom. I obtained them single and double, yellow, pink, salmon and orange. Having put a lot of work into this bit of rose pioneering, I thought we might introduce two of the hybrids, and sent them to the Royal National Rose Society's trials. No interest was expressed, and I accepted the fact that they were not yet suitable for gardens, although of great botanical interest.

I had a saying about breeding our own lines, that whatever is in is bound to come out again – some day. In the case of R. *persica* this was not true, because it was locked in; but I never lost hope of opening the way.

I moved from Hitchin in 1977, promising to return for the breeding; and settled in Southwold. It had taken forty years since I left Ireland to live again by the sea, which still exalts me. I miss seeing the roses every day. Against that, I have been able to deploy at long last my second love, which is writing. And every summer, Betty and I are back in the glass-house, scheming, sweating and pollinating; and in the rose field, selecting the future introductions and breeding stock. The younger members of the family, including my sons Robert and Philip, are directors of the business, growing and selling the roses every year. They are making a fine job of it, and all is well in Hitchin as I write, touch wood!

Breeding roses; writing; and Southwold: it seems to me I have the best of three worlds. And the clock has ticked on to mark half a century since I first went out to work. This year I have completely re-organized the hybridizing house to embark on a number of new projects, which ought to keep us busy until old Father Time says, in a friendly way I trust, 'Come along.'

Bibliography

GENERAL

AMERICAN ROSE SOCIETY, *et al. Modern Roses 6*, 1965; *Modern Roses 8*, 1980.
ELLWANGER, H. B. *The Rose*, 1882.
FOSTER-MELLIAR, Rev A. *The Book of the Rose*, 1905 (third edition).
HARKNESS, Jack. *Roses*, 1978.
—— *The World's Favorite Roses*, 1979.
—— *The Rose Directory*, 1982.
JÄGER, August. *Rosenlexikon*, 1936 (issued 1970).
KRÜSSMAN, Gerd. *Rosen, Rosen, Rosen*, 1974.
MCGREDY, Sam, and JENNETT, Séan. *A Family of Roses*, 1971.
SCHULTHEIS, Gebr. *Deutsches Rosen-Buch*, 1889.
SHEPHERD, Roy E. *History of the Rose*, 1954.
THOMAS, Dr A. S. *Knowing, Growing and Showing Roses*, 1975.
YOUNG, Norman. *The Complete Rosarian*, 1971.

1 GUILLOT

D'OMBRAIN, Rev H. H. 'French Rosarians', *The Rosarian's Year-Book*, 1893.
—— 'Hybrid Tea Roses', *The Rosarian's Year-Book*, 1895.
NATIONAL ROSE SOCIETY. 'Report of the Committee', *The Rosarian's Year-Book*, 1894.
PAUL, William. *The Rose Garden*, 1848.
WYATT, L. Arthur. 'Landmarks in Roses — Title in Dispute', *The Rose*, Winter 1962–63.
—— 'Tea-Scented Roses, A Survey', *The Rose Annual*, 1975.

Also unpublished notes kindly furnished by L. Arthur Wyatt of Teddington, and information from M. Jean Pierre Guillot.

2 BENNETT

BORCHARD, Dr Ruth. *Oh My Own Rose*.
DARLINGTON, H. R. 'The Gold Medal Roses 1883–1918', *The Rose Annual*, 1932.
D'OMBRAIN, Rev H. H. 'The Rose and the National Rose Society in 1890', *The Rosarian's Year-Book*, 1891.
EASLEA, Walter. 'Hybridisation of Roses', *The Rose Annual*, 1910.

FOSTER-MELLIAR, Rev A. 'Recollections of Roses and Rose Showing', *The Rosarian's Year-Book*, 1899.

The Garden, 22 November, 1879. 'Pedigree Seedling Roses'.

The Gardener's Chronicle, 23 August, 1890. 'Mr Henry Bennett'.

GRAHAME, C. J. 'Does Exhibition for Money Tend to Demoralization?' *The Rosarian's Year-Book*, 1895.

GRAY, Alexander Hill. 'Rose Jottings', *The Rosarian's Year-Book*, 1890 and 1891.

HOLE, Rev S. Reynolds. *A Book about Roses*, 1909 (25th impression).

KEYNES, WILLIAMS & Co. Advertisement in *The Rosarian's Year-Book*, 1901.

NAYLOR, Maj Gen R. F. B. 'The History, Development and Growth of the National Rose Society', *The Rose Annual*, 1965.

PAUL, George. 'Development of the Hybrid Tea Rose', *The Rosarian's Year-Book*, 1896.

PEMBERTON, Rev Joseph H. *Roses, Their History, Development and Cultivation*, 1908.

—— 'A Sprig of Rosemary', *The Rose Annual*, 1924.

—— 'Fifty Years of Rose Development', *The Rose Annual*, 1926.

ROYAL HORTICULTURAL SOCIETY. *Dictionary of Gardening*, 1956.

WYATT, L. Arthur. 'Vignette', *The Rose*, Autumn 1961.

—— 'Two Centuries of Roses', *The Rose*, Autumn 1965.

Also correspondence and unpublished notes kindly furnished by the Rev John P. Adams of Stapleford; Charles Quest-Ritson of Warminster; and L. Arthur Wyatt of Teddington.

3 PERNET-DUCHER

CURREY, Jesse A. 'Rose Culture in Oregon, USA', *The Rose Annual*, 1916.

DARLINGTON, H. R. 'Twenty-Four Roses for General Garden Cultivation', *The Rose Annual*, 1910.

—— 'The Hybrid Teas of the Past Ten Years', *The Rose Annual*, 1921.

EASLEA, Walter. 'Pernetiana Roses', *The Rose Annual*, 1921.

FELTON, R. F. 'Report of the Conference on "Roses for the Garden"', *The Rose Annual*, 1912.

GAUJARD, Jean. 'The Roses of France', *The Rose Annual*, 1950.

—— 'My Masterpiece', *The Rose Annual*, 1953.

HILL, E. G. 'Notes on My Visit to California', *The Rose Annual*, 1924.

KINGSLEY, Rose G. 'Some New Roses at Lyons', *The Rose Annual*, 1910.

MOLYNEUX, Herbert E. 'The Nickerson Awards, 1908', *The Rose Annual*, 1909.

—— 'The New Seedling Roses of 1913', *The Rose Annual*, 1914.

PAGE, Courtney. 'Mr George Paul, VMH', *The Rose Annual*, 1920.

PARK, Bertram. 'The Yellow Roses', *The Rose Annual*, 1961.

PARKIN, John. 'The Imperfections of Our Modern Roses', *The Rose Annual*, 1922.

PENZANCE, Lord. 'Experiments in Rose Hybridization', *The Rosarian's Year-Book*, 1892.

ROUSSET, Guy, *et al.* *La Rose de A à Z*, 1976.

TAYLOR, George M. 'The Newer Foreign Roses', *The Rose Annual*, 1922.

WADDELL, Dr A. R. 'A Milestone in the Evolution of Pure Colour in Roses', *The Rose Annual*, 1924.

WHEATCROFT, Harry. 'Francis Meilland', *The Rose Annual*, 1959.

WILLIAMS, Dr A. H. 'Roses for Market', *The Rose Annual*, 1912.

WYATT, L. Arthur. 'Quest for Gold', *The Rose*, Spring 1964.

—— 'Distant Cousins', *The Rose*, Autumn 1964.

—— 'The Wizard of Lyon', *The Rose Annual*, 1965.

—— 'Bagatelle', *The Rose*, Autumn 1966.

Also correspondence and unpublished notes kindly furnished by L. Arthur Wyatt of Teddington.

4 DICKSON

ASHCROFT, Robert W. 'The House of Dickson', *Town and Country News*, 18 December, 1925.

BUNYARD, E. A. 'Who's Who in the Rose Garden', *The Rose Annual*, 1937.

COWLEY, Herbert E. 'Two Days' Festival of Roses: The Summer Show', *The Rose Annual*, 1926.

DARLINGTON, H. R. 'The Gold Medal Roses 1883–1918', *The Rose Annual*, 1932.

DICKSON, Alex. 'A Symposium on Hybrid Perpetual Roses', *The Rosarian's Year-Book*, 1894.

—— 'The Hybridisation of Roses', *The Rose Annual*, 1909.

DICKSON, Alex. 'My Masterpiece', *The Rose Annual*, 1954.

DICKSON, A. P. C. 'Dazzled by Colour — But Not Blind to Form', *The Rose Annual*, 1964.

—— 'My Highlights of the Year', *The Rose Annual*, 1966.

—— 'Rose Breeding', *The Rose Annual*, 1969.

DICKSON, Alexander & Sons. Advertisements in *The Rosarian's Year-Book* and *The Rose Annual*.

D'OMBRAIN, Rev H. H. 'The Rose and the National Rose Society in 1889, 1893, 1897, 1900', *The Rosarian's Year-Book*, 1890, 1894, 1898 and 1901 respectively.

—— 'Mr George Dickson, of Newtownards', *The Rosarian's Year-Book*, 1891.

FLEXMAN, D. L. 'Around the Nurseries', *The Rose Annual*, 1951.

GRAHAME, Charles J. 'Alexander Dickson Junr.' *The Rosarian's Year-Book*, 1896.

GRAY, Alexander Hill. 'Rose Jottings', *The Rosarian's Year-Book*, 1893.

HARVEY, N. P. 'Irish Roses', *The Rose Annual*, 1954.

NATIONAL ROSE SOCIETY. 'Report of the Council for the Year 1913', *The Rose Annual*, 1914.

NORMAN, Albert. 'Great Roses', *The Rose Annual*, 1952.

PIPER, A. 'Some Hybrid Perpetuals and Hybrid Teas of Recent Years', *The Rosarian's Year-Book*, 1897.

RABAN, Nigel. 'The Men Behind the New Roses', *The Rose Annual*, 1972.

THORN, W. C. 'What's in a Name?' *The Rose Annual*, 1961.

WHEATCROFT, Harry. 'Alex Dickson, VMH, DHM', *The Rose Annual*, 1976.

Unattributed. 'The War of the Roses', *The Northern Whig*, 8 May, 1908.

Also notes kindly supplied by L. Arthur Wyatt of Teddington.

5   McGREDY

BARTLETT, A. Cecil. 'The Autumn Show', *The Rose Annual*, 1928.

EDLAND, H. 'The Trial Ground 1963', *The Rose Annual*, 1964.

FLEXMAN, D. L. 'Around the Nurseries', *The Rose Annual*, 1951.

McGREDY, Sam. 'Facts and Figures', *The Rose Annual*, 1955.

—— 'Roses and Rosarians', *The Rose Annual*, 1956.

—— 'Dreaming Roses', *The Rose Annual*, 1957.

—— 'Derriaghy', *The Rose Annual*, 1958.

—— 'In Search of New Roses', *The Rose Annual*, 1959.

—— 'The Happy Wanderer', *The Rose Annual*, 1965.

—— 'Field Selection of Seedlings', *The Rose Annual*, 1969.

—— 'Report from New Zealand', *The Rose Annual*, 1976.

—— 'A Hand-Painted Family Tree', *The Rose Annual*, 1978.

McGREDY, Samuel & Son. Advertisements in *The Rose Annual*.

NATIONAL ROSE SOCIETY. 'Report of the Council', *The Rose Annual*, 1935.

OPPENHEIMER, Herbert. 'The Trial Ground in 1929', *The Rose Annual*, 1930.

PAGE, Courtney. 'Rose Mermaid', *The Rose Annual*, 1920.

—— 'New Roses of 1919', *The Rose Annual*, 1920.

—— 'Samuel McGredy', *The Rose Annual*, 1922.

—— 'Rose Hybridization', *The Rose Annual*, 1935.

PRICE, B. W. 'Some Impressions of the Provincial Show, Wolverhampton', *The Rose Annual*, 1923.

RABAN, Nigel. 'The Men Behind the New Roses', *The Rose Annual*, 1971.

ROYAL HORTICULTURAL SOCIETY. *Dictionary of Gardening*, 1956.

SQUIRES, R. D. 'Carry on Painting, Sam', *The Rose Annual*, 1983.

THORN, W. C. 'What's in a Name?', *The Rose Annual*, 1961.

Unattributed. 'Samuel McGredy', *The Rose Annual*, 1927.

6   JACKSON & PERKINS

BOERNER, E. S. 'The Newark Rose Garden', *The Rose Annual*, 1957.

—— 'The Future of the Rose', *The Rose Annual*, 1959.

McGREDY, Sam. 'Dreaming Roses', *The Rose Annual*, 1957.

NICOLAS, Dr J. H. 'A Study of Rose Stocks', *The Rose Annual*, 1933.

—— 'Canned Roses', *The Rose Annual*, 1935.

Osborn, Arthur. 'Some Impressions of Rose Growing in America', *The Rose Annual*, 1936.

Raban, Nigel. 'The Men Behind the New Roses', *The Rose Annual*, 1974.

Thorn, W. C. 'What's in a Name?', *The Rose Annual*, 1961.

Wheatcroft, Harry. 'An American Journey', *The Rose Annual*, 1954.

Wyatt, L. Arthur. 'Eugene S. Boerner', *The Rose*, Autumn 1966.

Also information supplied by the Jackson & Perkins Company and L. Arthur Wyatt of Teddington.

7 PEMBERTON

Cowley, Herbert. 'Two Days' Festival of Roses: The Summer Show', *The Rose Annual*, 1926.

—— 'The Summer Jubilee Show', *The Rose Annual*, 1927.

Darlington, Mrs H. R. 'Rose Literature of the Past Fifty Years', *The Rose Annual*, 1926.

D'Ombrain, Rev H. H. 'The Rose and the National Rose Society of 1896', *The Rosarian's Year-Book*, 1897.

—— 'The Rev Joseph H. Pemberton', *The Rosarian's Year-Book*, 1898.

Foster-Melliar, Rev A. 'Recollections of Roses and Rose Showing', *The Rosarian's Year-Book*, 1899.

Holland, Edward J. 'The Past Presidents', *The Rose Annual*, 1926.

Hollis, Leonard. 'Rev Joseph Hardwick Pemberton', *The Rose Bulletin*, 1973.

Molyneux, H. E. 'The New Seedling Roses of 1913', *The Rose Annual*, 1914.

National Rose Society. 'Report of the Conference on "Roses for the Garden"', *The Rose Annual*, 1912.

—— 'Report of the Council for the Year 1929', *The Rose Annual*, 1930.

Page, Courtney. 'The New Seedling Roses of 1917', *The Rose Annual*, 1918.

Pemberton, Rev J. H. *Roses, Their History, Development and Cultivation*, 1908 and 1920.

—— 'Rose Perfumes', *The Rose Annual*, 1917.

—— 'The First Show of the National Rose Society', *The Rose Annual*, 1918.

—— 'The Crystal Palace Rose Show', *The Rose Annual*, 1919.

—— 'Recollections', *The Rose Annual*, 1922.

—— 'The Adaptability of the Rose', *The Rose Annual*, 1923.

—— 'A Sprig of Rosemary', *The Rose Annual*, 1924.

—— 'Nur Mahál', *The Rose Annual*, 1925.

—— 'Fifty Years of Rose Development', *The Rose Annual*, 1926.

—— Advertisements in *The Rose Annual*.

Thomas, Graham S. 'The "Hybrid Musk" Rose', *The Rose Annual*, 1968.

Wylie, Ann P. 'The History of Garden Roses', *Journal of the Royal Horticultural Society*, LXXX (1), January 1955.

Unattributed. 'Rev Joseph H. Pemberton', *The Rose Annual*, 1927.

Also notes and information furnished by the Rev Richard Grinsted of Havering and L. Arthur Wyatt of Teddington.

8   POULSEN

COVELL, Charles Vernon. 'A Rose Yank in Europe', *The Rose Annual*, 1954.
DARLINGTON, H. R. 'Some Roses of Recent Introduction', *The Rose Annual*, 1930.
—— 'The Diamond Jubilee of the National Rose Society', *The Rose Annual*, 1936.
DICKSON, A. P. C. 'D. T. Poulsens Planteskole 1878–1978', *The Rose Annual*, 1979.
LEVY, Lewis. 'The Newer Dwarf Polyanthas', *The Rose Annual*, 1933.
MCGREDY, Sam. 'Svend Poulsen', *The Rose Annual*, 1975.
MCGREDY, Samuel & Sons Ltd. Advertisements in *The Rose Annual*.
POULSEN, Niels Dines. 'Rose Growing in Denmark', *The Rose Annual*, 1964.
POULSENS PLANTESKOLE, D. T. *D. T. Poulsens Planteskole 1878–1978*.
POULSEN, Svend. 'My Masterpiece', *The Rose Annual*, 1954.
PYLE, Robert. 'Thirty Days Rose Hunting in Europe', *The Rose Annual*, 1948.
RABAN, Nigel. 'The Men Behind the New Roses', *The Rose Annual*, 1972.
TAYLOR, George M. 'Some Roses of Recent Introduction', *The Rose Annual*, 1932.
THOMAS, H. H. 'The Autumn Rose Show', *The Rose Annual*, 1926.
WYATT, L. Arthur. 'Landmarks in Roses — Northern Lights', *The Rose*, Autumn 1965.
WYLIE, Ann P. 'The History of Garden Roses', *Journal of the Royal Horticultural Society*, LXXIX (12), December 1954.

9   KORDES

KORDES, Wilhelm. 'Report of the International Rose Conference', *The Rose Annual*, 1939.
—— 'Roses in Germany', *The Rose Annual*, 1949.
—— 'The Problem of Winter Hardiness', *The Rose Annual*, 1952.
—— 'My Masterpiece', *The Rose Annual*, 1953.
—— 'Breeding for Hardiness', *The Rose Annual*, 1958.
—— *Roses*, 1964. (English translation of *Das Rosenbuch*.)
—— 'The History of Rosa kordesii, Wulff', *The Rose Annual*, 1965.
LEGRICE, E. B. 'The Development of Modern Yellow Roses', *The Rose Annual*, 1972.
—— 'Wilhelm Kordes', *The Rose Annual*, 1977.
RABAN, Nigel. 'The Men Behind the New Roses', *The Rose Annual*, 1971.
SKINNER, H. F. 'Minna Kordes', *The Rose Bulletin*, 1980.
THORN, W. C. 'What's in a Name?', *The Rose Annual*, 1961.
WYATT, L. Arthur. 'Landmarks in Roses — Queen of Queens', *The Rose*, Winter 1964–65.
—— 'Landmarks in Roses — Northern Lights', *The Rose*, Autumn 1965.

WYLIE, Ann P. 'The History of Garden Roses', *Journal of the Royal Horticultural Society*, LXXX (1), January 1955.

Also information kindly supplied by W. Kordes Söhne.

10   DOT

ALLEN, E. F. 'A Tribute to the Late Pedro Dot', *The Rose Annual*, 1978.
COGGIATTI, Stelvio. 'A Newsletter from Italy', *The Rose Bulletin*, 1974.
DOT, Pedro. 'Roses in Spain', *The Rose Annual*, 1950.
FITCH, Charles Marden. *The Complete Book of Miniature Roses*, 1977.
HARKNESS, Jack. 'The Spanish Contribution', *Country Life*, 1 July, 1982.
LECKY, Capt H. S. 'Where is the Garage?', *The Rose Annual*, 1941.
MACGREGOR, John C. *A Portfolio of Rose Hips*, 1981.
NICOLAS, Dr J. H. 'The Rose in Europe, 1936', *The Rose Annual*, 1937.
OPPENHEIMER, Herbert. 'The Trial Ground in 1930', *The Rose Annual*, 1931.
PAGE, Courtney. 'The Trial Ground in 1931', *The Rose Annual*, 1932.
RABAN, Nigel. 'The Men Behind the New Roses', *The Rose Annual*, 1973.
RIGG, Charles H. 'Symposium on the Best Twelve Climbing Roses for Walls', *The Rose Annual*, 1938.
ROUSSET, Guy, *et al. La Rose de A à Z*, 1976.
WARNER, Chris. 'A Day out in Spain', *The Rose Annual*, 1981.
WHEATCROFT, Harry. 'Pedro Dot Martinez', *The Rose Annual*, 1977.

11   TANTAU

DOBSON, Beverly R. *Combined Rose List*, 1983.
RABAN, Nigel. 'The Men Behind the New Roses', *The Rose Annual*, 1972.
ROUSSET, Guy, *et al. La Rose de A à Z*, 1976.
TANTAU, Mathias. 'My Masterpiece', *The Rose Annual*, 1956.
WYATT, L. Arthur. 'Landmarks in Roses — Queen of Queens', *The Rose*, Winter 1964–65.

Also information kindly supplied by Rosen Tantau.

12   MEILLAND

MEILLAND, Francis. 'My Masterpiece', *The Rose Annual*, 1953.
—— 'Patents, Trade Marks and Nomenclature', *The Rose Annual*, 1954.
MEILLAND, Francis and Alain. *Hommage à Francis Meilland*, 1976.
RABAN, Nigel. 'The Men Behind the New Roses', *The Rose Annual*, 1972.
RIDGE, Antonia. *For Love of a Rose*, 1965.
WHEATCROFT, Harry. 'Francis Meilland', *The Rose Annual*, 1959.

Also information kindly supplied by Universal Rose Selection — Meilland.

13 MOORE

FITCH, Charles Marden. *The Complete Book of Miniature Roses*, 1977.
MOORE, Ralph S. 'Rose Breeding Around the World', *Gardeners' Chronicle and New Horticulturist*, 11 April, 1969.
—— *The Story of Moore Miniature Roses*, 1974.
—— *The Breeding and Development of Modern Moss Roses*, 1978.
RABAN, Nigel. 'The Men Behind the New Roses', *The Rose Annual*, 1973.

Also information kindly furnished by Ralph S. Moore.

14 LeGRICE

ENGHOLM, B. C., *et al. Report of the Committee on Transactions in Seeds*, HMSO, 1960.
FLEXMAN, D. L. 'Around the Nurseries', *The Rose Annual*, 1952.
HOLLIS, Leonard. 'Leading Rose Personalities', *The Rose*, Winter 1963–64.
LeGRICE, E. B. 'In Search of a New Rose', *The Rose Annual*, 1937.
—— 'Roses of Tomorrow', *The Rose Annual*, 1949.
—— 'My Masterpiece', *The Rose Annual*, 1953.
—— 'A Week from a Hybridist's Note Book', *The Rose Annual*, 1954.
—— 'Strains Produced in Rose Hybridizing', *The Rose Annual*, 1956.
—— *Rose Growing Complete*, 1965.
—— 'Choosing the Right Rose Parents', *The Rose Annual*, 1966.
—— 'Breeding Blue and Brown Roses', *The Rose Annual*, 1969.
—— 'Rose Breeding Around the World', *Gardeners' Chronicle and New Horticulturist*, 21 and 28 March, 1969.
—— 'Fifty Years a Rose Grower', *The Rose Annual*, 1970.
—— 'The Development of Modern Yellow Roses', *The Rose Annual*, 1972.
—— 'Henry Morse & Sons', *The Rose Bulletin*, 1973.
—— 'The Highlights of the First 100 Years of the RNRS', *The Rose Annual*, 1977.
—— Unpublished correspondence.
LeGRICE, E. B. (Roses) Ltd. Advertisements in *The Rose Annual*.
—— Catalogue, 1981.
RABAN, Nigel. 'The Men Behind the New Roses', *The Rose Annual*, 1971.

15 JAPAN

McGREDY, Sam. 'The Happy Wanderer', *The Rose Annual*, 1965.
SUZUKI, Seizo. 'Roses in Japan', *The Rose Annual*, 1981.
SUZUKI, Seizo, *et al. Roses in Colour*, 1983.

Also information kindly supplied by Toru F. Onodera and Seizo Suzuki.

16 COCKER

COCKER, James & Sons. Catalogue, 1880–81.

COCKER. Advertisements in *The Rosarian's Year-Book* and *The Rose Annual*.

D'OMBRAIN, Rev H. H. 'The Rose and the National Rose Society in 1898', *The Rosarian's Year-Book*, 1899.

HARKNESS, Jack. 'The Second Step', *The Rose Annual*, 1968.

—— 'Breeding with Hulthemia persica (Rosa persica)', 1976.

—— 'Alec Cocker, SHM', *The Rose Annual*, 1978.

MAXWELL, Sir Herbert. 'Cocker's Nursery', *Scottish Gardens*, 1911.

PEMBERTON, Rev J. H. 'Recollections of Some New Roses of 1899', *The Rosarian's Year-Book*, 1900.

—— 'Rose Test Gardens', *The Rose Annual*, 1920.

PIPER, A. 'Some Comments on the New Roses', *The Rosarian's Year-Book*, 1899.

RABAN, Nigel. 'The Men Behind the New Roses', *The Rose Annual*, 1974.

Unattributed. 'Roses', *Aberdeen Chamber of Commerce Journal*, Spring 1960.

—— 'Rose Breeding — R. persica (Hulthemia persica)', *The Rose Annual*, 1977.

Also information kindly supplied by Mrs Anne Cocker.